FASHION AND MUSEUMS

Benjamin
Redhead
27.6.24

Dress, Body, Culture

Series Editor: Joanne B. Eicher, ***Regents' Professor*****,** ***University of Minnesota***

Books in this provocative series seek to articulate the connections between culture and dress which is defined here in its broadest possible sense as any modification or supplement to the body. Interdisciplinary in approach, the series highlights the dialogue between identity and dress, cosmetics, coiffure and body alternations as manifested in practices as varied as plastic surgery, tattooing, and ritual scarification. The series aims, in particular, to analyze the meaning of dress in relation to popular culture and gender issues and will include works grounded in anthropology, sociology, history, art history, literature, and folklore.

ISSN: 1360-466X

Previously published in the series

Helen Bradley Foster, *"New Raiments of Self": African American Clothing in the Antebellum South*
Claudine Griggs, *S/he: Changing Sex and Changing Clothes*
Michaele Thurgood Haynes, *Dressing Up Debutantes: Pageantry and Glitz in Texas*
Anne Brydon and Sandra Niessen, *Consuming Fashion: Adorning the Transnational Body*
Dani Cavallaro and Alexandra Warwick, *Fashioning the Frame: Boundaries, Dress and the Body*
Judith Perani and Norma H. Wolff, *Cloth, Dress and Art Patronage in Africa*
Linda B. Arthur, *Religion, Dress and the Body*
Paul Jobling, *Fashion Spreads: Word and Image in Fashion Photography*
Fadwa El Guindi, *Veil: Modesty, Privacy and Resistance*
Thomas S. Abler, *Hinterland Warriors and Military Dress: European Empires and Exotic Uniforms*
Linda Welters, *Folk Dress in Europe and Anatolia: Beliefs about Protection and Fertility*
Kim K.P. Johnson and Sharron J. Lennon, *Appearance and Power*
Barbara Burman, *The Culture of Sewing*
Annette Lynch, *Dress, Gender and Cultural Change*
Antonia Young, *Women Who Become Men*
David Muggleton, *Inside Subculture: The Postmodern Meaning of Style*
Nicola White, *Reconstructing Italian Fashion: America and the Development of the Italian Fashion Industry*
Brian J. McVeigh, *Wearing Ideology: The Uniformity of Self-Presentation in Japan*
Shaun Cole, *Don We Now Our Gay Apparel: Gay Men's Dress in the Twentieth Century*
Kate Ince, *Orlan: Millennial Female*
Nicola White and Ian Griffiths, *The Fashion Business: Theory, Practice, Image*
Ali Guy, Eileen Green and Maura Banim, *Through the Wardrobe: Women's Relationships with their Clothes*
Linda B. Arthur, *Undressing Religion: Commitment and Conversion from a Cross-Cultural Perspective*
William J.F. Keenan, *Dressed to Impress: Looking the Part*
Joanne Entwistle and Elizabeth Wilson, *Body Dressing*
Leigh Summers, *Bound to Please: A History of the Victorian Corset*
Paul Hodkinson, *Goth: Identity, Style and Subculture*
Leslie W. Rabine, *The Global Circulation of African Fashion*
Michael Carter, *Fashion Classics from Carlyle to Barthes*
Sandra Niessen, Ann Marie Leshkowich and Carla Jones, *Re-Orienting Fashion: The Globalization of Asian Dress*
Kim K. P. Johnson, Susan J. Torntore and Joanne B. Eicher, *Fashion Foundations: Early Writings on Fashion and Dress*
Helen Bradley Foster and Donald Clay Johnson, *Wedding Dress Across Cultures*
Eugenia Paulicelli, *Fashion under Fascism: Beyond the Black Shirt*
Charlotte Suthrell, *Unzipping Gender: Sex, Cross-Dressing and Culture*
Irene Guenther, *Nazi Chic? Fashioning Women in the Third Reich*
Yuniya Kawamura, *The Japanese Revolution in Paris Fashion*
Patricia Calefato, *The Clothed Body*
Ruth Barcan, *Nudity: A Cultural Anatomy*
Samantha Holland, *Alternative Femininities: Body, Age and Identity*
Alexandra Palmer and Hazel Clark, *Old Clothes, New Looks: Second Hand Fashion*
Yuniya Kawamura, *Fashion-ology: An Introduction to Fashion Studies*

Regina A. Root, *The Latin American Fashion Reader*
Linda Welters and Patricia A. Cunningham, *Twentieth-Century American Fashion*
Jennifer Craik, *Uniforms Exposed: From Conformity to Transgression*
Alison L. Goodrum, *The National Fabric: Fashion, Britishness, Globalization*
Annette Lynch and Mitchell D. Strauss, *Changing Fashion: A Critical Introduction to Trend Analysis and Meaning*
Catherine M. Roach, *Stripping, Sex and Popular Culture*
Marybeth C. Stalp, *Quilting: The Fabric of Everyday Life*
Jonathan S. Marion, *Ballroom: Culture and Costume in Competitive Dance*
Dunja Brill, *Goth Culture: Gender, Sexuality and Style*
Joanne Entwistle, *The Aesthetic Economy of Fashion: Markets and Value in Clothing and Modelling*
Juanjuan Wu, *Chinese Fashion: From Mao to Now*
Brent Luvaas, *DIY Style: Fashion, Music and Global Cultures*
Jianhua Zhao, *The Chinese Fashion Industry*
Eric Silverman, *A Cultural History of Jewish Dress*
Karen Hansen and D. Soyini Madison, *African Dress: Fashion, Agency, Performance*
Maria Mellins, *Vampire Culture*

FASHION AND MUSEUMS

Theory and Practice

Edited by

MARIE RIEGELS MELCHIOR
AND
BIRGITTA SVENSSON

Bloomsbury Academic
An imprint of Bloomsbury Publishing Plc

B L O O M S B U R Y

LONDON • NEW DELHI • NEW YORK • SYDNEY

Bloomsbury Academic
An imprint of Bloomsbury Publishing Plc

50 Bedford Square
London
WC1B 3DP
UK

1385 Broadway
New York
NY 10018
USA

www.bloomsbury.com

BLOOMSBURY and the Diana logo are trademarks of Bloomsbury Publishing Plc

First published in 2014
Reprinted 2014

British Library Cataloguing-in-Publication Data
A catalogue record for this book is available from the British Library.

ISBN: HB: 978-1-4725-2524-6
PB: 978-1-4725-2766-0
ePDF: 978-1-4725-6792-5
ePub: 978-1-4725-6793-2

Library of Congress Cataloging-in-Publication Data
Fashion and museums: theory and practice / edited by Marie Riegels Melchior and Birgitta Svensson.
pages cm. — (Dress, body, culture)
ISBN 978-1-4725-2524-6 (hardback) — ISBN 978-1-4725-2766-0 (paperback) — ISBN 978-1-4725-6792-5 (epdf) 1. Costume museums. 2. Museum exhibits—Social aspects. I. Melchior, Marie Riegels, 1974- editor of compilation. II. Svensson, Birgitta, 1948- editor of compilation.
NK4701.8.F37 2014
746.9'2075—dc23
2013045231

Series: Dress, Body, Culture, 1360466X

Typeset by RefineCatch Limited, Bungay, Suffolk
Printed and bound in Great Britain

CONTENTS

LIST OF ILLUSTRATIONS

Introduction

Chapter 1

Chapter 2

Chapter 3

Chapter 4

Chapter 5

Chapter 6

Chapter 7

Chapter 8

Chapter 9

Chapter 10

Chapter 11

Chapter 12

Conclusion

NOTES ON CONTRIBUTORS

Anna Dahlgren is senior lecturer at the Department of Art History at Stockholm University and was formerly post-doctoral researcher at the Nordiska Museet in Stockholm. Recent publications include *Representational Machines: Photography and the Production of Space* (Aarhus University Press 2013, co-edited) and *Ett medium för visuell bildning. Kulturhistoriska perspektiv på fotoalbum 1850–1950* (Makadam 2013).

Ingebjørg Eidhammer is curator at the Norwegian Museum of Science and Technology. She trained as a historian at the Norwegian University of Science and Technology in Trondheim, and worked at the National Archives before she started at the Museum of Science and Technology in 2010. There she works on educational and archival projects. Her research interests include, among others, textile history, industrial history, museology, and communication.

Jessica Glasscock is a research associate at the Costume Institute at The Metropolitan Museum of Art, as well as a writer and college instructor. Her fields of research are twentieth-century fashion, subcultural style, and futurism in fashion. Her written work includes the books *Striptease: From Gaslight to Spotlight* (2003) and *American Fashion Accessories* (2008) (written in collaboration with Candy Pratts Price). She was a co-curator of the retrospective "Stephen Sprouse: Rock on Mars" at Deitch Projects and creator of the lecture series "Form Follows Fashion" at Parsons, The New School for Design, where she has been a fashion history instructor since 2003.

Rosemary Harden is curator of the Fashion Museum in Bath, where she has worked for over twenty years. The Fashion Museum holds, develops, and preserves a world-class collection of historical fashionable dress, and presents informative and engaging exhibitions and displays, providing opportunities for audiences locally and globally to engage with the museum's collections. Rosemary has organized a number of exhibitions including "Women of Style" (2000), "The Diana Dresses" (2010) and "Laura Ashley: The Romantic Heroine" (2013).

Anne-Sofie Hjelmdahl holds a PhD in museology from the University of Oslo. She has worked at cultural history museums and done research on material culture, ritual dress, and types of body art among young people. Her thesis concerns how museums relate to the body and human life, and uses the field of dress history in museums as a case study. She defended her thesis *Liv i museet – Kunstindustrimuseet i Oslo gjør kropp med moteklær, 1928–1960* in 2013 at the University of Oslo.

Jeffrey Horsley is an independent curator and exhibition-maker. He has recently completed a PhD at London College of Fashion investigating innovative presentation modes for fashion in the museum. His research fields focus on exhibition design, the presentation of fashion, and contemporary menswear. Jeff has contributed to Amy de la Haye and Judith Clark's book *Exhibiting Fashion: Before and After 1971* (Yale University Press 2013), and is editor of displaymode.net, an online forum examining fashion presentation in the museum and commercial fields.

Harold Koda has been the curator in charge of the Costume Institute at The Metropolitan Museum of Art since 2000. His recent exhibitions and publications include *Schiaparelli and Prada: Impossible Conversations*, *The Model as Muse: Embodying Fashion*, *Poiret*, *Dangerous Liaisons: Fashion and Furniture in the Eighteenth Century*, *Chanel*, and *Goddess: The Classical Mode*. He first worked at the Metropolitan as an exhibition assistant to the Costume Institute's special consultant, Diana Vreeland, working on exhibitions including "The Glory of Russian Costume" (1976) and "Vanity Fair" (1977). He worked for eleven years at the Edward C. Blum Design Laboratory of the Fashion Institute of Technology as associate curator, and curator in the costume collection, then as director of the Design Laboratory from 1979 to 1992. He was the curator of "Balenciaga" (1986), and worked on exhibitions including "Jocks and Nerds" (1989) and "Halston: Absolute Modernism" (1991). In his early tenure at the Metropolitan as associate curator, he worked closely with the late Richard Martin, then curator in charge, on twelve acclaimed exhibitions, including "Diana Vreeland: Immoderate Style" (1993), "Madame Grès" (1994), and "Christian Dior" (1996). In 2000, he served as co-curator of "Giorgio Armani" (2000) at the Solomon R. Guggenheim Museum in New York.

Marianne Larsson holds a PhD in ethnology from Stockholm University. She is a researcher and curator at Nordiska Museet in Stockholm with a main focus on cultural history, gender, and social classes. Her research fields are clothing and outdoor living. She is currently working on a research project concerned with issues of tourism, cultural heritage, nationalism, and globalization. Among her latest publications is *Män i baddräkt: en kroppslig kulturhistoria* (Nordiska Museet 2011).

Marco Pecorari is completing his PhD in contemporary fashion theory at the Centre for Fashion Studies at Stockholm University. His thesis aims to show the epistemic potentiality of a category of contemporary fashion ephemera, and contributes to the methodological discussion on the role of objects in building knowledge on fashion. He has recently published a chapter titled "'Zone in between': The Ontology of a Fashion Practice," in *Couture Graphique: Fashion, Graphic Design and the Body* (Terra 2013).

Julia Petrov is an instructor at the School of Creative and Critical Studies at the Alberta College of Art and Design in Calgary, Canada. Her PhD on the history of fashion exhibitions in museums was granted by the School of Museum Studies at the University of Leicester, UK. Her research interests and teaching experience lie in the fields of visual and material culture, textiles and dress, and museology. She has worked in costume and textile collections for over ten years, and is co-editor of *The Thing About Museums* and *Narrating Objects, Collecting Stories* (both Routledge 2012)

Ingeborg Philipsen is director of Museum Amager, Denmark and holds a PhD in history from the University of Copenhagen, with a main interest in the Cold War era and the Bilderberg Organization from 1952 to 1977. Since 2010 she has been working at Museum Amager and has developed her research interests mainly in past and present dress and identity issues.

Tone Rasch is curator at the Norwegian Museum of Science and Technology. She is an art historian from the University of Oslo. Since 2000 she has worked at the Norwegian Museum of Science and Technology with a particular focus on the museum's photo archive. Her research interest is textile history and fashion, mainly everyday clothes. She has published articles about textile design, textile production, and fashion photography, such as "Home production" and "Norway" for Volume 8 (*West Europe*) of the *Berg Encyclopedia of World Dress and Fashion Dress* (Berg 2010) and "Making Clothes Desirable in Norway: Images from Sohlberg Foto in the Late 1960s," in *Images in Time* (Wunderkammer 2011).

Marie Riegels Melchior holds a PhD and is assistant curator at Designmuseum Danmark. She trained as a European ethnologist and between 2001 and 2002 was a Polaire Weismann Fund fellow at the Metropolitan Museum of Art. Her main research interests are fashion and dress museology, twentieth-century Danish Fashion history, and the relationship between fashion, nation, and globalization. Recent publications include "From Design Nations to Fashion Nations? Unpacking Scandinavian Fashion Dreams" (*Fashion Theory* 15(2) 2011) and the monograph *Dansk på mode! Fortællinger om design, identity og historie i og omkring dansk modeindustri* (Museum Tusculanum Press 2013).

Birgitta Svensson is professor of European ethnology at Stockholm University and Nordiska Museet. She is also permanent secretary of the Royal Swedish Academy of Letters, History and Antiquities. Among her latest publications is the co-edited volume *Markeringar och maskeringar. Att visa eller dölja sin kropp* (Nordiska Museet 2012).

José Teunissen is professor of fashion theory at ArtEZ Institute of the Arts (Netherlands) and a freelance fashion curator. She is also chair of the research network CLICKNL/Next Fashion in Dutch Creative Industries. Her publications include: *Global Fashion, Local Tradition* (Terra 2005), *The Power of Fashion* (Terra 2006), *Fashion & Imagination* (d'jonge Hond 2009) and *Couture Graphique* (Terra 2013).

Kirsten Toftegaard is curator at Designmuseum Danmark and keeper of the fashion and textile collection. She has curated several major exhibitions at the museum. Her research field has in recent years focused on eighteenth-century textile and fashion. Her other main research area is twentieth-century Danish fashion and textiles, especially printed textiles. Since 2005 she has been a member of Conseil du CIETA (Centre Internationale d'Études des Textiles Anciens) representing Denmark. Recent publications include a contribution to *Fashionable Encounters: Perspectives and Trends in Textile and Dress in the Early Modern Nordic World* (Ancient Textile Series 14, Oxbow Books 2014).

INTRODUCTION: UNDERSTANDING FASHION AND DRESS MUSEOLOGY

Marie Riegels Melchior

This book presents contemporary academic information on fashion and museums, past and present, as more museums worldwide, with a range of foci spanning art, design, and cultural history, pay attention to fashion as a subject for display. The book discusses and attempts to understand why museums have suddenly acquired an interest in fashion, what museological implications fashion may hold for the museum institution, and what can be learned from past and present experiences of fashion in museums. We are proud to present a new generation of intelligence emerging from the research environments of younger academic disciplines such as museum studies, fashion curatorship,[1] and fashion studies,[2] combined with new research from experienced curators of both key historic fashion museum institutions (including the Costume Institute at The Metropolitan Museum of Art in New York and the Fashion Museum in Bath, England) and new, unconventional, fashion-focused museums (such as Dragør Museum in Denmark and the Norwegian Museum of Science and Technology).

As the chapters of the book demonstrate, the analytical foundations of the field have been laid by the writings of earlier pioneers, in particular the critical reflections by Professor Lou Taylor (Brighton University), Dr. Valerie Steele (director of the museum at the Fashion Institute of Technology in New York) and Dr. Alexandra Palmer (senior Nora E. Vaughan curator at Royal Ontario Museum). Their work has shown how to seamlessly bridge the gap between the theories and practices of academia and museums. Collectively, their main research interests have included the history of fashion and dress in European and North American museums (Steele 1998; Taylor 2004), the rise of the fashion exhibition (Steele 2008), and the methodological challenges of physically handling fashion, dress, and textiles in a museum context (Taylor 1998; Palmer 2008). However, as the book reveals, for a new generation of scholars the key research questions have slightly changed; they now focus on the ways that museums have become ideal platforms for fashion display, on fashion's potential for other areas of museum practice outside the exhibition, and fashion's role in developing and transforming the museum as a twenty-first century cultural institution.

The redirection of research interests in fashion in museums was highlighted at the 2011 conference "Public Wardrobe: Rethinking Dress and Fashion in Museums" held at Nordiska Museet in Stockholm and organized in collaboration with Designmuseum Danmark in Copenhagen. Symptomatic of the current interest in fashion in museums, the two Nordic museums found it important to scrutinize the subject matter, as both had recently and publicly declared a fashion focus as part of their strategic development plans. By framing the conference under the title of "Public Wardrobe," the intention was to drive the discussion towards new understandings, due to the growing popularity of fashion in museums and how it could be linked to the traditional objective of museums to collect, document, keep, research, and display tangible objects for public good, education, and access. Furthermore, the conference asked which specific "public" is addressed when fashion is displayed and collected in museums, as well as how the display of fashion can strategically build an all-inclusive public profile, which for many publicly supported museums is a standard requirement. The content of this book constitutes the majority of papers presented at the conference.

Before introducing the structure and content of the book, this introduction focuses on the overall research questions to follow and will elaborate on the analysis by introducing the concepts of fashion museology and dress museology. These two concepts are seen as key to understanding the recent developments of fashion in museums and the challenges museums have to address when including fashion as part of their scope. The concepts have been developed through the research project "Fashion in Museums" for Designmuseum Danmark, based on eleven case studies of European and North American museums with a specific fashion focus.[3]

The attraction of the new, the obvious, and the popular

The question of why fashion has become significantly popular in museums seems at first to offer an almost obvious conclusion: it is a fashion. Like other areas of society, it can be argued that museums are embedded in the discourse of fashion and the attraction of the new. The Swedish ethnologist Orvar Löfgren uses the term "catwalk economy" to describe the contemporary invasion of the fashion industry and its catwalk technologies into the corporate world (Löfgren 2005). The catwalk economy poses an equally strong influence over the museum, as many museums are operating more like businesses in order to sustain their economic demands as government funding wanes. Yet in this context the definition of fashion is not limited to the connotation of a commercial strategy of producing and selling new commodities. In the museum sphere, fashion must be understood as something far more complex, entailing also the tangible objects produced by industry and the historically determined fashion system—that is, a specific system of production, distribution, and consumption of dress (Entwistle 2000).

The apparent success of the focus on fashion, considering its growing role in many museum exhibition programs, is also led by the achievements fashion seems to have made for international mega-museums such as The Metropolitan Museum of Art in New York and the Victoria & Albert Museum (V&A) in London. As curator in charge of the Costume Institute at The Metropolitan Museum of Art, Harold Koda (in collaboration with the Costume Institute's research associate, Jessica Glasscock) relates in Chapter 1 of this book, the museum became an international trendsetter for exhibition strategies and display methods in the early 1970s. Since the turn of the twenty-first century, new specialized fashion museums have developed and followed this example. These include MoMu—Mode Museum Province Antwerp (established in 2002), the Fashion and Textile Museum in London (established in 2003), Museo de la Moda in Santiago, Chile (established in 2006), and MUDE—Museo do Design et da Moda in Lisbon (established in 2008). Of course, museums are not the only institutions to embrace the display of fashion; fashion is increasingly being displayed in a highbrow, museum-like manner (in some cases with assistance from professional museum curators) as a favored strategy for associating cities and even countries with the image of fashion (e.g. Beard 2011) and as a way for fashion corporations to represent their own history and dress archive in a less commercial way (as in the case of the Italian fashion house Valentino and its virtual Valentino Museum, launched in 2011). In reverse, the museum is also becoming a commercial boutique concept for selling previous seasonal collections, as in the case of the Danish fashion company Wood Wood and their Wood Wood Museum store (opened in Copenhagen in 2012). This commercial potential, however, seen from both ends of the link between fashion and museums, has been met by strongly negative reactions among art critics as well as fashion research scholars. Museums are regarded as non-commercial spaces, and the entrance of fashion, particularly high-end contemporary fashion, makes museums a part of the fashion system, another channel for the display of the fashion industry (Anderson 2000).

Yet another explanation for the popularity of fashion in museums is found in "Dress and Fashion Museums," a review article in the 2010 *Berg Encyclopedia of World Dress and Fashion* by director and chief curator Akiko Fukai of the Kyoto Costume Institute. Fukai claims that, to understand fashion in museums, it is necessary to consider its connection to a new, broader perception of what

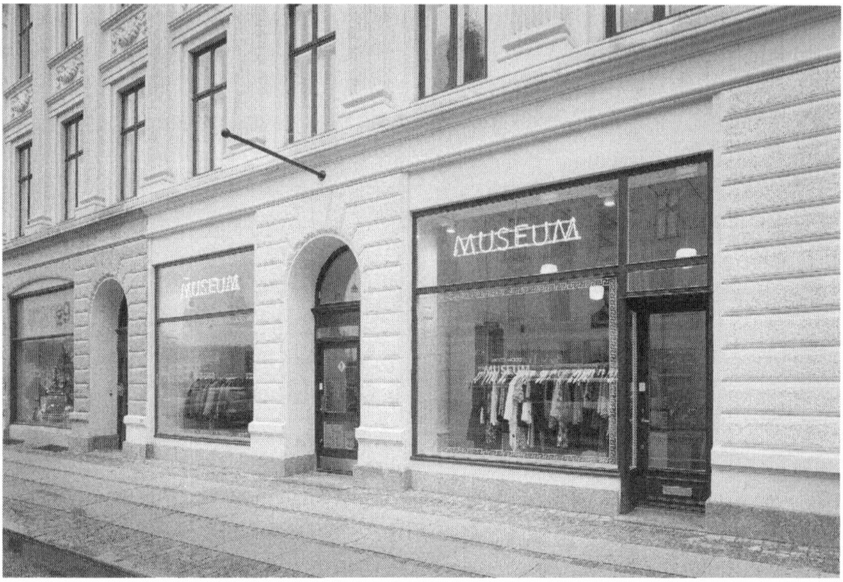

Figure I.1 The Wood Wood Museum shop, Copenhagen, reversing the popularity of fashion in museums as a commercial strategy for selling past collections of clothes. Courtesy of Wood Wood.

constitutes art, as well as a growing academic interest in the young discipline of fashion studies (Fukai 2010: 288). In other words, the popularity of fashion in museums is encouraged by both economy and intellectual enterprise, where the latter takes its starting point not in the fashionable objective (e.g. in disciplines of fashion history and dress history) but in an image-based analysis of fashion phenomena, resulting in fashion exhibitions built on spectacular scenography that visually illustrate an analytical narrative, with the fashionable objects placed like props for display. This development draws the contours of a shift from what I term "dress museology" to "fashion museology."

However, further conclusions have arisen in my own research project, "Fashion in Museums." It can be discussed how economically profitable it actually is for museums to have a fashion focus. The Costume Institute at The Metropolitan Museum of Art is an exception, no doubt, most recently due to the success of "Party of the Year," a fundraising event organized in collaboration with the publishing house Condé Nast and held to coincide with the opening of the annual special exhibition.[4] For other museums, the reality is more likely the opposite. The focus on fashion does not generate money so much as visibility. Fashion is eye-catching, and when it is on display in museums, it is more likely to attract media attention. As such, the value-adding potential of fashion in a museum context does not directly benefit the museum economically, but rather invests the museum with economic growth potential due to diverse media attention often followed by increasing visitor numbers. Nevertheless, the revenue gained from higher ticket sales hardly compensates for the cost of producing museum fashion exhibitions and running museum fashion or dress departments. Instead, fashion makes the museum newsworthy, both in general publications and in specialized fashion media such as magazines, blogs, and other social media platforms. In this way, museums reach more diverse media channels and potentially attract visitors who are not regular museum-goers. That being said, the reality is once again different for museums not located in large international cities. In the case of the Bowes Museum in the rural countryside of Durham County in northern England, the introduction of a new permanent display of fashion and textiles has not drawn the attention of visitors in large numbers comparable with big city museums, although it has generated more attention as such—as well as equally important network possibilities with the fashion industry, companies, and related people.[5]

Another capacity of fashion in museums (of which curators are very conscious) is its unique potential to produce presence within the context of interpreted meaning, while also appealing to people who consciously stage their personal appearance.[6] The advantage of dress, whether fashionable or not, is that it is easy to understand without extensive knowledge of art history, literature, sociology, or other intellectual disciplines, and can instead be read through its bodily syntax—how the body is concealed, revealed, or imaged. For example, the casual viewer is often amazed by the narrow waistlines of nineteenth-century corsets and can almost feel the pressure of the tight lacing on the body, relating to the feelings of women from that era—"Clothes are the shorthand for being human," in the words of Claire Wilcox, the senior curator of Fashion at the V&A (cited in Taylor 2004: 1). Museum visitors easily engage with dress, giving legacy to fashion heritage in museums. In this sense, it can be argued that fashion is popular culture and part of everyday life in modern, contemporary society. Yet fashion may also occupy an in-between position that is not necessarily beneficial to the subject area in a museum context. Fashion is not art, nor a matter of concern to the primary public responsibility of art museums. However, due to the evident interest of museum visitors in fashion (given the often record-breaking visitor numbers) and the growing research interest in the discipline of fashion studies, fashion has become increasingly legitimized as museum-worthy.

We may thus conclude that the strength of fashion in museums is its public engagement; it heightens the appeal of the museum and thereby gives it access to new audiences, both in terms of age and socioeconomic background. Not surprisingly, as I found in my own research, fashion is also selected as an effective strategy by museums in order to achieve the decades-old "new museology" paradigm, which still provides the model for museum politics and the goal of greater social inclusion among visitors (Vergo 1989). This is paradoxical in itself, as the goal of new museology was never intended to be achieved through popular culture (such as fashion), but rather through the communication of critical thinking that would deconstruct the existing modernist authority of the museum and thus open it up to representations of multiple truths and interpretations of past and present society, art, and culture.

To understand fashion in museums, and the transformations of museum practices catalyzed by fashion, it is useful to introduce the concepts of fashion museology and dress museology. Fashion museology describes the focus of museums on fashion and the declaration of new museum ideologies in what can be seen as a reaction to the new museology paradigm, stressing instead a very different fascination with the new. At this point, a history of fashion and dress museology will be instrumental in developing a critical discussion and thus a deeper analysis of the current developments of fashion in museums.

Fashion and dress in museums: past and present

As Taylor, Steele, and Palmer have argued, fashion in museums is, with very few exceptions, a late twentieth-century phenomenon. This relatively short history provides additional context for its recent prominence. However, the historic development of fashion in museums is inextricably linked to the presence of dress and dress accessories in museums. In that respect, dress museology and fashion museology have a largely shared history, briefly structured in at least three different periods of time, from the early introduction of dress for the sake of dress itself in museums to the establishment of both dress and fashion as part of the scope of art and culture in museums.

In the western world, the first initiatives of art museums to take a particular interest in collecting dress on its own merits began primarily in the late 1930s, in the years just before the Second World War. At that time, the focus was less on "fashion" than on "dress," or what would then be called "costume" in English-speaking contexts. In the second period, from the 1960s to the 1990s, fashion became apparent in museums as representative of popular culture and avant-garde design. The third period, from the late 1990s until today, shows the intensified focus on fashion in museums, the development of new specialized fashion museums, the spread of fashion exhibitions even to museums without a fashion or dress collection, and the display of fashion in spectacular visual shows modeled on the less critical high-profile haute couture fashion shows in Paris or more critical art installation-like displays.

The first period

The early stages of fashion in museums can be seen as starting with the introduction of dress into art museums as an accepted item for collection. This was the case, for example, at the V&A and the Gallery of Costume at Platt Hall in Manchester, despite the divergent characters of their collections. It would not be unusual to find textiles within the collections of art museums in the early twentieth century, particularly those focused on decorative arts, such as the V&A. Often these textile collections were the foundation for the emerging dress collections, as clothing would be collected due to the quality of the fabric or representation of a crafting technique. To be sure, collecting clothing in the early twentieth century was not unusual for cultural historic museums. By 1930, for instance, the main Nordic cultural historic museums (the National Museum in Copenhagen and Nordiska Museet in Stockholm) had well-established dress collections, as did several provincial museums of cultural history. These dress collections, however, consisted mostly of clothes from the pre-industrial era, representing how people dressed from lower to upper-class in the seventeenth, eighteenth, and nineteenth centuries across social and geographic divisions.

In the years just before and during the Second World War, however, art museums became interested in building dress collections and allowed existing dress collections to enter the museum, as in the cases of the Costume Institute and The Metropolitan Museum of Art (see Chapter 1 for further details on the merge between The Museum of Costume Art (founded in 1937, renamed The Costume Institute in 1943) and The Metropolitan Museum of Art) or the Gallery of Costume and the Manchester City Art Galleries. In both cases, the collections were focused on the style, cut, and material of dresses—the aesthetic value as well as the design—more than on the social and cultural meaning inscribed in the objects by their former wearers, with the exception of style icons or other kinds of early "fashionistas." Often the collections served as a laboratory for contemporary fashion designers and therefore the fashion industry. In the display of clothing at the time, these meanings materialized in the mounting of the garments on dress forms to highlight the objects themselves and their aesthetic value, whereas they were shown on lifelike mannequins with historically correct postures and wigs when the aim was to represent past ways of living and dressing, as Dr. Anne-Sofie Hjemdahl explains in Chapter 7 of this book based on her historic studies of several Nordic museums and their exhibition strategies.

The first period, then, was not dominated by a precise fashion museology but rather by a dress museology. The building block of this approach was the single, tangible object, often one piece of clothing or an accessory. The scholarly work carried out in museums began with the collection of clothing; the factual description and documentation of single pieces of clothing became the aim of what was later known as "dress history" or "dress studies" (Tarrant 1996; Taylor 2004). Not surprisingly, this practice has been very important for the formulation of international guidelines for handling dress in museums, known as ICOM (Costume Committee's Guidelines for Costume).[7] If fashion was of interest in this context, it was viewed as an ideal type, as an attribute of clothing defined either by the users or by a renowned fashion designer, and as the creation of a new style (in late nineteenth-century or early twentieth-century dress).

The second period

During the 1960s and 1970s, the subject of fashion in art museums gained significantly more interest. In these years the V&A founded its specific fashion focus, revealed to the public in the 1971 special exhibition "Fashion, an Anthology by Cecil Beaton," curated by the legendary British fashion photographer Cecil Beaton (1904–1980). The exhibition introduced new standards of display techniques similar to contemporaneous fashion boutique decorations, using abstract, modern mannequins and sensorial gimmicks, such as the spray of perfumes from select fashion houses.[8] Almost ten years earlier, the British collector Doris Langley Moore established the Museum of Costume in Bath, known as the Fashion Museum since 2007. Across the Atlantic, the Fashion Institute of Technology in New York opened with a study collection of clothing that would later form the basis of the Institute's Design Laboratory (later museum), founded in 1967.[9] The influence of that era's popular culture cannot be underestimated, as it went hand in hand with the recognition of fashion as an important part of the collective cultural heritage guarded by public museums.

In this second period, the Costume Institute in New York was heavily shaped by Diana Vreeland (1903–1989), the fashion editor of *Harper's Bazaar* from 1939 and editor-in-chief of American *Vogue* from 1963 to 1971. As a special consultant for the department, Vreeland curated fifteen special exhibitions on fashion between 1972 and 1989. The Vreeland exhibitions were, like the V&A's Cecil Beaton exhibition, highly staged and imaginative shows rather than representations of past histories. Vreeland has often been described as translating her editorial language into a museum curatorial one (Clark and Frisa 2012). In consequence, the faithfulness to the display of historical fact was less a priority than the expression of the creative talent of the fashion designer and the imagination of the given fashion world. As a curator, Vreeland came to represent the shift in focus from the single tangible object to the dream of fashion through the display of high-end, often avant-garde fashion design, a change received with varying opinions. Vreeland's exhibitions were popular among visitors, but museum curators and art critics received her work with skepticism (Steele 2008: 10–15).

It can be argued that in the second period, it gradually became clear that fashion in museums consisted of a front-stage and back-stage perception and handling of clothing. The handling of garments back-stage was formed and shaped by the standards expressed in the ICOM guidelines, as a distinct dress museology. The front-stage display of fashion was shaped and inspired by the experience of commercial fashion shows, the styling of fashion editorials, focusing less on the actual piece of clothing and more on the creation of a visual impression, a narrative to engage and evoke the feelings of the visitor. This distinction demonstrates what I call "fashion museology."

The third period

In the third period, the contemporary phase, the museum's affinity for fashion is exploding in popularity, and it seems more appropriate to conceptualize this tendency as a fashion museology. The connotation of fashion has expanded from a collection of tangible objects to encompass a discourse influencing the perceptions of museum practice. Fashion has now become a strategic focus for museum management teams appealing to new visitor populations as well as broad media attention. As Valerie Cummings makes clear in her critique of what she sees as a current divide between collections of dress and textiles in museums and the new academic interest and interpretation of fashion, this consequently threatens the survival of departments and specialized museums of costume and textile (Cummings 2004: 74). The interest in fashion continues to center on audience-friendly contemporary fashion designers or twentieth-century fashion history. These interpretations of fashion are believed to make the museum livelier and more eye-catching. At the same time, these exhibitions often compromise the ICOM guidelines for proper handling of clothing in a museum context—for example, not displaying fiber-based objects behind dust-protective glass or not restricting daylight or electric light in the exhibition gallery to the recommended maximum of 50 lux. This can, though, be justified if the objects on display (as in museum contemporary high-end or avant-garde fashion exhibitions) are loaned from private collections or corporate fashion houses, allowing museums to waive ICOM display restrictions. But, as a consequence, the museum collection risks becoming secondary to the special exhibition program, potentially raising a controversy between dress museology and fashion museology. In this respect, the relatively new Fashion and Textile Museum in London (established in 2003) is an interesting case: only a few years after opening, the management decided to barely keep a collection in order to cut costs related to staff and space, instead focusing on front-stage activities such as special exhibitions based on loaned pieces and the museum educational program.[10]

In this third period, fashion in museums is further characterized by an often hagiographic gaze on a selected and therefore celebrated fashion designer—a heritage, perhaps, of the days of Diana Vreeland's curation and her first solo designer display in 1983 on the fashion designer Yves Saint Laurent (Steele 2008: 12). The representation of fashion designers in museums makes them into artists; the narrative of their exhibitions communicates the gifted talent and creative vision that have shaped the objects displayed. Curators' critical voices—typical of contemporary art curators but not, traditionally, of dress and textile curators—rarely come forward in this kind of exhibition, and the fashion designer may even be involved in the actual exhibition-making process. As Marco Pecorari explains in the third chapter of this book, this is the case in many of the exhibitions focused on designers in the specialized fashion museum MoMu in Antwerp, as the museum's chief curator and director find it their obligation to present, analyze, and contextualize a personal narrative in collaboration with the fashion designer. The critical curatorial potential thus risks being reduced to extended marketing initiatives. Indeed, corporations desire the ultimate control of their historical legacy through the medium of the museum and the extreme use of marketing terms in the public display of fashion. Such initiatives can alternatively be viewed in more positive terms as they do give access to otherwise private, archival material that researchers and fashion designers may find useful.

A new curatorial approach to fashion exhibitions, meanwhile, is also coming to light in this third period, tracing back to the young discipline of fashion studies and fashion curation. The work of Judith Clark, an architect by training and an independent fashion curator, is instrumental to this approach. Her main debut exhibition (or rather fashion installation), "Spectre: When Fashion Turns Back," demonstrated new curatorial directions when shown at MoMu in 2004 and the V&A in 2005. Based on the critical analysis of late twentieth-century avant-garde fashion design by fashion theorist Caroline Evans (2003), the display of the narrative became a three-dimensional tableau full of props, from the historical dress objects of museum collections to new commissioned objects by an avant-garde jeweler (Naomi Fines) and drawings by a fashion illustrator (Ruben Toledo), in order to appeal to the visitor's curiosity. The approach not only showed a new way of installing fashionable clothing but also pointed to a different division of labor between the academic fashion theorist, the museum curator, and the "new" fashion curator in the making of fashion exhibitions. In short, the first delivers the analysis, the second functions more as a keeper of the collection, and the latter, the scholarly trained installation artist, erects the exhibition.

After this brief review of the history of dress and fashion in museums from the 1930s until the present, the contemporary situation of fashion in museums must be contextualized by a distinction between the concepts of dress museology and fashion museology. I would argue, in fact, that the difference between the two is precisely what marks the interest of museums in fashion. For museums, dress museology pertains to the actual material and practice of collecting dress: when done properly, it is costly and often requires large, climate-controlled storage facilities and rigorous handling and maintenance practices. Fashion museology, in contrast, emphasizes the visibility of the museum through the staging of spectacular shows, primarily creating unique visitor experiences and only secondarily raising collecting possibilities. It is a temporary, front-stage-dominated practice, believed to have a long-term influence on the museum's recognition by an increasing number of visitors, rather than building the museum collection and ultimately the preservation of fashion heritage; some institutions, such as the Costume Institute, the V&A, and the Museum at the Fashion Institute of Technology, manage to invest in both the scholarship of dress history and fashion studies, which should be considered the ideal.

As such, fashion museology is a transformation of dress museology and an outcome of recent developments in more general museum practices. Fashion museology has its outset in dress, as fashion is first and foremost perceived as a specific type of clothing in a museum context. On the other hand, fashion museology draws further on the fashion industry for the staging and visual performance of fashion as an integrated formula for exhibition displays. Fashion

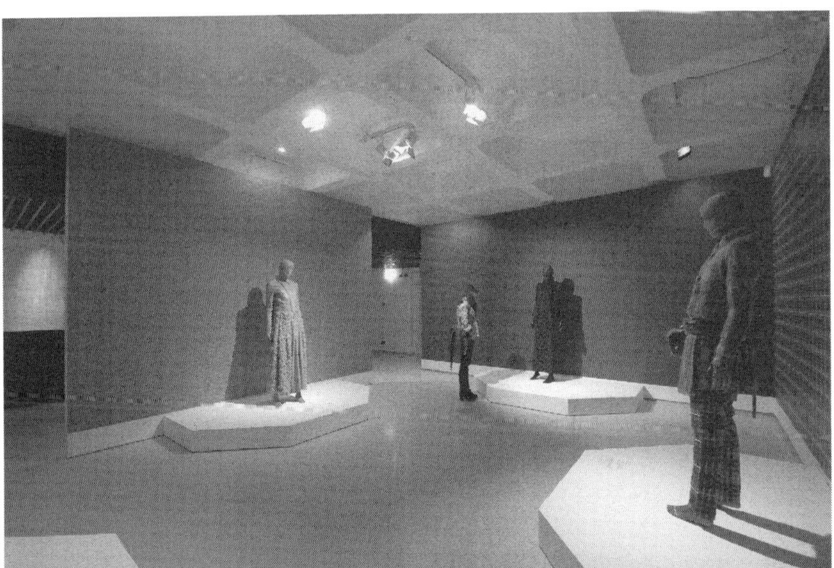

Figure I.2 Fashion museology on display. Jun Takahashi fashion design blending into the exhibition wall, shifting the focus of the garment to the concept of fashion design. "Future Beauty: 30 years of Japanese fashion," The Barbican Centre, London, 2011. Photography: Lyndon Douglas.

museology concerns the museum's front-stage and builds relationships with new visitors and commercial partners (investors, sponsors, and product developers). In short, fashion museology concerns not only the methods of handling dress in a museum context but, more importantly, the purpose of the museum and its immediate relevance to people and society.

Fashion museology as a "new museology" controversy

How can we further understand the presence of fashion in museums, the relationship between dress and fashion in museums, and the tendency of museum management and curators to favor fashion over dress? It is a celebration of the "new," a paradigm characteristic of our time, according to French philosopher Gilles Lipovetsky (1994). In cultural institutions for the preservation and reflection of cultural heritage, such as the museum, the theme of fashion seems to dust the museum off and make it inviting, dynamic, and attractive. In many ways, the intent parallels the ideological movement of critical museum studies under the heading of "new museology," a program for reflective museology, a critical approach to museum practices, and a constant focus on the democratic duty to interact with visitors, especially new ones (Vergo 1989).

However, fashion museology and the fashioning of the museum institution seem to relate more to what has been termed the "new museum" ethos (Message 2006). The oft-cited paradigm of the new museum is the Guggenheim Museum in Bilbao, opened in 1997. The new museum constitutes a new physical institution defined not by the category of objects in its collection but rather by its image of newness. As museum scholar Kylie Message states, new museums:

> [. . .] seek to blur disciplinary boundaries, and promote interpretation according to a wide and inclusive scope of reference. [The] image of newness refers to the style of architecture, the approaches towards installation, and the modes of publicity circulating around the museum, rather than to what is exhibited. [. . .] While the term "new" refers thus to a particular style of museum that has emerged recently, it also and, more importantly, indicates a desire for museums to appear relevant and appealing to contemporary society.
>
> Message 2006: 604

In other words, the new museum could be seen as a "fashioned" museum, styled by a star architect and subject to strategic branding in order to rejuvenate a place—in Bilbao, the design of Canadian-American architect Frank Gehry and the display of modern art marked the city's transition from industrial depression to supposedly post-industrial coolness. Furthermore, in the Bilbao case, the museum's fashion profile was established through the 2001 special exhibition on Italian fashion designer Giorgio Armani, with star curation by Harold Koda from The Metropolitan Museum of Art's Costume Institute in New York and exhibition design by the notable visual artist Robert Wilson.

Fashion makes museums appear relevant and appealing to contemporary society. The challenge is that while fashion exhibitions make museums attractive, they do not necessarily make museums reflective or particularly critical, nor do they transform museums into forums for the debate required to sustain and build democratic societies; as Steele has rightly stated, though, there is potential for innovative scholarship to communicate a nuanced understanding of fashion (Steele 2008: 25). However, this indicates a dilemma of fashion in museums: on the one hand, fashion gives museums, new or old, the potential to appear relevant, attract broader media attention, and generate greater visitor numbers with broader demographics. On the other hand, it can be questioned what relevance fashion exhibitions have beyond the entertainment value of the display of a fashion designer's creativity or the joy of beauty expressed via clothing and body adornment. New museology's aim of reflection on our cultural heritage and its multi-vocality is as yet unfulfilled by fashion in museums, except in rare instances. Instead, fashion in museums has become an alternative to new museology—a fashion museology—driven by the so-called "catwalk economy," throwing light on what I would call a new museology controversy. The aim of future fashion museology must be to sharpen its critical edge, particularly in the practice of fashion curatorship. As the topic of fashion engages non-standard museum-goers, from the museum's perspective it can become a lens through which our past and present can be told and explored in a much more nuanced way. Increasing research in fashion through fashion studies as an academic discipline should promote such development; however, it may cause immediate friction and dispute the control of corporate sponsorships of museums. The challenge, as always, is to find the right balance of compromise in order to collaborate in the literal meaning of the word, as well as to develop the critical scope of genuine research.

Past dress—future fashion?

The trajectory of fashion in museums appears to move from a previous focus on dress to a present focus on fashion, from a focus on the object to a focus on the experience of exhibitions and other front-stage, public museum activities. Furthermore, as in the Fashion and Textile Museum in London, the goal of building a collection has become less important; the museum has chosen to work with contemporary loaned pieces for the production of new temporary displays and dedicate its employees' time to developing and executing exhibition and educational programs. This reveals the tension between the museum as a center for knowledge and object preservation and the museum as an institution for cultural entertainment and storytelling. By calling on fashion, the museum also calls on certain expectations from visitors accustomed to commercial experiences of fashion in high-end concept stores, fashion magazines, and television shows, where it is possible to either touch and try on the latest fashion or encounter fashion in an edited and overtly styled manner. Museums must deliver the spectacle of fashion consumption and the fashion world in order to entice the visitors, but they must also develop and guard what is signified by museum value. A key question arises: what can museums do that fashion houses, concept stores, magazines, television programs, and books cannot? Perhaps museums can present objects with a sense of authenticity and tell stories with a scholarly basis. More importantly, though, museums can provide context through visual and material experiences where a critical research-based approach can strengthen the significance of the institution. Acclaimed international fashion research is currently flourishing in international academic publications, but it must shape and develop the messages communicated by museums far more than it does now.

Fashion museology has a convincing potential to make the contemporary museum into a democratic institution of knowledge, education, and entertainment in combination, engaging visitors on many levels. As this book demonstrates, fashion unarguably has a place in museums and an important role to play in opening the museum to new visitors, but one that should be carefully guarded and developed by the scholarship of the field; it cannot remain simply a quick fix for front page media coverage with a spectacular image of a sexy, high fashion dress.

Introducing the book

The chapters that constitute this edited book on fashion and museums will continue the discussions introduced here, both generally and in specific case analyses and experiences of practice. The combination of contributions mixes historic approaches with writing on the contemporary, developing a varied and complex gaze on fashion as well as dress in theory and practice in museums.

The first section of the book, titled "The Power of Fashion: When Museums Enter New Territory," begins with a presentation of the evolving history of the Costume Institute by curator in charge Harold Koda and research associate Jessica Glasscock. In detail, Koda and Glasscock introduce one of the world's leading fashion collections, documenting exhibition practices from its early days in the 1900s, as the wardrobe collection of a community theater, until the beginning of the twenty-first century. The Costume Institute sets many precedents for other fashion museum departments in terms of the changing practices of fashion in museums and the historic tie between fashion in museums and the fashion industry that helps define its purpose and support its development economically. In Chapter 2, Professor José Teunissen of the ArtEZ Institute of the Arts (Arnheim, the Netherlands) reflects on the practices of major museums that highlight fashion in order to discuss why museums are ideal platforms for the display of contemporary avant-garde fashion design. In Chapter 3, Marco Pecorari (a PhD candidate at Stockholm University's Center for Fashion Studies) concentrates on the specialized fashion museum MoMu in Antwerp, questioning and discussing its practice of interpreting what Pecorari terms "contemporary fashion history." In Chapter 4, Anna Dahlgren, Senior Lecturer in Art History at Stockholm University, turns the focus towards fashion photography and its entrance into the new museum constellation, demonstrating the power of fashion in museum front-stage activities; her further scrutiny highlights contradictions in museological practices, raising questions about genre definition and collecting practices particularly in terms of fashion photography in Swedish museums.

The second section, "Fashion Controversies: When Bodies Become Public," highlights the challenges of fashion in a museum context, raising a number of substantial questions particularly in terms of gender issues, collecting policies, and the perception of the ideal body promoted through display methods. For instance, in Chapter 5, Dr. Julia Petrov of the School of Creative and Critical Studies at Alberta College of Art and Design in Calgary, Canada, discusses the gender inequality embedded in museum fashion and dress collections and display traditions, and thus questions the extent to which museums meet their purpose as public wardrobes and the obligations to which museums are held. In Chapter 6, Dr. Marianne Larsson from Nordiska Museet in Stockholm looks at the representation of gender and class through the early nineteenth-century female ski wear in the museum collection, and explores how a fashion focus contradicts a focus on ordinary people's everyday wear. In Chapter 7, Dr. Anne-Sofie Hjemdahl of the University of Oslo continues the historical perspective by analyzing the different ways in which display mannequins have been used in fashion and dress exhibitions, as well as the kinds of body types produced by museums in their aim to present dress and fashion in the museum context. In particular, Hjemdahl is concerned with the mannequin system known as "the Swedish System" developed in the 1930s at Nordiska Museet.

The third section of the book, "In Practice," comprises a selection of case studies on the developments, challenges, and future directions for fashion in museums, as seen from the museum practitioners' points of view. In Chapter 8, museum manager Rosemary Harden from the Fashion Museum in Bath unfolds the history of the museum and its collecting and exhibition strategies, showing that the concepts of back-stage and front-stage are essential in increasing the museum's attraction. Harden explains how the storage of the nineteenth-century dress collection was turned into an exhibition, not only improving conditions for the collection but also making the back-stage an attractive front-stage display. In Chapter 9, Kirsten Toftegaard, curator and keeper of the fashion and textile collection at Designmuseum Danmark, investigates what happens to textile and dress collections when fashion becomes the new buzz, as in her institution. In Chapter 10, museum director Ingeborg Philipsen of Museum Amagermuseet in Denmark explains her exhibition strategy for exhibiting dress practices when high-end fashion design is not a display option, in order to attract a younger audience to the museum. In Chapter 11, the curators Tone Rasch and Ingebjørg Eidhammer from the Norwegian Museum of Science and Technology describe the reverse: they use the perspective of fashion to stimulate the museum's educational program and students' understanding of the industrialization process by presenting fashion as a personal issue as well as a developing technology for better production and trade. In Chapter 12, Dr. Jeffrey Horsley points to a future of fashion exhibitions, through a hypothetical autobiographical fashion exhibition type that would reflect society's current celebration of the individual and perhaps suppress the glamor of the high-end fashion designer displays that now dominate fashion in museums. It is a promising future scenario, but also a provocative one, as it pushes the boundaries of who is the museum expert and what is the value of their work.

In the last and concluding chapter of the book, Birgitta Svensson, holder of the Hallwyl professorship and chair in European Ethnology at Nordiska Museet and Stockholm University, gives some reflections on how this book can inspire future discussions and practices of fashion and museums.

Notes

1. London College of Fashion introduced in 2006 an MA in fashion curation.
2. Fashion studies as an independent academic discipline at MA and PhD levels was first introduced in 2006 at Stockholm University. A few years later, Parsons, The New School for Design, in New York introduced the first MA program in fashion studies in North America. Lund University in southern Sweden in 2012 launched a fashion studies program at BA level. These programs can be seen as a continuation of earlier established study programs in costume or dress history. However, these are founded within a different academic scope of a post-modern, anti-positivist, theoretically-informed approach to the study of fashion interested in meaning, power and identity.
3. The research project was conducted at Designmuseum Danmark in 2011–2012. The eleven case studies include the Costume Institute at The Metropolitan Museum of Art in New York, the Museum at the Fashion Institute of Technology in New York, Mode Museum Province Antwerp, the V&A and the Fashion and Textile Museum, both in London, the Fashion Museum in Bath (UK), the Gallery of Costume in Manchester (UK), the Bowes Museum in Barnard Castle (UK), Snibston Discovery Museum in Coalville (UK), the Nordic Museum in Stockholm, and Röhsska Museum in Gothenburg, Sweden.

4 For example, in 2011 the Costume Institute raised 10.8 million US dollars from the fundraising event "Party of the Year" at the opening of the "Alexander McQueen: Savage Beauty" special exhibition (according to an interview with Harold Koda on May 12, 2011).

5 According to an interview with keeper of textile at the Bowes Museum, Joanna Hashagen, April 6, 2011.

6 According to interviews with curators of fashion and their feedback from exhibition visitors in the museum visitors' books, e.g. interview with managing director and curator at the Fashion Museum in Bath (UK), Rosemary Harden, March 2, 2011, interview with senior curator of fashion at the V&A, Claire Wilcox, March 9, 2011, and with the director of the museum at the Fashion Institute of Technology in New York (USA), Dr. Valerie Steele, May 13, 2011.

7 See: www.costume-committee.org.

8 According to Amy de la Haye's presentation, "Constructing Histories and Re-constructing an Exhibition: Fashion: An Anthology by Cecil Beaton (1971)," at the conference "Developments in Dress History," Brighton University, December 8–10, 2011.

9 According to Steele, the museum at the Fashion Institute of Technology developed out of the Edward C. Blum Design Laboratory founded at the Brooklyn Museum in 1915 as a teaching collection. The collection was later made into two separate collections, one belonging to the Brooklyn Museum and the other to the Museum at the Fashion Institute of Technology (Steele 2008: 9).

10 According to an interview with the Fashion and Textile Museum curator Dennis Nothdruft, February 11, 2011.

References

Anderson, Fiona (2000), "Museums as Fashion Media," in: *Fashion Cultures: Theories, Explorations and Analysis*, edited by Stella Bruzzi, pp. 371–389, London: Routledge.

Beard, Nathaniel Dafydd (2011), "From Out of the Box," in: *Address: Journal for Fashion Writing and Criticism*, 1, pp. 8–17.

Clark, Judith and Maria Luisa Frisa (2012), *Diana Vreeland after Diana Vreeland*, Venezia: Marsilio.

Cummings, Valerie (2004), *Understanding Fashion History*, New York: Costume and Fashion Press.

Entwistle, Joanne (2000), *The Fashioned Body: Fashion, Dress and Modern Social Theory*, London: Polity.

Evans, Caroline (2003), *Fashion at the Edge. Spectacle, Modernity, and Deathliness*, New London: Yale University Press.

Fukai, Akiko (2010), "Dress and Fashion Museums," in: *Berg Encyclopedia of World Dress and Fashion*, volume 10, edited by Joanne B. Eicher, Oxford: Berg, pp. 280–294.

Lipovetsky, Gilles (1994), *The Empire of Fashion*, Princeton, NJ: Princeton Univeristy Press.

Löfgren, Orvar (2005), "Catwalking and Coolhunting: The Production of Newness," in: Orvar Löfgren and Robert Wilim (eds), *Magic, Culture and the New Economy*, Oxford: Berg, pp. 57–71.
Message, Kylie (2006), "The New Museum," in: *Theory, Culture and Society*, 23(2–3), pp. 603–606.
Palmer, Alexandra (2008), "Untouchable: Creating Desire and Knowledge in Museum Costume and Textile Exhibitions," in: *Exhibitionism*, edited by Valerie Steele and Alexandra Palmer, special issue of *Fashion Theory: The Journal of Dress, Body & Culture*, 12(1), pp. 31–63.
Steele, Valerie (1998), "A Museum of Fashion is More Than a Clothes-Bag," in: *Fashion Theory: The Journal of Dress, Body & Culture*, 2(4), pp. 327–335.
Steele, Valerie (2008), "Museum Quality: The Rise of the Fashion Exhibition," in: *Exhibitionism*, edited by Valerie Steele and Alexandra Palmer, special issue of *Fashion Theory: The Journal of Dress, Body & Culture*, 12(1), pp. 7–30.
Tarrant, Naomi (1996), *The Development of Costume*, London: Routledge.
Taylor, Lou (1998), "Doing the Laundry? A Reassessment of Object-based Dress History," in: *Fashion Theory: The Journal of Dress, Body & Culture*, 2(4), pp. 337–358.
Taylor, Lou (2004), *Establishing Dress History*, Manchester: Manchester University Press.
Vergo, Peter (1989), *The New Museology*, London: Reaktion Books.

SECTION 1

THE POWER OF FASHION: WHEN MUSEUMS ENTER NEW TERRITORY

1

THE COSTUME INSTITUTE AT THE METROPOLITAN MUSEUM OF ART: AN EVOLVING HISTORY

Harold Koda and Jessica Glasscock

The first appearance of the Costume Institute's collection was not in a museum, but rather in a Lower East Side Settlement House in Manhattan, New York. Consisting of the wardrobe of a community theater, the early 1900s "collection" costumed the productions of the philanthropic sisters Irene and Alice Lewisohn, who offered the adults and children of the Lower East Side classes in dancing, pantomime, and diction as well as their own festival dances and performances. These daughters of a copper baron were able to finance and build the Neighborhood Playhouse in 1915 as part of the Henry Street Settlement House. Though now better known as one of the first off-Broadway theaters in New York, the Neighborhood Playhouse was originally built as an expression of Settlement movement idealism, with Alice Lewisohn noting that "[t]he festivals and dramatic work of the settlement have grown out of the belief that every one should have a share in the world's treasures of imagination and poetry, and in return contribute something to the interpretation of human experiences" (*New York Times* 1915: 100).

By 1927 the sisters were less engaged with the philanthropic endeavor of the Settlement House and more intrigued with the possibilities of the world of professional theater. They moved their Neighborhood Playhouse company and wardrobe uptown to be more proximate to Broadway. The sisters were joined by Aline Bernstein, daughter of the stage actor Joseph Frankau. Bernstein was initially interested in a career as an actress, but had pursued the study of portraiture with the influential Ashcan School painter, Robert Henri, instead. She also made costumes for the Neighborhood Playhouse to increasing acclaim. When a *New York Times* profile was written about her in 1927, Bernstein's study of historic costume was noted, an interest that was surely buoyed by exposure to the many examples of period and regional dress Irene Lewisohn had acquired by the 1920s. Lewisohn's collection had by then become so extensive and its contents increasingly valued for their rarity that she began to solicit support for a costume museum. On May 3, 1937, the viability of the idea was substantiated with the opening of a temporary exhibition of the newly designated Museum of Costume Art that consisted primarily of material from the Lewisohn collection. Held in the Maison Française at Rockefeller Center (a space temporarily donated by Nelson Rockefeller), the exhibition was "designed to present a picture of the activities that will take place when the Museum of Costume Art has its permanent building" (Jewell 1937: 21). The exhibition was also designed to interest and engage American fashion designers and Seventh Avenue in the study of historic costume.

Ambition and innovation in a vagrant collection

By 1938, 400 objects had been assembled and Bernstein was presenting a series of talks on costume history. Lewisohn headed the Museum's committee, planning it as "a source of authentic information and inspiration to stylists, couturiers, designers, and manufacturers" (*New York Times* 1937: 28). They were joined by textile authority M.D.C. Crawford, who had been instrumental in starting the Design Laboratory (the Brooklyn Museum of Art's costume study collection), the production designer Lee Simonson, and Ethel Frankau, a vice president of the department store Bergdorf & Goodman Company (and Aline Bernstein's sister). A second provisional exhibition by the Museum resulted in 4,500 visitors in only two weeks and the organizers were encouraged in their search for adequate facilities for the collection. In 1939, larger quarters in Rockefeller Center were established along with an ambitious program of education, collection, preservation, and exhibition of "the clothes of all ages and all peoples." Soon, the Museum had amassed 1,400 costumes and its first full-blown exhibition "A Cycle of American Dress" was complemented with loans from individuals and institutions. The show was well received by the public (an extended run was required), but the reviewer at the *New York Times* opined that perhaps it had some unfulfilled potential:

> If only the Museum of Costume Art, housed now in the International Building at Rockefeller Center, had been established nearer to the Metropolitan, or even under the same roof, the exhibition of eighteenth and nineteenth century clothes and the Metropolitan's exhibition of paintings, "Life in America," could be seen more closely in relation one to the other [. . .] I have worn down the pavement dashing between the two museums.
>
> Harris 1939: X7

The collection that drew museum-goers to the small Rockefeller Center space had been installed by Aline Bernstein and Polaire Weissman on the recently introduced Greneker Studios mannequins. Conceived in 1937 by Lillian Lidman Greneker, an architect with a husband who worked in theater publicity, the mannequins were the first with movable parts including carpenter-made joints and rubber ribs. Already embraced by New York department stores, the flexible mannequins lent themselves to the demands of the display of historic costume as well. Topped with wigs made by Weissman and with stylized eye make-up, the mannequins stood alone against light walls or in stiff tableaux with minimal props. The "Cycle of American Dress Part I" exhibition was followed by two more of the series as the collection grew.

In the same period, the Museum of Costume Art was strengthening its relations with the fashion industry, especially in its role as a study collection for top American designers like Adrian (1903–1959) and Hattie Carnegie (1880–1956). The long tenure of then titled "executive technician" Polaire Weissman had begun, and Seventh Avenue fashion designers were being invited in to teach standing room only master classes based in the collection. By the end of 1941, the Museum of Costume Art numbered 4,500 pieces including the addition of three privately held folk and period costume collections. The availability of the collection's historic costume to American designers was especially useful in the aesthetic blackout of the Second World War, as the American fashion industry's long reliance on the "inspiration" of Paris fashion was precluded during the German occupation of France. This would prove to be a benefit to both the American fashion industry and the young Museum. In a situation of mutual benefit, the Museum offered its expertise in assisting the fashion industry through the privations of the Second World War, which saw shortages of silk, new wool, and chemical dyestuffs, among other things, in return for the support of their facility. The Museum responded during the war years with exhibitions on East Asian traditional costume (featuring an "economical use of cloth" (*New York Times* 1942a: 13), on textiles both synthetic and sustainable ("100 percent spun rayon, which had been made from spruce" (*New York Times* 1942b: 21), and on fastenings and embellishments (to address the zipper shortage).

By the Museum's fifth anniversary, over 5,000 objects had been acquired, and over 50,000 visitors had seen its exhibitions without nearly enough room for the collection or its management. The Museum was relocated to East 50th Street in 1943 before plans began to merge the Museum's collections, rechristened The Costume Institute, with The Metropolitan Museum of Art. Irene Lewisohn had passed away before her museum found its home, but the Institute was in good hands as the deal that had been struck between The Metropolitan and the costume scholars of the Museum of Costume Art introduced a new cast of contributors to the cause.

Early exhibitions at The Metropolitan Museum of Art

First came Dorothy Shaver, then vice president of Lord & Taylor, who was introduced in the announcement of the formation of the Costume Institute in December 1944 as "Chairman of the committee that developed the plan of uniting the two museums." Businesswoman Shaver noted at the time that The Metropolitan's plan showed "a desire on the part of a great museum to serve effectively the American fashion industries" (*New York Times* 1944: 20). As a natural extension of her work as a fashion industry executive, she had been on an advisory committee for the Museum of Costume Art since 1940. Shaver's tenure at Lord & Taylor had seen the implementation of "The American Look" program in 1932, where she had promoted over sixty American designers, including Elizabeth Hawes and Lilly Daché, by representing their work throughout the department store. In Shaver, the Costume Institute had an industry powerhouse (she would become president of Lord & Taylor the following year) as an ally who would orchestrate the primary funding of the Institute by the fashion industry.

Also a part of the Costume Institute's newly formed executive committee was the indefatigable publicity agent Eleanor Lambert. Like Shaver, Lambert was a champion of American designers. She was also responsible for introducing the International Best Dressed List (she took over the French version during the Second World War) and the twice-yearly fashion weeks that grouped individual designer shows into a condensed format for journalists. Lambert had supported the Institute since its birth in 1937 and shared the founders' conviction that fashion was an art form. Her gift for drawing a crowd along with Shaver's financial know-how resulted in the birth of "The Party of the Year" fundraiser from which all Costume Institute funding continues to be drawn.

Early Costume Institute exhibitions, before its permanent offices and galleries were established at the Metropolitan, emphasized its potential as a resource to the contemporary fashion industry. "Hats and Headdresses" was promoted in terms of "spring trends." "American Fashions and Fabrics," the last exhibition before the Institute's inaugural exhibition, was as much a textile industry showcase as the culmination of Lee Simonson's project to invite fashion designers to explore and be inspired by Museum objects. The resulting display had contemporary fabrics mounted above and alongside the art objects that had inspired them (a beige plaid based on the "wrappings of an Egyptian mummy's shroud" was among the results) (Pope 1945: 20). Of more interest to the press, however, were the repeated promenades of the resulting gowns to the public, set in the Greek and Roman galleries of the Museum.

However, the possibilities of The Metropolitan Museum of Art's embrace of the Costume Institute were not fully explored until the department's formal opening in December 1946 when a little over 100 years of fashion were paired with 5,000 years of art history in a display of dress from the late eighteenth century through to the end of the nineteenth century alongside Museum treasures from all departments. Billed as "a panorama of fashion sources," The Metropolitan's artworks and decorative arts surrounded the resplendent collection of dress assembled by the Museum of Costume Art in a chronologically ordered series of nine tableaux representing daily life. Curated by Eleanor Lambert, and again featuring the installation work of Polaire Weissman, the opening exhibition set a formula for display that would be revisited regularly in the early years of the Costume Institute.

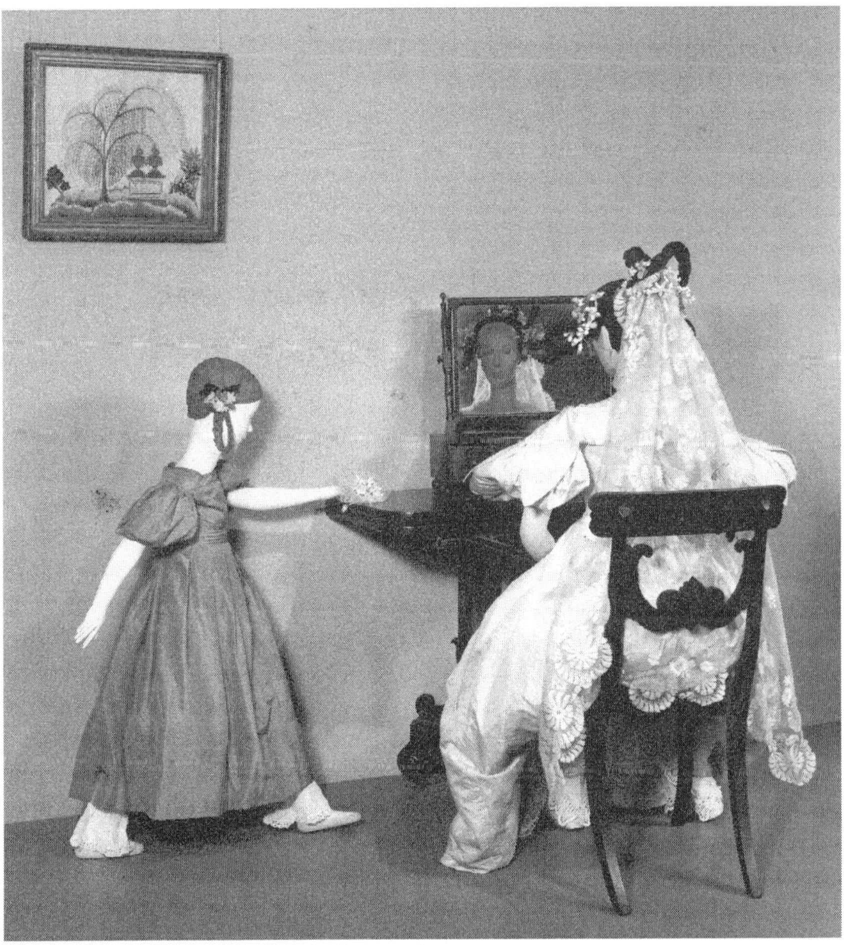

Figure 1.1 A small scene from the third of nine tableaux from the Costume Institute's opening exhibition in 1946. Titled "The Sentimental 1830's," it featured a classical figure from both the designer runway and the museum plinth: the bride. Image © The Metropolitan Museum of Art.

In 1949, the Costume Institute returned to its origins in the theater with "Behind American Footlights," an exhibition of theatrical costume arranged by Polaire Weissman and founder Aline Bernstein. Though nearly choked with old photographs, sketches, and theatrical ephemera, the most appealing part of the exhibition drew on Bernstein's experience as a scenic and costume designer offering striking tableaux for the costumes, replete with framing curtains, furniture settings, and playful large-scale scenic elements. The vignettes of "Behind American Footlights" not only suggested the potential for the display of fashion in the context a fantastical sensibility (such as the one behind Bernstein's successful theatrical career), but also marked the apogee of her involvement with the Institute. The next exhibition, "Adam in the Looking Glass," focused on menswear which again juxtaposed period dress with appropriate furniture and decorative arts examples. Curated by Polaire Weissman in collaboration with the estimable A. Hyatt Mayor of The Metropolitan's Drawings and Prints collection, evocative allusions were made to men's portraiture from The Metropolitan's collection. The mannequins were shown with masks, enlarged reproductions of men's faces taken from period prints, giving the figures the appearance of life-sized paper dolls.

Most of the aforementioned exhibitions included elements of contemporary fashion on display as well. Indeed the Costume Institute's strong connection to the fashion industry was unabashed at this time. "Adam in the Looking Glass" featured a number of women designers' interpretations of the future of menswear. Another exhibition, "From Casablanca to Calcutta," offered synthetic textiles inspired by the various Eastern originals. Though "Behind American Footlights" did not feature such a direct tie-in, the show itself was quite contemporary in its presentation of recent Broadway costumes.

The display methodologies set forth in the early Costume Institute exhibitions were repeated in the 1950s and 1960s. Installation styles ranged from relatively sedate exhibitions featuring blank-faced mannequins against white walls, to more vivid presentations with lifelike figures fully detailed and accessorized in the period rooms or posed in front of paintings featuring related dress. Art historical themes were dutifully explored, but alternated with themes originating from the details of textile and dress (ribbons, floral patterns, regional traditions). These early years contributed to the formulation of the various methodologies employed to situate fashion history in a museum context. Though some scholars had related the history of fashion to the history of art (in the work of costume historian James Laver, for example), and institutions such as the Brooklyn Museum had active costume and textile departments, costume studies and fashion history had not until the post-war period been integrated into the sweeping scope of The Metropolitan Museum of Art. To the great pleasure of both the museum's public and the fashion design community, the Institute's dedicated constituency, the early era of Costume Institute shows accomplished this.

The Costume Institute was so successful that by 1968, enough money had been raised for a major renovation of its offices, storage facilities, and galleries. Consequently, the Institute closed its doors for nearly four years. In 1971, the "new" Costume Institute opened with the "Fashion Plate" exhibition curated by Adolph "Dus" Cavallo, who had replaced the retired Polaire Weissman. Cavallo's exhibition juxtaposed lifelike mannequins against blow-ups of related period fashion prints. His next exhibition, "Untailored Garments," examined the cut of clothes and was a conceptual and radically abstract presentation. Some garments were draped on full figures, but skirts and *dhoti* were shown on torso-less hip and leg mounts, and many examples were presented two-dimensionally on T-stands and kimono racks in the manner of traditional regional garment display. As in the prior decades of the Costume Institute's history, Cavallo exploited the wide range of exhibition effects available and best suited to his curatorial intentions. His brief scholarly and academically grounded tenure ended in 1972 with the unexpected appointment of Diana Vreeland as special consultant to the Institute by the Museum's director, Thomas Hoving.

The Vreeland era

Hoving had been convinced that Vreeland could transform the department by emphasizing its relevance to contemporary life, and enliven its presence through the kind of "blockbuster" exhibitions that he himself had introduced to other departments of the Museum. Vreeland had been a fashion editor at *Harper's Bazaar* from the 1930s until 1961 when she was made editor-in-chief of *Vogue*. Her leadership at *Vogue* was marked by a taste for strong graphics, the photography of Richard Avedon and Irving Penn, and the worlds of both the elite establishment and pop culture trendsetters. While *Vogue* promoted Seventh Avenue designers and manufacturers, it was also heavily Francophile, and in features on the haute couture and the more avant-garde ready-to-wear, Vreeland's predilection for novelty and an aspirational world of fantasy was both pronounced and emphatic. Eventually, she was to be dismissed from her position of leadership at *Vogue* as much for her increasing estrangement from the realities of the evolving demographics of her readership as for her relaxed relationship to budgetary constraints. She was not the most obvious candidate to animate the basement galleries of the Costume Institute, and there were some who saw in her arrival the Museum's apparent endorsement of entertainment and theater at the cost of seriousness and scholarship. However, the Museum's director envisioned the possibility that the charismatic editor's projects might be anchored by the academic rigor and experience of the curatorial team at her disposal.

Her first exhibition was a monographic survey of the work of the Spanish couturier, Cristobal Balenciaga. Unlike any costume exhibition seen previously in the US, Vreeland created an immersive experience beyond the simple presentation of the garments either as artworks placed in isolation within sparse white-walled galleries or as cultural artifacts shown "naturalistically" with contextual elements of furniture or narrative backdrops. The Balenciaga exhibition was to establish a template for the Costume Institute exhibitions that followed. Mannequins were contemporary and abstracted, often with dramatic positioning and animated gestures, and shown bald without wigs or any other simulations of "hair." Naturalistic mannequins had their faces obscured by stockings pulled completely over their heads, or were painted in vivid hues selected to coordinate or contrast with the garments being shown. Vreeland felt that nothing dated a style more than the hair and make-up of a given period, and argued that a design worthy of consideration as artwork should be considered "timeless" in its aesthetic power and relevance, and never be consigned simply to the era of its origination. For this first effort, she had the walls of the galleries lacquered in rich high gloss enamels in colors associated with Spain and Balenciaga. Directional spotlighting with colored filters created strong pools of light in the hot pink, camellia leaf green, and blood-red rooms. Music was piped into the galleries with selections intended to evoke the designer's heritage. Open bottles of Balenciaga's perfume, Le Dix, were placed in the air conditioning vents to scent the galleries in the theory that nothing evoked the emotional connection of a memory more than sounds and smells. Finally, in a quintessential Vreeland flourish, a knight on horseback, Don Quixote, suited up for battle by the Museum's Arms and Armor Department was placed as the centerpiece of the exhibition with a wake of adoring señoritas in Balenciaga cocktail and evening dresses.

"The World of Balenciaga" debuted in 1973, a year after the groundbreaking Victoria and Albert (V&A) exhibition, "Fashion: An Anthology," guest curated by the society photographer, Cecil Beaton. Fredrick Vreeland, Vreeland's younger son, saw the London exhibition and described it in detail to his mother. "It influenced her," he said recently. Photographs bear this out: the use of bald, contemporary mannequins in animated poses in King's Road boutique-like environments. Surprisingly for someone known for her over-the-top aesthetic, Mrs. Vreeland seems to have digested the aggressive, striving hipness of the Beaton effort, and tamed it by simplifying its components. Like *Vogue* in the 1960s, the galleries were dramatic and graphic, but clarified in their aesthetic.

Her later series of historical costume exhibitions such as "The Glory of Russian Costume," "The Manchu Dragon," "The Imperial Style: Fashions of the Hapsburg Era," "The Belle Époque," "Costumes of Royal India," and "Diaghilev" were similarly treated. On occasion, draped fabrics, curtains, wallpapers or scenic views were used as backdrops for the tableaux, and mannequins over time were occasionally styled with wigs created out of materials such as papier mâché or nylon tulle that suggested the volume of hairstyles without literally reproducing the quality of hair. The artificiality of such efforts saved these effects from violating completely Vreeland's original edict precluding lifelike mannequins. This latter development was due in part to the impact of the 1980 Kyoto Costume Institute exhibition, "Evolution of Fashion: 1935–1895," with creative input from Robert Currie, the display director of Henri Bendel, and his assistant, Stephen de Pietri. Currie's ability to create a sense of naturalistic interaction with his mannequins, and de Pietri's extraordinary styling gifts, together with the decision to suggest hair for the eggshell-white period mannequins through a simple application of cut paper strips were to impact international costume displays thereafter.

As Vreeland became too frail to directly control the increasingly complex coordination of The Costume Institute exhibitions, her concepts and detailed directions were channeled through Katell le Bourhis. Le Bourhis, well-read, a lover of history, but also someone as passionate about conveying the excitement of fashion as her mentor, continued the general aesthetic approach established by Vreeland in her heyday. But le Bourhis also contributed a stronger emphasis on historical research and scholarship. Upon Mrs. Vreeland's death in 1989, the responsibility for the Costume Institute exhibition calendar reverted to the curators, but it cannot be said that the display techniques ever repudiated the Vreeland era practices, or the innovations in mannequin presentation coming from the Kyoto Costume Institute. Jean Druesedow, Caroline Goldthorpe, and Beth Alberty for the most part focused on themes originating from strengths in the collection, though Goldthorpe's "From Queen to Empress," with Queen Victoria as its subject, continued the tradition of shows heavily reliant on loan material.

The academic and the cinematic

Of the immediate post-Vreeland exhibitions, "The Age of Napoleon" and "Theatre de la Mode," organized by le Bourhis, generated the most public interest. Perhaps because of this, Philippe de Montebello, the director at the time, tasked her to reconfigure the Costume Institute galleries for a different kind of programming. Reducing the department's gallery footprint to a quarter of its original size, the intention was to have a workable, rotational gallery similar to those of the Museum's other departments with light-sensitive works such as photography, prints and drawings, and Asian art. Five permanent vitrines were installed to allow for pieces from the collection to be rotated after a three-month display period. In a sense, the presentation arranged by formal elements devised by le Bourhis such as "Geometry," "Florals," and "Black and White," without reference to period or culture, allowed for a freedom of selections for each space. In addition, the use of slate gray mannequins, against gray walls, was intended to give added focus to the objects on view without scenographic distraction. Le Bourhis, however, left prior to the opening of her new installation to become director of the Musée de la Mode in Paris, and Richard Martin, the art historian and director of the Shirley Goodman Resource Center at the Fashion Institute of Technology, became curator-in-charge.

His first change was to repaint the gallery walls a chalk white. He also argued that because no collection could constantly rotate its works based on any fixed themes without soon having to resort to secondary and tertiary examples, the Institute would begin a cycle of thematically varied installations. The advantage to this would be that different portions of the collection could be highlighted, and the subjects of the exhibitions could generate renewed interest three times a year. His fear was that one "permanent" exhibition, even with a constant substitution of objects, would not allow for sufficient interest to encourage return visitors or the development of a wider audience with new enticements.

Given the restrictive spaces of the vitrines, initial installation variations under Martin with styling by his associate curator, Harold Koda, were restricted to the mode of presentation of the mannequins. "Infra-Apparel" emphasized the coldness of the gray fiberglass forms inherited from le Bourhis by giving each mannequin a sculpted hairstyle in crushed aluminum mesh; "Bloom" (an expansion on the theme of le Bourhis' floral gallery) had headdresses molded from dried leaves; and "Two-by-Two" utilized wigs constructed of paper twine. Martin's exhibition "Wordrobe/Wardrobe" and his last effort, "Rock Style," with Myra Walker as the exhibition's organizer, played with lighting effects and incorporated neon signage, but walls were painted in various colors, and there was ambient music *à la* Vreeland.

When the Museum partnered with the Kennedy Library for its exhibition on Jacqueline Kennedy, guest curator Hamish Bowles took a traditional approach to his installation and his mannequins. The Kyoto Costume Institute had several years before in its exhibition on eighteenth-century dress created astonishing head treatments of carefully folded plastic mosquito screening. The Kennedy signature bouffant was replicated in that material. Large, mural-sized photographic blow-ups were peppered through the space as backdrops, and the sound that filled the galleries emanated from old television footage shown on monitors from the early 1960s.

With the return of Koda as curator-in-charge of the Costume Institute in 2000, the most significant development has been a decade of collaborations with theatrical and film production designers to create a diversity of *mise-en-scènes* for the Costume Institute installations. Opera set designer, Jean-Hugues de Chatillon, created the backdrops for "Poiret: King of Fashion," with animations developed by SoftLab projected onto scrims to reveal the modernist innovations of Poiret's pattern-making. In perhaps the most imaginative interpretation of traditional mannequins-in-a-period-room installation, Patrick Kinmonth, a production designer for opera and theater and more recently a design curator, created the mannequins, originated the narratives, and developed the scenography for "Dangerous Liaisons: Fashion and Furniture in the Eighteenth

Century." In a lavish installation in the Wrightsman Galleries, the Museum's French period rooms, Kinmonth covered the period mannequins in muslin with human hair wigs. The final effect was poised between the abstract and the naturalistic. Working with his partner, Antonio Monfreda, and curator, Andrew Bolton, on "Anglomania: Tradition and Transgression" in the Aitken Galleries, the Museum's English period rooms, Kinmonth and Monfreda utilized realistically modeled lacquer-white mannequins with exaggerated Day-Glo hairstyles by Julien d'Ys. The approach was deliberately anachronistic with juxtapositions of eighteenth-century and nineteenth-century works and contemporary fashions. John Mayer, an Academy Award winning set designer, did the elaborate installations for "Model as Muse," with photographic backdrops, and a recreation of the private room at Studio 54. Nathan Crowley, also a production designer for film, was responsible for "Superheroes," "American Woman," and "Schiaparelli and Prada: Impossible Conversations." Each of his installations responded to the content of the exhibition, with the painted backdrops of "American Woman" the most traditional and scenographic, and the spare installation of "Schiaparelli and Prada" the most high-tech, with its glossy and minimal architectural framework showcasing huge high-definition screens displaying videos by movie director Baz Luhrmann. The videos of the two designers, Schiaparelli played by Judy Davis and Prada as herself, in an imaginary conversation was based on Schiaparelli's actual words taken from her autobiography, *Shocking Life* and the real-life responses by Prada.

"Savage Beauty," Bolton's exhibition on the work of Alexander McQueen, was the Costume Institute's most elaborate, multi-media installation created and coordinated by the team responsible for all of the late designer's runway presentations. Bolton had wanted the emotional power and impact of McQueen's shows, without replicating any of them literally. By knitting his curatorial concept of the different galleries with the McQueen team's experience and understanding of what the designer might have imagined, "Savage Beauty" transcended the simple presentation of great artworks. The immersive environment, operatic and animated by videos, holograms, rotating platforms, one-way mirrors, and a soundtrack based on effects originated by McQueen, became a word-of-mouth sensation. The most important aspect of the exhibition's success, however, was in the power of the works themselves. If there is one lesson a review of the Costume Institute's decades of exploration and experimentation of various installation techniques and mannequin treatments teaches us (however they support curatorial narratives and conceits or help to engage and inform the viewer), it is that, in the end, there is simply no substitute for inspiring content and the compelling artistry of the works themselves. Scenography and installation techniques can amplify the public's understanding of works, but it is the ability of pieces of compelling creative distinction or virtuosity to astonish and amaze that finally determines the most memorable exhibition experience.

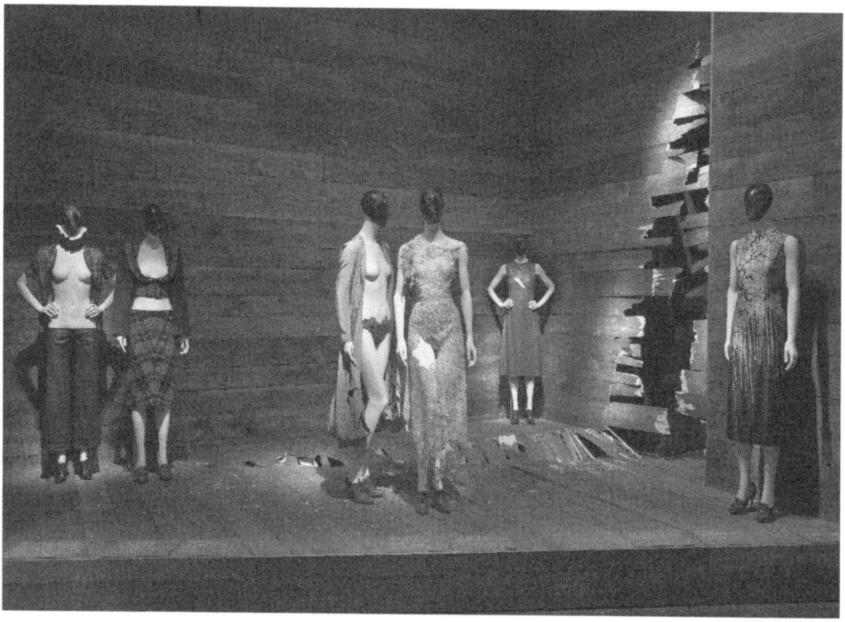

Figure 1.2 A gallery from the exhibition "Alexander McQueen: Savage Beauty" featuring work from McQueen's "Highland Rape" collection of fall/winter 1996–1997. Andrew Bolton curated the exhibition which featured set design by longtime McQueen collaborators Gainsbury & Whiting, as well as headpieces by Guido Palau. Image © The Metropolitan Museum of Art.

References

Harris, Ruth Green (1939), "How Americans Dressed: Museum of Costume Art Recalls the Brave Spectacle of Decades Now Long Sped," in: *New York Times*, July 23, 1939, p. X7.

Jewell, Edward Alden (1937), "Artists Congress Opens Show Today," in: *New York Times*, April 16, 1937, p. 21.

New York Times (1915), "The Neighborhood's Year," in: *New York Times*, October 10, 1915, p. 100.

New York Times (1937), "Costume Exhibit Opens: Includes Garments From Many Nations and Books About Them," in: *New York Times*, May 4, 1937, p. 28.

New York Times (1942a), "Garments of Korea, India and Other Lands Illustrate Simple, Economical Use of Cloth," in: *New York Times*, April 17, 1942, p. 13.

New York Times (1942b), "Fabrics From Trees Shown at Museum," in: *New York Times*, July 16, 1942, p. 21.

New York Times (1944), "Costume Branch for Metropolitan," in: *New York Times*, December 12, 1944, p. 20.

Pope, Virginia (1945), "Results of Union of Museums Strikingly Seen at Style Show," in: *New York Times*, March 21, 1945, p. 20.

2

UNDERSTANDING FASHION THROUGH THE MUSEUM

José Teunissen

"Until fairly recently, most museum exhibitions of clothing tended to be antiquarian in their approach and chronological in their organization. Typically, these exhibitions consisted of a display of upper-class women's fashions, organized to show the temporal succession of styles," writes fashion scholar and museum director, Valerie Steele (2008: 10) in the academic journal *Fashion Theory*'s themed issue, "Exhibitionism." This has indeed been the approach for almost all pre-1970s fashion and dress museum presentations. Fashion and fashion history were presented as a historic succession of styles. History was most likely brought to life through actual outfits whose fabrics, detailing, and origins were key; the historic context of the garment was illustrated by reference to the wearer's background (Taylor 1998: 317).

A turning point occurred in the 1970s when Diane Vreeland, an ex-editor of American *Vogue*, became special consultant to the Costume Institute of New York's Metropolitan Museum of Art and started curating exhibitions (Palmer 2008: 32; Steele 2008: 10). Vreeland drastically changed the presentation form of the Costume Institute by employing stylized, lifelike mannequins, window-dressing techniques, and dramatic lighting (Palmer 2008: 32). She hoped that these theatrical techniques would bring more "life" into the exhibition and entice a larger public.[1] Even more significantly, however, Vreeland curated her exhibitions from a contemporary perspective. She considered it important that the clothing on display have an up-to-date look, even if this look was not historically accurate: the result had to be attractive and recognizable to the wider public. "Everything must look *Now*," was her credo, and it was one to which she sacrificed historical accuracy (Dwight 2002: 210; Palmer 2008: 42). For instance, in displaying the clothing for the 1980 special exhibition "The Manchu Dragon: Costumes of China" she took her guide not from the symbolism of the clothing, but quite consciously gave the outfits the layered look and mix-and-match style that was typical of the 1980s and therefore conformed with the taste of the times (Steele 2008: 190). Vreeland gave her subject visual contemporaneity, as it were, by adapting it to the fashion tastes and aesthetics of the moment. In doing so, actual history—the sartorial aspect—was sometimes given short shrift.

In *Fashion Theory*'s themed issue, curators such as Alexandra Palmer (Royal Ontario Museum, Canada) and Valerie Steele (The Museum at the Fashion Institute of Technology, New York) distance themselves in part from this approach. While they have great admiration for the seduction perspective and for the visual forms of thematization, they lament the lack of depth and accuracy. "People need to be seduced into really seeing and identifying with fashion before they can begin to learn about it. Museum visitors are also becoming ever more visually sophisticated, and exhibition design is increasingly important," says Steele. "At the same time, I believe that a significant percentage of museum visitors really want to learn something when they see an exhibition. There is no reason why exhibitions cannot be both beautiful *and* intelligent, entertaining *and* educational" (Steele 2008: 14).

Steele therefore concludes that a good contemporary fashion exhibition should be both entertaining and seductive in form, historically accurate in content, and provide insight into the phenomenon of fashion. But in what way might a fashion exhibition legitimately place clothing objects in a new and broader context? How and why have museums become established as an ideal platform for avant-garde fashion presentations since the 1980s?

These are the central questions addressed in this chapter. First, an analysis of several fashion exhibitions of the last decades will make clear that both fashion scholars and museums have started understanding fashion from a broader perspective. In addition, literature and more specifically the studies of fashion curator Richard Martin (2009) and philosopher Gilles Lipovetsky (1994) help to bring forward why and how the fashion system from the 1960s on underwent major changes and started to evoke overtly political and cultural comments on society and the fashion system. Finally I will argue that avant-garde fashion designers have altered the fashion system from presenting a feminine ideal into a conceptualization of fashion as a system (a formal approach to the design process and the construction of fashion) (Martin 2009; Teunissen 2009), storytelling (to reveal clothing with traces and emotions) (Vinken 2009), and a focus on experiential design (a process where the non-visual imagery becomes as important as the product itself) (Lipovetsky and Manlow 2009). These elements in particular, with a strong resemblance to the art world, make contemporary museums, and particularly the specialized fashion museum, the ideal environment for understanding an avant-garde fashion presentation.

Establishing fashion as a cultural phenomenon in art museums

When "Streetstyle: From Sidewalk to Catwalk" opened at London's Victoria & Albert Museum (V&A) in 1994, it was one of the most significant fashion exhibitions to be based on cultural theory and the book *Subculture* by Dick Hebdige (Steele 2008: 23).[2] For the first time, the starting point was not a series of collected garments and artifacts but an underlying vision. The exhibition showed how since the 1950s a variety of youth cultures had been creating distinctive identities for themselves using self-selected clothing, looks, and music. In displaying this variety of clothing cultures and lifestyles, the display was effectively portraying the processes of democratization and individualization that had marked the 1960s fashion system; it showed perfectly how the transience and fickleness of fashion trends reveal deeper, underlying societal processes—in short, it illustrated how fashion functions as a cultural phenomenon. Up to this point, using an exhibition to reveal concepts and societal processes had been the almost exclusive preserve of the visual arts; using dress and fashion in this way was new to the art museum world. Right up to the 1960s, museum dress and fashion collections were usually part of the domain of the applied arts department within these museums. Most collections were composed of luxurious, exclusive pieces donated by elitist families.[3] For each fashion object, careful research was carried out into crafting techniques and tailoring and into who had worn it and on what occasion. Dress and fashion, in short, were collected as separate historic and aesthetic artifacts, described in terms of style, form, fabric, craft, and the personal history of the wearer (Taylor 1998: 317).

The context of fashion: a new and thematic approach

In the 1960s, when fashion was democratized and transformed from an exclusive luxury product for the elite into a clothes culture accessible to the masses, the museum world was forced to adjust its perspective. After all, what would have to be collected in order to follow and display the most important developments in contemporary fashion—haute couture? The newest Paris *prêt-à-porter*? Street fashion? More important still, how was this contemporary fashion to be studied? It would no longer be sufficient to focus on the clothing object itself; an eye would have to be developed for the societal and political context of clothing, and for the fact that fashion was now being expressed in a number of disciplines.

This interest in context has been widely shared by museums, including fashion museums, in recent decades. Fashion, like media, was now seen as an interesting form of popular visual culture, which gave expression to essential aspects of our social culture (Lipovetsky 1994: 149). This new approach also had an influence on the exhibition of historic dress; this was now given a broader, more thematic approach, and sometimes mixed historic clothing with modern fashions. For instance, in 1999 the Kyoto Costume Institute of the National Museum of Modern Art in Kyoto held an exhibition, "Visions of the Body: Fashion or Invisible Corset," curated by the Japanese fashion scholar Akiko Fukai, which showed historic corsets in combination with a Stockman (1997) bodice by the avant-garde Belgian fashion designer Martin Margiela. This wearable Stockman corset, made out of the same linen as the Stockman mannequin, created an alternative corset; a bodice on which you could start the process of designing by adding pieces of fabric and loose drapery. It was Margiela's avant-garde answer to the revival of haute couture where the British fashion designers Alexander McQueen (working at the time for the fashion house of Givenchy, Paris) and John Galliano (working for the fashion house of Dior, Paris) reinvented and explored traditional craftsmanship in combination with a mix-and-match styling and experimental design methods. In this manner Fukai's exhibition underlined major changes in the fashion industries of the mid-1990s where haute couture became the most important vehicle for creativity. About the exhibition Fukai stated: "The exhibition is an attempt to re-evaluate the future relationship between clothes and the body, focusing on how artists interpret parts which fashion has not yet actualized clearly. What comes out is the multi-structure of fashion culture [. . .] The corset is fashion, in other words, a social framework which always exists within" (Fukai 1999: 193).

Fukai's exhibition was focusing on understanding fashion as a cultural phenomenon. The exhibition Steele devoted to the corset at about the same time, "The Corset: Fashioning the Body" (2000) at The Museum at the Fashion Institute of Technology in New York, was chiefly concerned with "the changing *meanings* of the corset in society" (Steele 2008: 26). In both exhibitions, dress and fashion objects were given a central role but at the same time they formed part of, and were embedded within, a broader sociocultural historic narrative. It made the public aware not only of how the shape and aesthetics of the corset had changed over time, but also of the cultural values and the body-imagery going along with it.

> [. . .] it is too simple to say that it [*The Corset: Fashioning the Body* (2000) JT] is just a question of fashion versus liberation and that the corset is not to be taken simply as an instrument of the oppression of women. The corset is something the meaning of which people in different times and places have reconstructed themselves and which in fact is continuing to be part of the vocabulary of fashion and of the body-imagery.
>
> Steele 2004: 77

Contextualization of fashion in a museum

In the exhibitions I curated in Utrecht's Centraal Museum[4] in the period 2000–2005 I invariably took as a starting point a current fashion theme whose underlying layers I wished to bring to the surface. In 2000 I curated with Ida van Zijl an exhibition on "Droog & Dutch Design" in which we showed how Dutch fashion designers such as Alexander van Slobbe and Viktor&Rolf were working within the same philosophy—Dutch modernism—as product designers like Hella Jongerius, Richard Hutten, and Marcel Wanders (Teunissen and Van Zijl 2000). For the exhibition "Woman by" (2003), nine fashion houses, including Maison Martin Margiela, Ann Demeulemeester, Dior, and Viktor&Rolf, were asked to design an installation which expressed their own vision of the feminine ideal in fashion and their idea of femininity (Teunissen 2004). With this exhibition I wanted not only to show that today's fashion designers were working with a very different image of women, but also to emphasize that for fashion designers like Martin Margiela and Hussein Chalayan the design concept comes first and the chosen model serves merely as a vehicle for its presentation. For example, Margiela's catwalk models are often blindfolded, so as not to distract the audience's eyes from the clothes. Hussein Chalayan developed an installation, *Kinship Journeys* (2003), in which a trampoline, a confessional booth, and a boat/coffin together represent the three essential phases of life. The three objects were originally made for the exhibition "Woman by," but were removed from the exhibition for two days to serve as décor for the presentation of the collection of the same name in Paris. On the one hand, the theme of "Woman by" made it clear that contemporary fashion design has become much more conceptual and that the design concept itself has taken center stage. On the other hand, it also showed how ideals of femininity, in today's post-feminist age, are defined in different ways by different fashion designers (Teunissen 2004: 63–77). Where Vivienne Westwood and Veronique Leroy presented classical femininity and the game of seduction as "empowerment" of the modern woman, Ann Demeulemeester depicted a feminist emancipated woman: delicate, soft, elfin-like who comes across tough and nonchalant at the same time.

The exhibition "Global Fashion, Local Tradition" (2005) illustrated how, while the internet has made fashion more global, it also calls on a sense of local identity by using regional crafts (Teunissen 2005). I occupied a professorship with ArtEZ in Arnhem during both exhibitions, and was able to carry out extensive research together with Fashion & Strategy MA students into both relevant literature and specific designers.

These exhibitions always took (crucial) objects as their foundation, but the underlying concepts and narratives were visualized by means of films, installations, lighting, and scenography—the most appropriate way to portray underlying layers and processes in contemporary fashion. In this way the

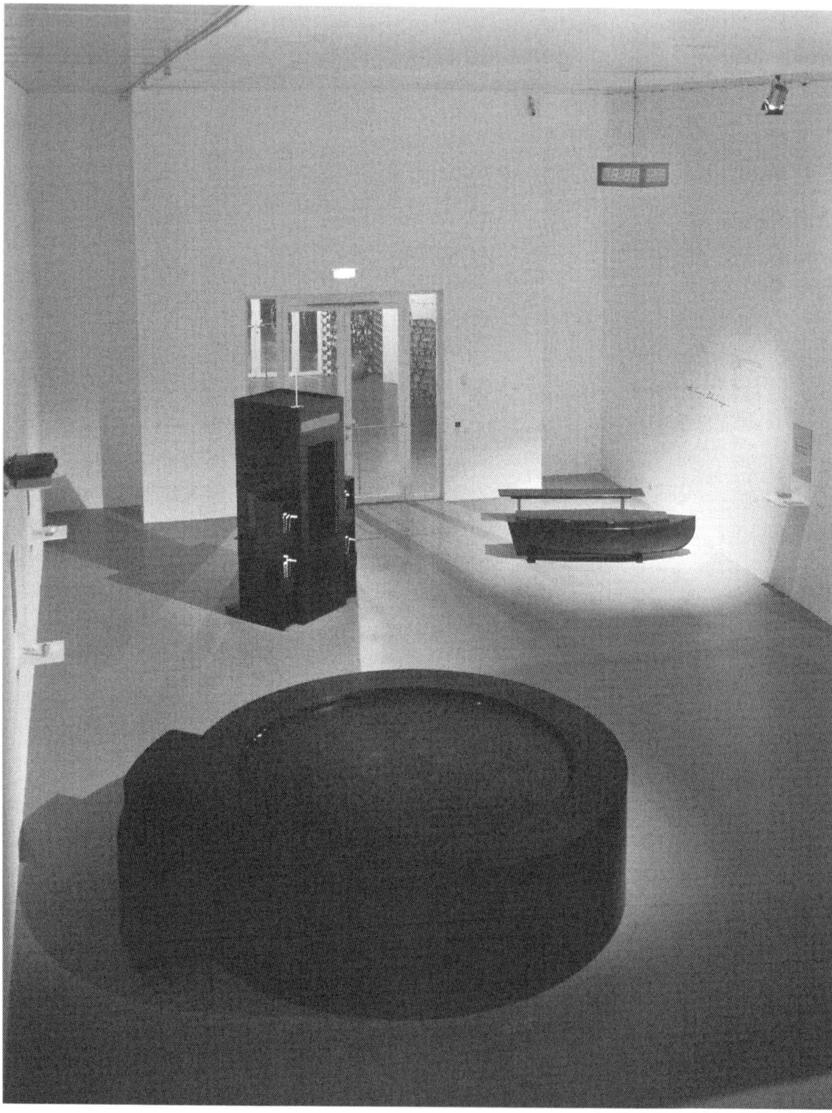

Figure 2.1 *Kinship Journeys* (2003) was specially developed by Hussein Chalayan for the exhibition "Woman by Hussein Chalayan." A trampoline, a confessional booth, and a boat/coffin represented together the three essential phases of life. Image and copyrights Centraal Museum Utrecht/Ernst Moritz.

exhibitions tried to be both entertaining and seducing in form, historically accurate in content, and provide insight into the phenomenon of fashion. In all cases the selected objects and their aesthetics remained crucial in the presentations, in that they were not merely a manifestation or illustration of an underlying idea (Haxthausen 2003; Steele 2008: 25). But what exactly changed in the fashion system during the 1960s and what was the impact for the museum at the beginning of the twenty-first century?

Fashion as popular culture: a new vision, a new approach

In the 1960s fashion became not just a mass-market product, it also became part of a popular visual culture in which the media played an important role. This made fashion more complex. While the object, the fashion designer, and the wearer had been important, now also the societal context in which fashion operated became of increasing importance (Teunissen 2009: 11). Suddenly, fashion was no longer all about the presentation of a feminine ideal and the display of wealth. A scenography of elegance had been replaced by a theatricality of meaning (Lipovetsky 2002: 8). Clothes allowed us not only to create our own identities, but to consciously propagate political ideals, as punks did with printed T-shirts. In the twenty-first century, fashion designer Hussein Chalayan used installations such as "Afterwords" (a/w 2000), "Kinship Journeys" (2003), "Readings" (2008), and "Micro Geography" (2009) in art museums to raise political and societal issues such as migration, alienation, and the effects of globalization on daily life. In short, I would argue, fashion could now deliver a message beyond an aesthetic expression of style. At the same time, the fact that fashion could arise on the street meant that it was no longer a product made by a designer for a consumer; this hierarchy disappeared and was replaced by a dialogue, an exchange between fashion designer and wearer, in which the media played a crucial role (Martin 2009: 27). These changes transformed fashion into an important phenomenon of our visual culture whose social impact and manifestations have become increasingly important (Lipovetsky 1994: 88).

In this way, from the 1960s onwards, fashion increasingly became an expression of ideas and concepts. The fashion avant-garde had escaped the straitjacket of the functional demands traditionally made by the applied arts: fashion had become the product of a design which was "attached" to the human body, but which also researched and explored its own relationship with this body, with identity, self-image, and environment. In doing so it had come to strongly resemble Pop Art and the performance art emerging in the visual arts (Teunissen 2009: 24). "In forming this liaison with art and in marrying Pop Art specifically, what did contemporary fashion accomplish? It became avant-garde in sensibility, it came under and drew from the thrall of popular culture, and it became the nexus of democratic social values and the clarifying aesthetic order of art" (Martin 2009: 27).

This new interdisciplinarity implied that fashion no longer ideally had to be presented on a catwalk or in a store: new fashion designs could also be launched in new and less commercial environments such as the street, the media, or the art museum.

Fashion studies and their influence on the fashion exhibition

The fashion developments of the 1960s also changed attitudes towards fashion in academic circles. Newer disciplines such as cultural studies, visual culture, and women's studies shared this new interest in fashion as part of popular culture. They started studying fashion much more as a cultural phenomenon than was the case in classic art history studies, in which the object itself, its history, and its place in dress history are central. Valerie Steele argues:

> Traditional art historical practice associated with the museum emphasizes close description and connoisseurship, while the so-called "new" art history as practised in the university draws on alternative approaches and methodologies derived from cultural studies. The new art history, in turn, helped give birth to what might be called the "new" fashion history, which also placed greater emphasis on analysing *meanings* of cultural objects and practices.
>
> Steele 2008: 25

This new approach towards fashion has been met with some suspicion by traditional museum curators trained in the discipline of dress history as a subdiscipline of art history, because the approach diverted attention from the object or artifact and its aesthetics radically towards the manifestation of an underlying idea, with the clothes themselves forming no more than an illustration (Haxthausen 2003; Steele 2008: 25). In this respect the exhibition "Malign Muses" (2004) curated by Judith Clark for The Mode Museum (MoMu) in Antwerp, later also appearing with the exhibition title "Spectres: When Fashion Turns Back" in London's V&A (2005), became heatedly debated among dress and fashion curators and researchers. Based on the ideas put forward in the book *Fashion at the Edge* (Evans 2003), which showed how experimental fashion designers of the 1990s depicted themes such as death, trauma, and alienation, Clark tried to visualize these ideas using a variety of installations; the clothing she had chosen to accompany the installation served as incidental illustrations rather than central exhibits. Not all her professional colleagues appreciated the move. "Ideas and settings dominated the clothes," complained Lou Taylor (2006: 17). Fashion researcher Christopher Breward, on the other hand, considered the exhibition a success and saw it as an effective new form of exhibition for fashion (Breward 2008: 91). The controversial point here was that the concept of the curator overshadowed the fashion objects themselves. The critical comment was directed towards an overly liberal interpretation and visualization, however compelling and inviting this may be.

Conceptual fashion: explaining the idea behind the object

Fashion designers themselves have been altering essential components of classical fashion since the 1970s. For Viktor&Rolf, the environment of an art museum or gallery has always been an ideal platform for the presentation of their ideas. "To us, fashion represents more than just cloth and form. We turn the phenomenon of fashion into its own subject matter. We have expressed and reflected on that very position in various ways through various media, in an art context but also within the context of fashion" (*T Magazine* 2008).

The question here is why these fashion designers have chosen the art museum as an ideal platform and how the art museum helped them to bring forward their concepts and ideas. And how do designers define the relationship between the exhibited object and the context?

In the early 1980s, the Japanese designers Yohji Yamamoto and Rei Kawakubo of Comme des Garçons were the first conceptual fashion designers. Both designers played with the traditional patterns of western clothing, mixing them with elements of Japanese clothing styles or combining them in unorthodox ways (Fukai 2006: 291), seeking and pushing the boundaries of the classic fashion garment. Like a modernist artist, Kawakubo had chosen a formal or formalistic starting point In her designs: "[. . .] just as abstraction in art usually depends on an underlying knowledge of traditional drawing skills, so pattern-making at Comme des Garçons is rooted in a thorough grounding in basic principles, which are then subverted' (Sudjic 1990: 31). The innovative thing about Rei Kawakubo was that she focused on the processes of clothing design and construction. She was one of the first designers to develop (together with architect Takao Kawasaki), shops and spaces in which the philosophy of her clothes could find ideal expression. It was a universe in which the product itself was given maximum attention, within an interior design, which could hardly be distinguished from a museum or gallery.

Fashion, storytelling, and experience design

Along with these experiments with form, themes such as melancholy, decay, and ageing made their introduction in contemporary fashion design from the 1980s onwards. Maison Martin Margiela started to focus on second-hand clothes, since these have already been "embodied" with life and therefore contain their own meanings. The fashion researcher Barbara Vinken suggested that after the 1980s avant-garde fashion design no longer focused on the "new," but designed "time" to display the signs of mortality that fashion had so stubbornly effaced in the past. In the postmodern age the awareness of transitoriness—long explored in detail in literature and the visual arts—was no longer excluded, but became an essential part of fashion. Fashion designers such as Alexander McQueen, Yohji Yamamoto, and Martin Margiela regularly revealed clothes' "traces and emotions." In addition, new presentation forms in galleries and museums were explored which brought these stories to the surface.

In the work of Viktor&Rolf the design concept is not at the forefront but the designs and the imaginary worlds they inhabit are inextricably linked. Since the start of their label in 1993 they often used museum and galleries for their fashion presentations: "[. . .] we always have mixed feelings when it comes to fashion exhibitions because somehow, life is taken out of the subject. But a museum show is also a more democratic way of showing fashion than a catwalk presentation. It allows us to explore perspectives and ideas beyond that format" (*T Magazine* 2008).

The retrospective exhibition "The House of Viktor&Rolf" (2008) for the Barbican Art Gallery in London, curated by the fashion design duo, illustrated perfectly how their designs and imaginary world are connected. At the heart of the exhibition was a 5-meter high dolls' house, inside which all their collections were recreated—in miniature—on classic porcelain dolls. Viktor&Rolf had created a fairy-tale with an unsettling effect, for their designs were not displayed in miniaturized versions alone; in adjoining rooms the original designs were displayed on the same, but now life-sized, dolls. For a viewing public accustomed to skinny models and equally skinny mannequins, seeing these dresses on large, chubby dolls was a shock. The macabre aesthetic—such beautiful dresses on such childish dolls' bodies—prodded the public into thinking anew about beauty ideals in fashion.

This exhibition illustrated clearly how the museum had become an ideal platform for fashion designers such as Viktor&Rolf. When Hussein Chalayan developed "Kinship Journeys" (2003) for the Centraal Museum he stated: "The aura of the museum, the installations, I need these in order to render my ideas visible" (Teunissen 2003: 68).

Summing up, for avant-garde fashion designers the museum or gallery appears to be a necessary component of their fashion brand's strategy; the world of the brand is complete and shown to best advantage when it appears in a museum or gallery in all its manifestations.

This encounter between museum and contemporary fashion design, I would claim, is both the result of and the reason for, the new exhibition practices of

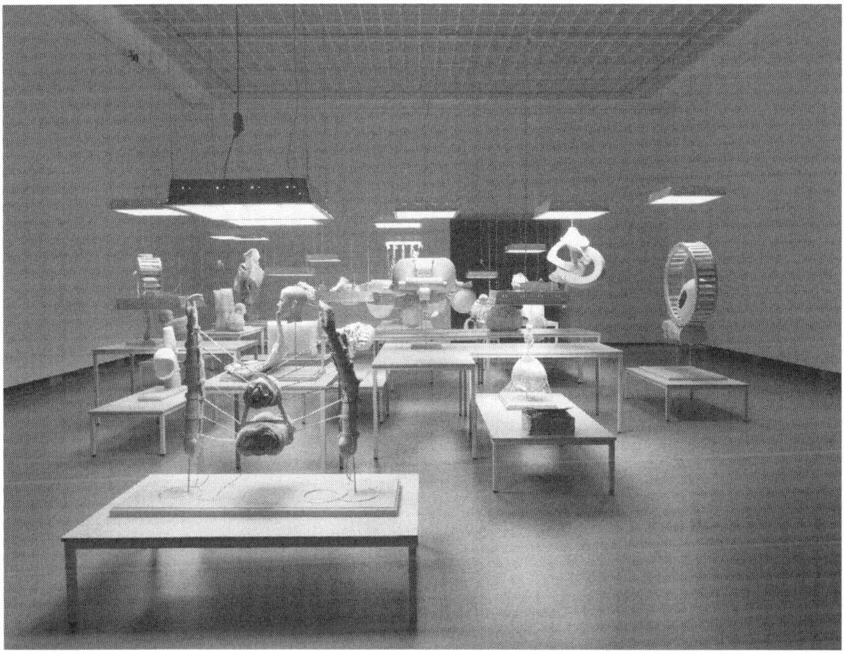

Figure 2.2 In the installation *No ~~References~~* (2008), the Belgium fashion designer Christophe Coppens explored the boundaries of accessories by dividing the body into thirty-three pieces and examining the possibilities for accessorizing each body without references to history, art, design, or fashion. Museum Boijmans Van Beuningen, Rotterdam. Loan from Han Nefkens' H + F Fashion on the Edge Foundation. Photography by Studio Hans Wilschut. Credit: B 611 1-32 (KN&V).

fashion presently. The tangible object—a wearable dress or installation—is given space center stage. But at the same time it is part of a broader conceptual, storytelling narrative of the designer. In form and approach these self-curated presentations do not differ from an exhibition curated by a museum curator. Only the viewpoint is different: where the museum curator is showing fashion objects in a broader cultural context, the fashion designer is primarily explaining the object and installation in the context of his or her own conceptual work.

Conclusion

In general, from the 1960s onwards, fashion transformed into an artistic expression of ideas and concepts. Fashion became the product of a design which was attached to the human body, but which also researched and explored its own relationship with this body, with identity, self-image, and the social environment. Fashion studies and new art history as well as the new fashion museums helped give birth to this new fashion narrative, which placed greater emphasis on fashion as a part of our media-driven and social culture and less on fashion as a tangible object.

Since a good contemporary fashion exhibition should, as modern curators agree on, be both entertaining and seductive in form, historically accurate in content, and provide insight into the phenomenon of fashion as part of a larger narrative, it seems no longer adequate to display clothing objects, as the classical museum did, only within the personal context of the wearer. The discussion now focuses on exactly how a fashion exhibition might legitimately place clothing objects in a new and broader context.

This approach has been met with some suspicion by museums and more traditional museum curators, because it diverts attention radically towards the manifestation of an underlying idea in fashion design, but as long as the object or installation is taken center stage a broader narrative is permitted.

For the fashion public the museum has become a "new" place for understanding the work of avant-garde fashion designers as well as for understanding fashion as part of our contemporary visual culture in the same manner as has been applied to understanding the visual arts. And (fashion) curators and museums have started to learn how to deal with fashion designers working like artists in very close contact and dialogue.

Notes

1 Clothing on mannequins, after all, looks dead; a problem in exhibiting clothing is that the living body is absent, and a substitute for it must be found.

2 The exhibition was accompanied by the publication of the book *Streetstyle* by anthropologist Ted Polhemus, who as its creator and curator interpreted the exhibition from an anthropological viewpoint.

3 In the Netherlands, the Rijksmuseum in Amsterdam, the Gemeentemuseum in Den Haag, and the Centraal Museum in Utrecht have extensive dress collections dating from the eighteen-century to the present day. There is also a separate museum of regional dress in Arnhem.

4 The Centraal Museum in Utrecht has one of the largest costume and dress collections in the Netherlands, and also collects contemporary fashion.

References

Breward, C. (2008), "Between the Museum and the Academy: Fashion Research and its Constituencies," in: *Fashion Theory*, Oxford: Berg, pp. 83–95.

Dwight, E. (2002), *Diana Vreeland*, New York: HarperCollins.

Evans, C. (2003), *Fashion at the Edge*, London: Yale University Press.

Fukai, A. (1999), "Visions of the Body," in: *Visions of the Body*, Kyoto: Kyoto Costume Institute, pp. 190–193.
Fukai, A. (2006), "Japan and Fashion," in J. Brand and J. Teunissen (eds), *The Power of Fashion: On Design and Meaning*, Arnhem: Terra/ArtEZ Press, pp. 288–314.
Haxthausen, C. (ed.) (2003), *The Two Art Histories – The Museum and the University*, Worcester, MA: Clark Studies in Visual Arts.
Lipovetsky, G. (1994), *The Empire of Fashion: Dressing Modern Democracy*, New York: Princeton University Press.
Lipovetsky, G. (2002), "More than Fashion," in: *Chic Clicks*, Ostfildern: Hatje Cantz Publishers.
Lipovetsky, G. and V. Manlow (2009), "The 'Artilization' of Luxury Stores," in: J. Brand and J. Teunissen (eds), *Fashion and Imagination*, Arnhem: d'jonge Hond/ArtEZ Press, pp. 154–168.
Martin, R. (2009), "Beyond Appearances and Beyond Custom: The Avant-garde Sensibility of Fashion and Art since the 1960s," in: J. Brand and J. Teunissen (eds), *Fashion and Imagination*, Arnhem: d'jonge Hond/ArtEZ Press, pp. 26–44.
Palmer, A. (2008), "Untouchable: Creating Desire and Knowledge in Museum Costume and Textile Exhibitions," in: *Fashion Theory*, Oxford: Berg, pp. 31–65.
Steele, V. (2004), "The Corset," in J. Brand and J. Teunissen (eds), *The Ideal Woman*, Nijmegen: SUN/ArtEZ Press, pp. 77–80.
Steele, V. (2008), "Museum Quality: The Rise of the Fashion Exhibition," in: *Fashion Theory*, Oxford: Berg, pp. 7–31.
Sudjic, D. (1990), *Rei Kawakubo and Comme des Garçons*, London: Westbourne Grove.
T Magazine (2008), "For the Moment | Viktor&Rolf," June issue.
Taylor, L. (1998), "Doing the Laundry? A Reassessment of Object-based Dress History," in: *Fashion Theory*, Oxford: Berg, 2(4), pp. 337–358.
Taylor, L. (2000), "Review of 'Spectres: When Fashion Turns Back'," in: *The Art Book*, 13(1), pp. 16–18.
Teunissen, J. (2003), "Woman by", Utrecht: Centraal Museum.
Teunissen, J. (2004), "Knocking Woman off her Pedestal," in: J. Brand and J. Teunissen (eds), *The Ideal Woman*, Nijmegen: SUN/ArtEZ Press, pp. 63–77.
Teunissen, J. (2005), "Global Fashion, Local Tradition," in: J. Brand and J. Teunissen (eds), *Global Fashion, Local Tradition*, Arnhem: Terra/ArtEZ press, pp. 8–23.
Teunissen, J. (2009), "Fashion and Art," in: J. Brand and J. Teunissen (eds), *Fashion and Imagination*, Arnhem: d'jonge Hond/ArtEZ Press, pp. 10–25.
Teunissen, J. and I. Van Zijl (2000), *Droog & Dutch Design*, exhibition catalog, Central Museum, Utrecht.
Vinken, B. (2009), "Fashion: Art of Dying, Art of Living," in J. Brand and J. Teunissen (eds), *Fashion and Imagination*, Arnhem: d'jonge Hond/ArtEZ Press, pp. 82–92.

3
CONTEMPORARY FASHION HISTORY IN MUSEUMS

Marco Pecorari

Between April 2010 and May 2011, Musée Des Arts Décoratifs in Paris presented two exhibitions entitled "Historie idéale de la mode contemporaine vol. I: '70–'80" and "Historie idéale de la mode contemporaine vol. II: '90–'00." Curated by Olivier Saillard, these two exhibitions were organized through a chronological narrative that showcased in diverse boxes the work of the most famous international fashion designers of the period: from Yves Saint Laurent and Thierry Mugler to Jean Paul Gaultier and Maison Martin Margiela. As explained in the catalog, the exhibition aimed to show fashion designers' ideas of fashion, interpreting them as the foundation of contemporary fashion history. Although these two exhibitions were not the first attempt to create a historical discourse on contemporary fashion, "Historie idéale de la mode contemporaine vol. I & II" represented one of the most recent and outspoken attempts, made by an established fashion museum, to systemize the concept of contemporary fashion history. Whereas the creation of fashion exhibitions and fashion museums focusing on contemporary fashion has represented a diffused phenomenon in the last thirty years (Steele 2008), Musée Des Arts Décoratif's exhibitions proposed an interesting neologism to reflect on. What do we mean by contemporary fashion history? How are fashion museums relating to this definition and to contemporary fashion at large?

Only a terminological issue?

As Alexandra Palmer argues, the continuous proliferation of alternative forms of exhibiting dress in connection with some specific economic and practical museological reasons brought many fashion museums to favor the exhibition of contemporary dress (Palmer 2008: 36). Such a turn from historical dress to contemporary dress brought diverse fashion museums to dismiss the important tradition of dress history while, at the same time, simplifying the current discussion on fashion history. Despite the important steps towards a critical approach to the concept of fashion history developed in museums and academia,[1] the international scenario still reports many examples of problematic approaches to the study of contemporary fashion history in museums. Examples of these misuses may be seen in the recent phenomenon of the transformation of many costume or dress museums into fashion museums, or in the proliferation of fashion museums that seem to emulate fashion industry practices rather than trying to critically analyze them.[2] As in "Historie idéale de la mode contemporaine vol. I & II," the use of terms like fashion, fashion history, or contemporary fashion history in exhibitions is often ambiguous and they are mostly used as unsaid synonyms for contemporary fashion design, contemporary fashion designers' creations or biographies. Furthermore, contemporary fashion designers' creations are often exhibited with similar methods used to exhibit historical dress, often reducing the discourse on contemporary fashion history into a hagiographic study of contemporary designers without a deep understanding of fashion design as a practice able to shape ideas on our contemporary society. Whereas the need to attract more audiences is both a clear and feasible reason behind this terminological change or behind designer focused exhibitions, these new nomenclatures hardly reflect an aligned curatorial strategy, showing an uncritical use of terms.

This chapter aims to explore these issues through the presentation of one of the most referenced fashion museums in the study of contemporary fashion: the Mode Museum in Antwerp (MoMu). MoMu is an interesting example to be observed as, since it opened in 2002, it has mainly focused on contemporary fashion and contemporary fashion designers. For this reason, my aim is not only to discuss the ways in which MoMu has used fashion design and designers in its museum practices but also to reflect on the possible effects of its practices in the understanding of contemporary fashion in fashion museums. This chapter is based on visits to the museum and its exhibitions (until September 2012), interviews with the director of the museum, as well as archival studies at the museum, including exhibition images, catalogs, and other documentary resources.[3]

Fashion designing the museum

MoMu officially opened on September 21, 2002 with "Backstage: Selection I." This exhibition aimed to reflect on the role of a fashion museum through staging MoMu's archive: acting as a sort of manifesto. The decision to stage the archive enshrined the multiple goals behind the creation of MoMu: from dedicating more attention to the visitor's experience by inviting them in the "behind the scenes,"

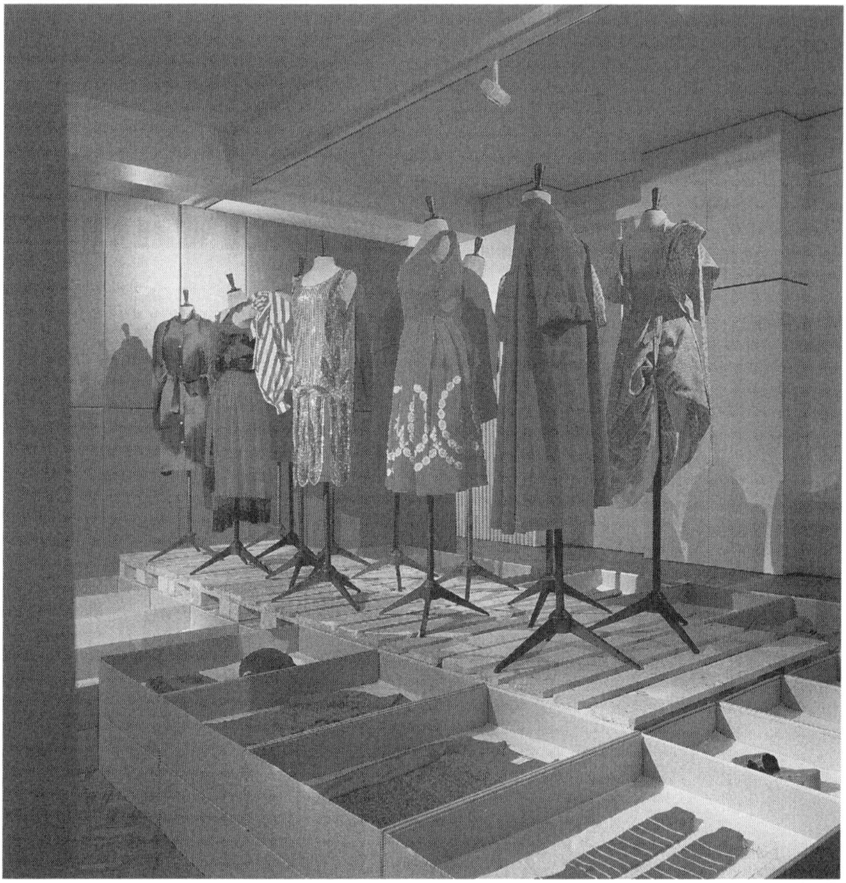

Figure 3.1 Backstage: Selection I, 2002. Image of the exhibition's hall. Copyright MoMu. Photography by Koen De Waal.

to exhibiting the archive as a living device and metaphor of a new approach to fashion history; passing through the introduction of spectacular and non-traditional scenographies that, in this case, performed the archive through the use of acid-free cardboard boxes where garments and other objects were showcased.

Created on the ashes of the Vrieselhof Museum (the old costume museum of Antwerp), MoMu did not only aim to create a rupture from the old museum but also from the international scenario of fashion museums. Since its first exhibition, the museum aimed to position itself in the international realm of fashion museums, strategically employing a different way to think about fashion in museums, and specifically orienting its exhibiting policy to contemporary fashion and fashion design. This decision was quite natural for this institution as its main mission was to institutionalize the work of the Antwerp fashion designers, who, at the beginning of the 1980s, started to attract international attention for their "resistance" to the established practices of the fashion system.[4] While a few scholars have already shown the role played by cultural institutions in the transformation of Antwerp into a fashion avant-garde city for touristic and commercial reasons (Martinez 2003), what has been overlooked is a deeper analysis of the museological formation and consequent practices of MoMu in order to better understand how this museum has become an international reference in only ten years. Indeed, the rise of MoMu has coincided with a specific museological strategy that, to some extent, brought the museum to mime the avant-garde role played by the Antwerp designers within the fashion system.

Firstly, the province of Antwerp decided to nominate as director Linda Loppa:[5] a fashion insider with no museological experience. Such a decision did not only indicate a drastic rupture with the previous traditional costume museum but also with the international atlas of fashion museums, following, to some extent, the controversial experience of Diana Vreeland as special consultant at the Costume Institute of The Met (Steele 2008; Clark and Frisa 2012). As the exhibition "Vreeland After Vreeland" held at Palazzo Mocenigo showed, the main legacy of Vreeland in fashion curating has been to introduce a new way of thinking about fashion in exhibitions, relying on her experience as editor of *Harper's Bazaar* and *Vogue* (Monti 2013). Similarly to Vreeland's experience, Loppa brought an "insider" view on fashion within a brand-new museum without the restriction and history of a more established institution like the Costume Institute of The Met. Such a lack of institutional heritage facilitated the strategies of Loppa who aimed to bring MoMu "very close to the fashion system, to be open to it, to look to the future and to help to shape it" (Furniss 2004).

Such proximity to the fashion system was reflected in many museum practices, starting with the decision to stage only temporary exhibitions every six months following the fashion industry's calendar. It was also decided to employ fashion professionals to collaborate with the museum. This was the case for the museum's scenographer Bob Verhelst, who previously collaborated with Maison Martin Margiela as visual merchandiser, or the graphic designer Paul Boudens, who constantly collaborates with many of Antwerp's designers. For MoMu, Boudens did not only create the museum's logo but also all the communication mediums of the museum: from posters to catalogs. The latter have been a quite distinctive work as they do not simply aim to report the images of the showcased objects but perform and deepen the exhibition, as in the case of the exhibition catalog for "Backstage: Selection I" where the cover resembles the boxes used for the exhibition's design and the sketches of the exhibition's design are included. Indeed, the decision to employ people working in the industry was not only due to the small size of Antwerp's fashion scene but also a conscious choice to align the realms of the museum and the designer.

Another relevant change that testifies to MoMu's affiliation to a new museology[6] is its constant challenge to improve the experience of visitors through curatorial decisions that resemble more the practice of commercialization of fashion rather than its musealization. While the museum favored the visual experience through the elimination of windows (when possible) and the captions in the exhibition hall,[7] the experience of visitors was on some occasions pursued through drastic and non-conventional decisions such as in the case of the retrospective exhibition on Yamamoto, "Dream Shop" (2007). Here the public could actually try the designers' creations in fitting rooms created within the exhibition hall.[8] Last but not least, the decision to dedicate 50 percent of the budget to the acquisition of contemporary fashion designers' garments avoided relying only on donations by private parties or fashion designers to build the contemporary fashion archive. This active collecting practice did not only include garments, accessories, and shoes but also a methodical collection of ephemera (invitations, catalogs, press releases, posters, etc.), audiovisual material, and other artifacts. Once again, this decision was stimulated by the nature of the three archives that constituted the base for MoMu's contemporary archive and that originally belonged to three "insiders" like Loppa, the fashion journalist Gerdi Esch, and the polyedric figure of Gert Bruloot. These three personal archives strongly contributed to "designing" MoMu's collection and more generally to its approach to contemporary fashion, as Debo argues in an interview published by the famous fashion blog "A Shaded View on Fashion by Diane Pernet."

> From the Belgian designers we not only collect the garments, but we also collect DVDs of their fashion shows, invitations, all the graphic work they make [. . .] books, invitations for special events, press releases. We do all this in order to give researchers complete overview of what the designers do, because fashion design is much more than only designing a garment or a collection. I see that a lot of bigger institutions, more traditional museums didn't think of all those ephemera. They just focus on the garment. [. . .] I guess we are one of the few museums that collect all these items.
>
> Belijanskin 2010

The above abstract helps to sum up two crucial considerations in the formation and nature of Antwerp's fashion museum. Firstly, it shows how MoMu acts as a gateway between the fashion industry and the public.[9] In fact, MoMu does not simply blur the boundaries between the industry and the museum but merges them, not only by adopting some practices of the industry but also by being formed by some current or former professionals. In this manner, MoMu becomes, or claims its role as, a unique or "one of the few," to use Debo's words, gatekeeper of contemporary fashion knowledge. Indeed, MoMu is a singular experience due to its closeness to the industry and for this reason it may act as an example for future investigations of the relationship between the industry and other cultural institutions like museum or academia.[10]

The second consideration that emerges concerns the museum's approach to fashion design and its practices. MoMu conceives dress within a process of creation of an idea of fashion design. As Debo argues, the museum is seen as "a context in which to place fashion, [. . .] which means not merely lingering on the final product—the piece of clothing—but paying as much attention to the artistic process" (Debo 2002: 11). This approach differentiates MoMu from more traditional methods of intending dress as the unique object of fashion in a museum: an approach that is often associated with dress history. By basing its approach on a specific idea of fashion design, MoMu proposes to employ the process of design as the idea on which to base its own approach to fashion. In this sense, the museum has not randomly adapted some practices used in the fashion industry but consciously employs and reflects this processual method of thinking about fashion in the museum: from the collecting to the exhibiting practices, passing through the transformation of the catalog, or by pushing the visitors' experiences. In this manner, MoMu mimes, in the fashion museum world, the role played by the Antwerp fashion designer in the fashion system. While designers like Van Beirendonck or Margiela problematize the practices and methods of fashion design, MoMu problematizes the ways fashion is approached in fashion museums. It employs the idea behind fashion design not only to represent fashion in exhibitions but also to critically re-translate it in the practice of the fashion museum.

Curating (with) the fashion designer

This blurring of the boundaries between museum and industry and the attention given to fashion design by MoMu is also reflected in one of the most peculiar curatorial strategies of the museum: inviting designers to curate (or co-curate) their own exhibitions. As the freelance curator Fiona Anderson argues, the collaboration between fashion designers and curators is undoubtedly an important aspect of fashion curation, and curators must embrace it in order to acknowledge the commercial character of the fashion industry (Anderson 2000). Such a practice is indeed implemented very often at MoMu: at present it has produced nineteen exhibitions of which ten have had a designer as curator.

The most diffused type of exhibition, involving the designer as curator, is the retrospective. In this area there have been established designers, like Maison Martin Margiela, new fashion designers like Bernhard Willhelm, and also students of the Academy whose works can be showcased in the downstairs gallery. As Debo affirmed on many occasions, MoMu does not wait for a designer to be established but looks at his/her capacity of expressing the "Antwerp fashion idea" (Debo 2011).

Far from being attempts to present the paradigm designer-as-artist, MoMu's retrospectives aim to recreate the idea of fashion that a designer develops through his/her work. The aim is to install, in the exhibition, the personal voice that characterizes Antwerp's designers. To achieve this, MoMu produces an impressive work on the exhibition's scenography. In this sense, MoMu's exhibition hall becomes a very dynamic and mutable space, especially when designers' retrospectives are hosted.

The best example of this spectacular scenography was probably "Het Totaal Rappel" (2007): the retrospective exhibition of Bernhard Willhelm. Indeed, Willhelm's exhibition revolutionized MoMu's exhibiting gallery thanks also to the work of the Swiss artists Tayo Onorato and Nico Krebs who curated the scenography. As Granata reports in her review (2009), Willhelm's references to carnival and the grotesque were rebuilt in the exhibition thanks to an impressive scenography that helped to deliver the designers' atmosphere. For example, in one exhibition room the curators created an enormous plastic mountain-like structure, housing Willhelm's collections which were decorated with small toys hanging all over the structure's walls. Moreover, a small toy train circled around the installed mountain. The atmosphere aimed to recall the childhood atmosphere that is a central element in the designer's creations.

The research of spectacle as a tool to recreate the atmosphere of designers' work does not always serve the purpose of a retrospective as it can be at odds with the crucial role played by the materiality of the objects. In many cases, the attempt to privilege the "feeling" of the designer's idea may overcome the explanation of the ways in which this feeling is embedded in the object. An example of this danger was "Moi, Veronique. Branquinho Toute Nue," held at MoMu in 2008. The exhibition consisted of a dramatic climax of rooms recalling the *Twin Peaks*' atmosphere used by the designer in her late collections and fashion shows. As the brochure reports, "the designer lets us look inside her ambiguous, suggestive world" and this statement sounds like the best explanation of the problem of having a designer as curator of his/her own exhibition. While the luxury of discussing and learning directly from the designer is a clear advantage for a museum, the danger of giving carte blanche to a designer may generate a lack of critical point of view, as the fashion scholar Stevenson (2008) argues.

This might also be the case for the last retrospective exhibition, "Walter Van Beirendonck: Dream the World Awake," which explored the last thirty years of work by the Antwerp designer. Visiting the show, it becomes difficult to differentiate MoMu's exhibition from Van Beirendonck's "Gallery window," which constitutes a section of his shop, placed a few hundred meters from the museum. The desire to recreate Walter's world distracts attention away from the very contribution that the designer generated in his thirty years of work in the fashion business. This becomes evident as the silhouettes confusingly occupy the main part of the space without any sort of path or internal dialogue that usually represents an important aspect of MoMu's exhibitions. Traditionally, an exhibition is developed through six different themes: fairy-tales, alien spirits, techno crafts, alterations, rituals, actions/reactions. However, on this occasion the itinerary of the exhibition was less articulated and visitors were not invited to any sort of conceptual articulation but were simply ask to admire the designer's creation from a very close position: the best element of the show. For the exhibition, MoMu interestingly commissioned a special project from the fashion photographer and founder of Showstudio.com, Nick Knight, who created a personal retrospective. The work consisted of a live broadcast shooting which created an impressive 360-degree print and video, showing once again how MoMu does not act as a canonical museum as it constantly blurs the boundaries between authorial and curatorial work.

Despite these curatorial issues, Van Beirendonck's exhibition was the most visited at MoMu with an average of 450 visitors per day. Once again, the enormous capacity of retrospective exhibitions to attract audiences must reflect the importance of the balance in contemporary fashion exhibitions between two elements: the objects and the exhibition design.[11]

This balance was probably totally achieved in the retrospective "20th The Exhibition: Maison Martin Margiela" (2008) which represented an interesting mixture between well-thought-out scenography and a clever selection of objects. If the idea of recreating a *trompe-l'oeil* effect in the exhibition rooms brought physical and conceptual dynamism to the exhibition, the selection of the themes and related showcased pieces gave to the visitor a clear and complete view on the designer's work. It may be a coincidence but the Margiela exhibition was entirely curated by MoMu's staff.[12]

The danger of the designer-curator is not only a lack of objectivity or critical view. The concept also relies on the disservice that such an exhibition may cause to the work of the designer. For example, Van Beirendonck's exhibition did not help people to understand his aesthetical and political contribution to contemporary culture, especially in relation to issues like gender identity or contemporary romanticism (see Debo 2011). In this sense, MoMu's example shows how fashion retrospectives are crucial opportunities to deliver the meaning of fashion as a contemporary cultural phenomenon: they are not simply an assemblage of spectacular garments or designers. The attempt to "curate with the designer" must be implemented by a "curation of the designer" as a critical action to explain his/her role in our contemporary visual culture. To some extent, MoMu has done this in the only two exhibitions that were curated by two Antwerp-trained fashion designers but were dedicated to specific themes and were not retrospectives. The first was "GenovaAnversaeviceversA" (2003) where the Italian Angelo Figus created an exhibition that narrated the historical commercial dialogues between the ports of Genova and Antwerp. The second was "Katarina Prospekt: the Russians by A.F. Vandevorst" (2005) where An Vandevorst and Filip Arickx showed their vision of Russia, through a selection of their creations and objects from the historic collection of the State Historical Museum in Moscow. In these two attempts, MoMu confirmed its approach to fashion designers as something more than simple dressmakers: as figures of contemporary culture, who create ideas through dress but also through other languages or formats such as exhibitions, for example.

The "new" fashion history and its objects

Another crucial way in which MoMu has used contemporary fashion design as a tool to read fashion history is through its objects produced within the process of design. In this sense, the most evident example was "Malign Muses: When Fashion Turns Back," curated by Judith Clark and held at MoMu in the 2004.[13] Created in collaboration with the Victoria & Albert Museum ((V&A) in London, "Malign Muses" was probably the exhibition that mostly clearly reflected on the practice of exhibiting contemporary fashion in museums as it aimed to reveal the relationship between contemporary fashion and its history. Outspokenly inspired by Caroline Evans' analysis of contemporary fashion in the book *Fashion at the Edge* from 2003, Clark staged the idea that contemporary fashion design is not simply a practice of creating dresses but can be read as a language through which to understand ideas of fashion. As Evans argues, contemporary creations "unlock the way in which the work of these designers—fragmented, episodic and emblematic—helps us to make sense of contemporary culture and its concerns" (Evans 2003: 13). Through a historicization of theory and specifically of works by Benjamin, Baudelaire, or Mallarmé, Evans does not simply read contemporary fashion poetics but produces an interesting method by which to read contemporary fashion ideas. Referring to Margiela's ragpickings or Galliano's spectacles, Evans explains how these two examples embody the two extreme poles of our modern and capitalist society. By doing this, the fashion scholar shows how designers act similarly to historians, creating ideas about our society by digging into the past and projecting it into the future. In this sense, fashion history is less seen as a chronological succession of events, objects, or people, but as a force that scrambles time in a constant tension between past, present, and future.

Evans' ideas on fashion history were spectacularly staged in Clark's exhibition that was divided into six thematic sections, aiming to explain diverse narratives belonging to contemporary fashion. The dress was considered as an element of a narrative and as such it assumed meaning only through its interaction with other objects. The object was not seen through a chronological succession of styles; the exhibition explained how fashion objects stimulate historical relations, which support our understanding of fashion mechanisms. Although this exhibition also attracted diverse critics on its misuse of objects (e.g. McNeil 2008), it may be seen as a three-dimensional manifesto of what has been defined as "new fashion history" (Anderson 2000; Steele 2008). This "new fashion history" develops a study of the mechanics of fashion where the past and the present are in constant dialectical dialogue, escaping any form of chronological progression, typically associated with dress history. Clark's exhibition revealed a process that, to some extent, was embedded in MoMu's approach to contemporary fashion history and outspokenly presented in "Backstage: Selection I and Patterns" (2003).

"Backstage: Selection I and Patterns" revoked the archive as a closed, dead repository of clothes and proposed it as an active, Derridian dimension where the contemporary dress is put in constant dialogue with the historical dress but with the other fashion materials (sketches, patterns, etc.). Similarly to the designers described by Evans, MoMu recognizes the archive as a place of constant historical re-elaboration, showing how materials' dialogues activate and suggest new creative processes of interpretation of fashion history. As Debo claims, MoMu interprets its collection "as a 'living' collection, a work in progress, conceiving the history of fashion not as a linear continuum but instead as a circular process" (Debo 2002: 11). This vision is not employed only in the historical reconstruction but it is constantly performed also in the curatorial strategies. In Maison Martin Margiela's exhibition, some mannequins were covered in calico clothes with the label "New Collection s/s '09. Presentation 2/10/08," waiting to be dressed with the creations of the last collection. Indeed, MoMu constantly challenges the exhibition's ontology and the role of the museum as a place where past, present, and future meet.

MoMu does not use only contemporary fashion designers or dresses as tools to unlock these historical dialogues but it has other objects belonging to the process of designing a garment. In this sense, the exhibition "Pattern/Patronen" (2003) represents the most clear example of how contemporary fashion design may be used to unlock fashion history. In this exhibition, MoMu concentrated on a technical element of fashion design as curators used the pattern to open up issues of fashion history. As Debo argues in the catalog: "From a technical standpoint, the pattern is a two-dimensional transition between the three-dimensional body and the finished piece of clothing. Every pattern carries within it the potential garment and, therefore, the potential body" (2003: 9).

The exhibition drew what I would define a "landscape of the pattern" which had two extreme poles: its physical technical element, on the one side, and its conceptual relation to the body, on the other side. In the exhibition, the pattern is recognized from its invisible but fundamental role in fashion design. The pattern was used for its translative capacity to decipher ideas of fashion and trigger multiple histories of fashion: from the role of the pattern-maker in design and his/

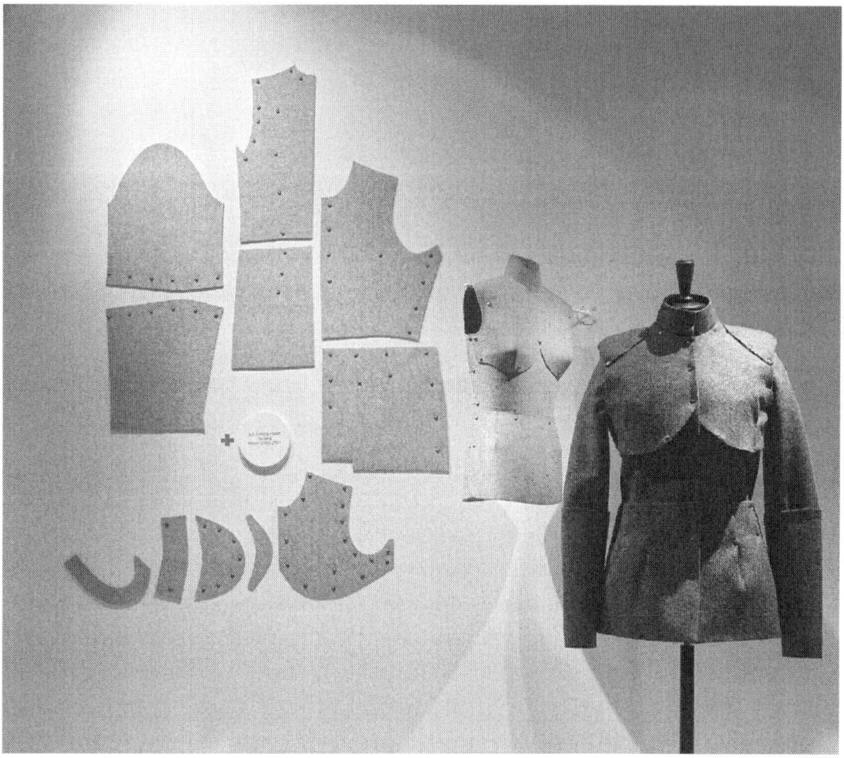

Figure 3.2 Patterns/Patronen, 2003. A.F. Vandevorst, a/w 2000/2001. Copyright MoMu. Photography by Koen De Waal.

her social condition, to the evolution of the measurement of the modern body; from the historical changing of pattern-making to patterns' capacity to translate designers' ideas into objects. In the exhibition, a technical ingredient of the design process showed not only how it is an element in the construction of a dress but that it can be used beyond its documentary function of helping to study the dress. MoMu's exhibition showed how a pattern can be used as a hermeneutical tool to unlock the heterogeneous nature of fashion as a phenomenon that deals with social identity, categorization of bodies, economic history, aesthetics, etc.

Concluding remarks

In this brief analysis of MoMu's experience, the aim has been to show the practice of a particular museum, which was created with a peculiar mission to institutionalize a specific category of contemporary fashion designers and concentrate on contemporary fashion. However, what has been shown is that MoMu has not simply celebrated this phenomenon by purely enhancing its value in the history of fashion design but uses its peculiar traits in order to perform its own practices. By doing so, I have shown how MoMu utilizes fashion design, its actors, and its materials as hermeneutical tools to read fashion history. The designers, contemporary fashion dresses, and fashion design may be used as tools to attract greater audiences, but also as tools to read past and current histories of fashion. MoMu's practices allow us to rethink the term "contemporary fashion history" in a more complex manner than just as a succession of recent fashion designers. In this sense, it can be useful to see this formula from the point of view of the philosopher Michel Serres, who argues that "contemporary" is a "multitemporal concept in which diverse times are compressed, related and folded together" (Serres and Latour 1990). Contemporary fashion history may be a complex neologism that helps to remind us how fashion and its practices compress past and present ideas of aesthetics, identity, economy, and society, and for this reason can be used to unlock these histories rather than hiding them. The recent work by the Galliera's director Olivier Saillard has gone in this direction, and he has started to use the practices, actors, or icons of the fashion industry to propose new performative and dynamic ways to read fashion history in museums. While in the exhibition "Models at Work" (2012) the catwalk became an archetype through which the study of a "history of model's pose" could be undertaken, in "The Impossible Wardrobe" (2012) Tilda Swinton carried and interpreted Galliera's historical pieces, portraying the fashion museum's conservator as a human device between past and present.

At the same time, it is important to highlight how MoMu's method has also reflected a common tendency of museums to concentrate on the production of contemporary fashion rather than on consumption or dissemination. The influence of Antwerp's designers brought MoMu to focus on a specific segment of contemporary fashion, partially overlooking other aspects of the wide scenario of contemporary fashion and its related history. If the work of the fashion designer may be used as a fruitful key to read our contemporary culture, this method could be enlarged to other forms of production, like mass-produced fashion, but also to the dissemination or consumption of contemporary fashion. To achieve this, fashion museums must concentrate more on other geographies of contemporary fashion: enlarging their discourses from the practice of producing high fashion to the analysis of our everyday practices of consuming and disseminating fashion. In this manner, the understanding of contemporary fashion history will not simply be unlocked through the work of designers and their creations but may be activated also through other contemporary fashion practices like the fashion buyer, mass market brands, the consumer, the fashion blogger, etc.

The enormous amount of material produced in the production, dissemination, and consumption of contemporary fashion could be used to produce new forms of museums where objects can become more important than the creator, brands can become more important than the product, the sketch more interesting than the final product, the consumer more important than the creator, and so on.[14] Basically, future fashion museums must actually understand contemporary fashion history as something that cannot be reduced merely to "some" objects or "some" names: a phenomenon that can be fully understood only through the dynamic exploration of its meanings and values.

Notes

1 To read more about this disciplinary debate see Taylor (1998) and Breward (2008).

2 An example of this change in the name is the former Museum of Costume in Bath, lately renamed the Fashion Museum. At the same time many museums have been instituted with the name "fashion museum" as in the case of the Fashion & Textile Museum in London (established in 2003), the Museo de la Moda in Santiago, Chile (established in 2006), or the Palazzo Morando—Costume Moda Immagine Milano (2010).

3 I would like to thank all MoMu staff, and in particular Birgit Ansoms, Kaat Debo, and Dieter Suls, for their patient and crucial help and support during my research.

4 To read more about the rise of the Belgian fashion designers see Evans (2003).

5 Linda Loppa is another fundamental figure in the affirmation of Antwerp as a fashion city. Graduated in fashion design at the Academy, she opened the first shop on international contemporary fashion, selling Japanese, Italian, and French creations. Always active in the fashion field, she began to teach at the Academy at the end of 1970s, becoming director in 1981.

6 Vergo (1989).

7 This decision was also taken due to the language problem as MoMu had to write its captions in three languages (Dutch, French, and English).

8 These garments of the exhibition did not belong to MoMu's collection but to Yamamoto's archive.

9 With the term "new museology" I refer to what Peter Virgo defined as a new approach to the study of museums as institutions that do not simply collect, conserve, study, and exhibit objects but as social institutions that must be examined also for their political, social, and economic purpose. To read more see Vergo (1989).

10 To read more about this relation see McNeil (2008).

11 To read more about the curatorial issue see Clark (2008), Frisa (2008), and Clark and Frisa (2012).

12 Pecorari (2008).

13 Although the exhibition is mostly known by the name "Spectres" used for its V&A appearance, here I will use the name that was given to the exhibition at MoMu.

14 This dynamic vision of the museum is rooted in the work of Raimonda Riccini; see Riccini (2003) and Maddalena Dalla Mura (2009).

References

Anderson, F. (2000), "Museum as a Fashion Media," in: S. Bruzzi and P. Church Gibson (eds), *Fashion Cultures: Theories, Explorations, and Analysis*, London: Routledge, pp. 371–389.

Belijanskin, T. (2010), "Interview with Kaat Debo, The Director of the Fashion Museum of the Province of Antwerp," in: *A Shaded View on Fashion by Diane Pernet*, published September 10, 2010, http://dianepernet.typepad.com/diane/2010/09/interview-with-kaat-debo-director-of-fashion-museum-momu-in-antwerp-by-tanja-beljanski.html [accessed 28 September 2012].

Breward, C. (2008), "Between the Academia and the Museum: Fashion Research and its Constituencies," in: *Fashion Theory: The Journal of Dress, Body & Culture*, 12: 83–93.

Clark, J. and A. de la Haye (2008), "One Object: Multiple Interpretation," in: *Fashion Theory. The Journal of Dress, Body & Culture*, 12, pp. 137–169.

Clark, J. and M.L. Frisa (eds) (2012), *Diana Vreeland after Diana Vreeland*, Venezia: Marsilio.

Dalla Mura, M. (2009), *Design e musei fra storia e nuovi approcci: Il contributo dei musei di scienza e tecnologia*, PhD thesis, doctoral programme in design sciences, supervisor: Raimonda Riccini, Doctoral School of the Università Iuav di Venezia, 20th cycle, a.y. 2008/2009.

Debo, K. (2002), "Backstage: The Fashion Museum," in *Backstage. Selection I*, Antwerp: MoMu, pp. 11–19.

Debo, K. (2003), "Patterns," in: *Patronen, Patterns, Patrons*, Antwerp: MoMu, pp. 9–19.

Debo, K. (2011), "Walter's World of Wonder," in: *Walter Van Beirendock. Dream The World Awake*, Antwerp: MoMu, pp. 15–27.

Evans, C. (2003), *Fashion at the Edge: Spectacle, Modernity and Deathliness*, New Haven, CT: Yale University Press.

Frisa, M.L. (2008), "The Curator's Risk," in: *Fashion Theory: The Journal of Dress, Body & Culture*, 12(2), pp. 171–180.

Furniss, J.A. (2004), "Fashion & Style: In Praise of Goddess," in: *The Independent*, June 1.

Granata, F. (2009), "Exhibition Review: *Het Totaal Rappel*—Bernhard Willhelm's Cabinet of Wonder," in *Fashion Theory: The Journal of Dress, Body & Culture*, 13, pp. 371–378.

Martinez, J.G. (2007), "Selling Avant-Garde: How Antwerp Became a Fashion Capital (1990–2002)," in: *Urban Studies*, 44, pp. 2449–2464.

McNeil, P. (2008), "We're Not in the Fashion Business: Fashion in the Museum and the Academy," in: *Fashion Theory: The Journal of Dress, Body & Culture*, 12, pp. 65–81.

Monti, G. (2013), "After Diana Vreeland. The Discipline of Fashion Curating as a Personal Grammar," in: *Catwalk: The Journal of Fashion, Beauty, and Style*, 1, pp. 63–90.

Palmer, A. (2008), "Untouchable: Creating Desire and Knowledge in Museum Costume and Textile Exhibitions," in: *Fashion Theory: The Journal of Dress, Body & Culture*, 12, pp. 31–63.

Pecorari, M. (2008), "Mestieri di Moda," in: *Wit Magazine*, October 2008, p. 11.

Riccini, R. (2003), "Le cose che ci fanno intelligenti," in: R. Riccini (ed), *Imparare dalle cose: la cultura materiale delle cose*, Bologna: Clueb, pp. 25–45.

Serres, M. and B. Latour (1990), *Conversations on Science, Culture and Time*, translated by Roxanne Lapidus, Ann Arbor, MI: University of Michigan Press.

Steele, V. (2008), "Museum Quality: The Rise of the Fashion Exhibition," in: *Fashion Theory: The Journal of Dress, Body & Culture*, 12, pp. 7–30.

Stevenson, N.J. (2008), "The Fashion Retrospective," in: *Fashion Theory: The Journal of Dress, Body & Culture*, 12, pp. 219–235.

Taylor, L. (1998), "Doing the Laundry? A Reassessment of Object-based Dressed History," in: *Fashion Theory: The Journal of Dress, Body & Culture*, 2(4), pp. 337–358.

Vergo, P. (1989), *The New Museology*, London: Reaktion Books.

4

APPRAISED, DISPLAYED, AND CONCEALED: FASHION PHOTOGRAPHY ON THE SWEDISH MUSEUM STAGE

Anna Dahlgren

Over the last twenty years fashion photography has been increasingly embraced by museums worldwide and its link to glamor, sex, and celebrity culture has attracted large audiences and considerable media interest (Williams 2008: 204). This chapter analyzes how a handful of Swedish museums who collect and display either fashion or photography have worked or positioned themselves in relation to fashion photography, since the turn of the nineteenth century and up to the present time. It is evident that fashion photography is simultaneously appraised, displayed, and concealed by museums. The aim of this chapter is to consider the historical and contemporary rationales for these different processes. Furthermore it seeks to discuss the relationship between collecting and exhibiting fashion photography in museums and how these practices may be connected to the social, economic, and historical factors of the production and consumption of these images. Finally, it considers the definition of fashion photography and its relationship with the collecting and exhibiting institutions.

Fashion photography as a definite genre emerged around the turn of the nineteenth century. The technique for making photographs of fashion had been available since the early nineteenth century, while the most prominent fora, fashion magazines such as *Harper's Bazaar* and *Vogue*, date back to the late nineteenth century. Nevertheless photography appeared later in fashion magazines. In fact the first fashion photographs appeared as late as 1892, in the French magazine *La Mode Pratique*.[1] The crucial prerequisite was the printing technique, which gradually improved from the 1880s and onward and successively photography replaced drawing as the primary tool for communicating fashion. By the 1910s photography increasingly appeared in fashion spreads in American, British, French, and German publications (Hall-Duncan 1979; Ducros 1998; Shinkle 2008). In Sweden this development came a bit later and the breakthrough for photographic illustrations in advertising and fashion did not occur until the late 1920s (Dahlgren 2007).

To date Sweden has no museum dedicated to fashion or photography, despite its significant history of textile production and fashion design, yet fashion photography is collected and displayed by several museums such as Röhsska Museet, Nordiska Museet, Malmö Museer, and Moderna Museet. The first two of these are dedicated to dress and fashion, the second, third and fourth have considerable photographic collections. Furthermore there is Fotografiska, a privately run exhibition hall. It is not a museum yet its physical size and ambitious exhibitions program makes it an important arena for displaying photography in Sweden.

Two art and design museums

Röhsska Museet, founded in 1916, is dedicated to fashion, design, and craft. It currently holds a collection of 50,000 artifacts; dresses and accessories and other artifacts from the fashion system, but the collection contains only a handful of fashion photographs.[2] In 2011 the museum held an exhibition on fashion photography. It was small but still ambitious, focusing on the Swedish fashion photographer Carl Bengtsson and comprising approximately forty photographs from the photographer's thirty-year long career.[3] Bengtsson has been acting as a fashion photographer since 1976 and his work has been published in international magazines like *Vogue* and *Elle* (Bengtsson 2011).

The museum of modern art in Sweden, Moderna Museet, holds on the other hand a large collection of photographic prints of which fashion photography is an integrated part. The photographic department, called Fotografiska Museet, was established in 1971. This happened some years after the Swedish state had bought the Helmut Gernsheim Duplicate Collection in 1964 and, the following year, the photo-historic collection of Helmer Bäckström. The collection comprises approximately 100,000 items dated from the 1840s until today, for the most part consisting of black and white prints from the twentieth century, among them some of the most prominent fashion photographs produced in Sweden and abroad with prints by Irving Penn, William Klein, and Helmut Newton as well as famous Swedish photographers like Sten-Didrik Bellander, Arne Wahlberg, Herman Bergne, and Kerstin Bernard.[4] All in all 168 prints are cataloged as fashion photography in the museum's database, but there are also additional fashion-related prints in the collection, yet not registered as such.[5] Moderna

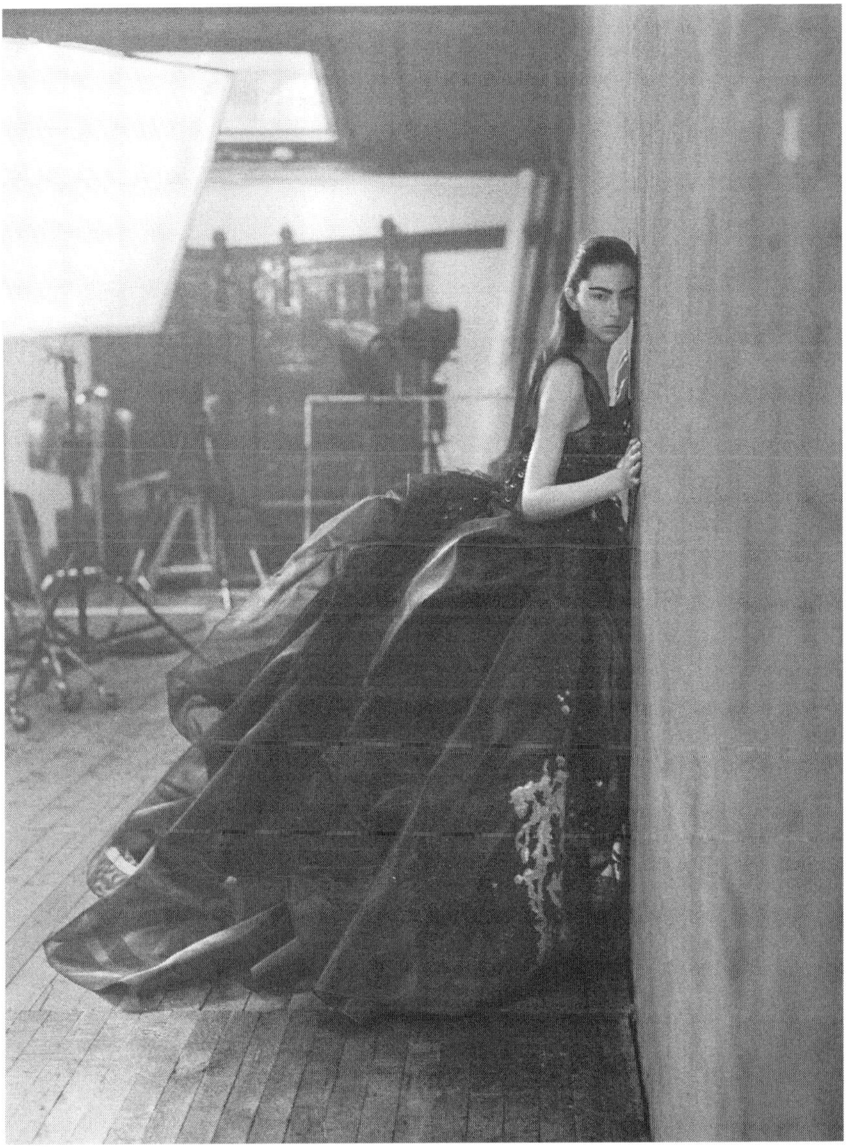

Figure 4.1 Carl Bengtsson had a solo show at the Swedish design museum Röhsska In 2011. He has been working as a fashion photographer since 1976. This image of Agnieszka Wichniewicz was made for Studio Sala, Paris, 2006. Photography © Carl Bengtsson.

Museet has a history of exhibiting fashion photography. In 1993 the exhibition "Catwalk" was held at the museum where the work of six contemporary Swedish fashion photographers—Mikael Jansson, Denise Grünstein, Carl Bengtsson, Patrik Andersson, Ewa Marie Rundquist, and Mattias Edwall—was exhibited.[6] In

2004 the museum held another exhibition that included fashion photography but also dress items, called "Fascination."[7] Over the years fashion photography has obviously also been exhibited in other shows, albeit not presented or cataloged as such. The most recent example is the large solo show of the French photographer Jeanloup Sieff who worked with fashion, advertising, reportage, and portraits throughout his professional career.[8] Thus Moderna Museet has a broad collection of photographs, yet the main part of them comprises vintage prints labeled "art photography." Put differently, Moderna Museet has an important collection of fashion photography but is not working with these images as primarily fashion photographs but rather as the work of different individual photographers or artists. A turn to cultural historical museums reveals other circumstances.

Two cultural historical museums

The cultural historical Nordiska Museet is the oldest among the four museums and as such it also has a long and diverse history of collecting photographs of dress and fashion. The collection of photographs at Nordiska Museet is diverse, a diversity that highlights the complexity of defining or delimiting what fashion photography is. Some scholars have argued that fashion photography is a part of the modern project, in other words a phenomenon that grew out of the late nineteenth-century industrialization and emerging media landscape around the turn of the nineteenth century. Others have argued that the term fashion applied to the aesthetic and presentation of dress and accessories long before the end of the nineteenth century (Breward 1995; Andersen 2006). Following Charlotte Andersen, fashion photography is more than images of fashion. It is rather images that make dress and other items look fashionable and modern—in short it is not only a genre defined by the image motif but also the way this motif is depicted (Andersen 2006: 27). In the cultural historical museum Nordiska Museet the genre of fashion photography in this sense is not pronounced. On the contrary all photographs of dress, whether they are originally press photographs, the result of a ethnographic fieldwork, or fashion photographs initially published in a fashion spread or advertising, are cataloged and used by the museum for the same ends, i.e. to document dress habits and changing design ideals.

To this end Nordiska Museet has been collecting photographs of different dress customs since its inauguration in 1873. Today the museum holds between 5 and 7 million photographs, of which images of dress items form a considerable part. Right from the start fashion items were an important part of the museum's collection. The very first photographs that were acquired were in fact photographs of costumes. In 1873, slightly less than 100 *carte-de-visite* photographs of men and women in Swedish folk costumes were acquired. The museum founder

Artur Hazelius wanted to preserve disappearing traditions and customs and to collect garments, particularly folk costumes but also upper-class fashion from older times. Thus, as well as collecting old and disappearing fashion items, photographs of the same artifacts were collected. As the collection grew, so did the need for documentation. Initially the artifacts in the collections were drawn by hand by an employed artist, but from the early twentieth-century photographers were hired for the same task.[9] These types of photograph are seldom seen in museum exhibitions or in writings on photohistory but are produced with great care being given to composition and lighting, and demand considerable technical skill (Born 1998: 227). The practice of internal and external documentation—of the collection and in fieldworks—continued into the twentieth century. Fashion photography was also included in the collection via the archives of individual photographers and companies. Thus Nordiska Museet's photographic collection also comprises the archives of individual photographers, image archives, and company archives with connections to fashion imagery.

Nordiska Museet has constantly been exhibiting fashionable costume. In February 2010 the new permanent exhibition on dress, called "The Power of Fashion: 300 Years of Dress," opened at Nordiska Museet and before that another permanent exhibition called "Paris—Stockholm" was on display between 1988 and 2009.[10] Fashion photography was explicitly exhibited for the first time in 2008, when the externally produced exhibition "Modebilder" was on display.[11]

The exhibition "Modebilder" toured and was thus also exhibited at Malmö Museer, which holds one of Sweden's largest photo collections. Malmö Museer has around 4 million photographs, some of which are images by some of the most prominent and successful commercial photographers in Sweden, like Georg Oddner, Karin Olofsdotter, and Åke Hedström. There are currently no exact data on the proportion of fashion photography in the collection, partly due to the fact that the photos are to a large extent not cataloged or arranged in any detail. Yet there are at least 14,000 estimated fashion photographs in the museum collection, photographs that were originally produced for fashion spreads or advertising.[12]

Collecting, displaying, and concealing

Despite the fact that museums like Nordiska Museet, Moderna Museet and Malmö Museer hold large collections of fashion photography they have scarcely displayed them in exhibitions. In the current permanent exhibition on fashion at Nordiska Museet representations of fashion, in the form of photographs, drawings, and moving images are scarce. The main focus is on dress, shoes, and accessories. In the adjoining catalog on the other hand the number of fashion photographs is considerably more. However, they are not presented or discussed as a mode of representation, but are rather used as documentation of different appearances in fashion (Eldvik 2009). In short their denotative content is mainly in focus. The fact that fashion representations are an important factor in fashion history and the fashion industry is not emphasized, and neither is the fact that fashion imagery has in itself a history of changing aesthetics and meanings (Andersen 2006).

Over the last twenty years, fashion photography has been increasingly embraced by museums worldwide.[13] Sweden nevertheless seems to have been lagging behind until very recently. Two large exhibitions on fashion photography have been on display in the country since 2009, both of them with loose connections to the national museum collections. It is telling that the latest large exhibition explicitly devoted to Swedish fashion photography, “Bilden av modet,” was based on the work of two freelance fashion writers' archival studies (Lewenhaupt and Lewenhaupt 2009), mainly in press archives. In other words, the material emanated from publications where fashion photographs had initially been reproduced, that is, neither from a photographer's archive nor a museum collection. Thus very few of the photographs that made up the exhibition came from museum collections and they were in the most part reproductions, i.e. not vintage prints.[14] It is also telling that the first major inventory of the international history of fashion photography exhibited in Sweden occurred at the privately run exhibition hall Fotografiska and not in any Swedish museum with a photographic collection. Between September 2010 and January 2011, around 200 photographic prints were exhibited, among them some of the most famous fashion photographs ever published by photographers such as Irving Penn, Horst P. Horst, George Hoyningen-Huene, Martin Munkacsi, and Helmut Newton. Needless to say, Fotografiska's exhibition “Fashion!—modefotografi genom tiderna” got a lot of attention in national media and had many visitors.[15] Yet Fotografiska has no collections but is run like a grand art gallery.[16] Tellingly the exhibition “Fashion!” was produced in cooperation with the gallery Camera Works in Berlin that produces exhibitions and books, and sells contemporary and historic photographic prints.[17]

To sum up, the relationship between collecting fashion photography and displaying fashion photography seems to be weak in the Swedish context.[18] There are currently many examples of fashion photography in Swedish museum collections, but it seems that they are not consciously cataloged as such. Most of them have come into the museum collections as part of individual professional photographers' oeuvres. In this sense the museums have primarily collected photographers and not consciously a particular genre, i.e. fashion. Other fashion photographs have entered the archives as documentation of textile and clothing manufacturing industries or department stores. The collection from the Swedish department store Nordiska Kompaniet now deposited at Nordiska is such an example. In includes 40,000 negatives and an uncounted number of prints produced between 1916 and 1963. The focus on industry and large companies in archives may be a bias in the reconstruction of the history of fashion photography. As pointed out by Tone Rasch, the main corpus of early twentieth-century fashion photography in Norway was made on commission by the textile industry (Rasch 2012: 22). Or, at least, this is the image of the field given by the museum collection, in this particular case, the collection at The Norwegian Museum of Science, Technology and Medicine. In fact this kind of bias holds for all archives and museum collections, as they are always a product of the ideological, historical, and administrative circumstances of the collecting institution (Schwartz and Cook 2002). Thus fashion photographs do exist in the museum collections but they are not visible as a coherent genre. Scattered around in the archives as they are, they turn out to be hard to present collectively. It seems that the demand of tracking such images in order to put together an exhibition outweighs the economic and personnel capacity of the museums.

It is striking that the main research for the exhibition and book, "Bilden av modet," on the Swedish history of fashion photography mentioned above, was being done in the commercial image archive ScanPix that among others things keeps the large press archive, "Pressens bild." Fashion photographs have typically been produced for publication in magazine reportage or adverts. In many cases the copyright of these commercial commissions was granted to the publishing houses or businesses that ordered them. Consequently, the image rights and in some cases also the physical prints left the photographer's archive and ended up in the publisher's archive or in the worst cases, in their trash bin. Historically, even by the photographers themselves, fashion and other commercial assignments were considered to have a short life span. The photographers may in some cases not even have kept the prints, while the commissioner in turn had no incentive to save the prints once they were published (Dahlgren 2009). To sum up, the remains of commercial photographic assignments are dispersed and many examples are definitely lost. As a consequence the magazines and printed adverts present a more full-bodied image of the history of fashion photography as they have been saved for posterity in a much more consistent way by the national library. In fact the fashion magazine may be considered as the prime archive of fashion photography. However, there is a drawback here: the names of the photographer, model, advertising agency, and other production data have historically almost never been printed in the publications. Consequently we have today a full body of anonymous fashion photographs in the illustrated press on the one hand, and a scattered and scarcely cataloged body of prints in different photographers' collections in museums and archives on the other hand. In relation to the great popularity of fashion in museums, this is a paradox. Keeping the visitor in mind, the museums create exhibitions, but care less about the back-office work of collecting and ordering fashion photography. Yet there are exceptions. Those images that have metamorphosed into art, such as the initially commercially produced photographs by Irving Penn, Richard Avedon, and Inez van Lamsveerde, to mention a few, are axiomatic in museum exhibitions. This in turn raises the question of how to define fashion photography and in consequence also how the genre could be presented in the public museum space.

The art of display

Every photograph that was not initially produced to be on display on an exhibition's wall in a gallery or museum defies, in one way or another, the display format. This holds true for fashion photography. It is also the case for press photographs whose meaning is produced by an amalgamation of image, byline, and editorial text, and for personal photographs that appear in albums and are heavily dependent on a particular pre-knowledge about the images and the oral stories told in conjunction with viewing.[19] Furthermore, the default presentation of these types of images is the "series." In fact the basic appearance of analogue photography is not the single image but instead the series, especially pronounced in the contact sheet (Ekeberg and Ostgaard 2008; Batchen 2011). This also holds true for the fashion context. Fashion photography has historically been produced to appear in fashion editorials for fashion magazines, printed ads, fashion company "look books" or business catalogs as an integrated part of graphic design and eventually editorial text. The question is then how these kinds of photographs could be presented on the gallery or museum wall. Normally the sizes of prints aimed for reproduction are relatively small, while prints produced for exhibitions or studio display are large. In other words, vintage fashion photographs normally do not match the viewing context of the museum or gallery. When working with displays of contemporary fashion photography this dilemma is easily solved as the photographers can make exhibition prints for the purpose. This was the case at the exhibition "Fashion!" at Fotografiska in Stockholm in 2010–2011. All photographs made by contemporary photographers were large, at least 30 × 50 cm, framed or mounted on a support. Even the prints from the early twentieth century were in fact framed, relatively large, and some possibly new prints. The only exception was Helmut Newton's polaroids from the mid-1970s. The fact that the majority of the photographs came from the gallery Camera Works in Berlin is symptomatic for the art-like presentation as it is a commercial agent that exhibits and sells contemporary as well as historical fashion photographs.[20] For obvious economic reasons there are incentives to consider fashion photography as art, as this raises the price for the individual print. Furthermore, fashion is a convenient way to expand the market for photography, in a time when it is depleted of the old masters working within the bounds of high art photography.

Another contemporary example of displaying fashion photography that in fact incorporates the different appearances of the genre and acknowledges the production and consumption circumstances can be found in the National

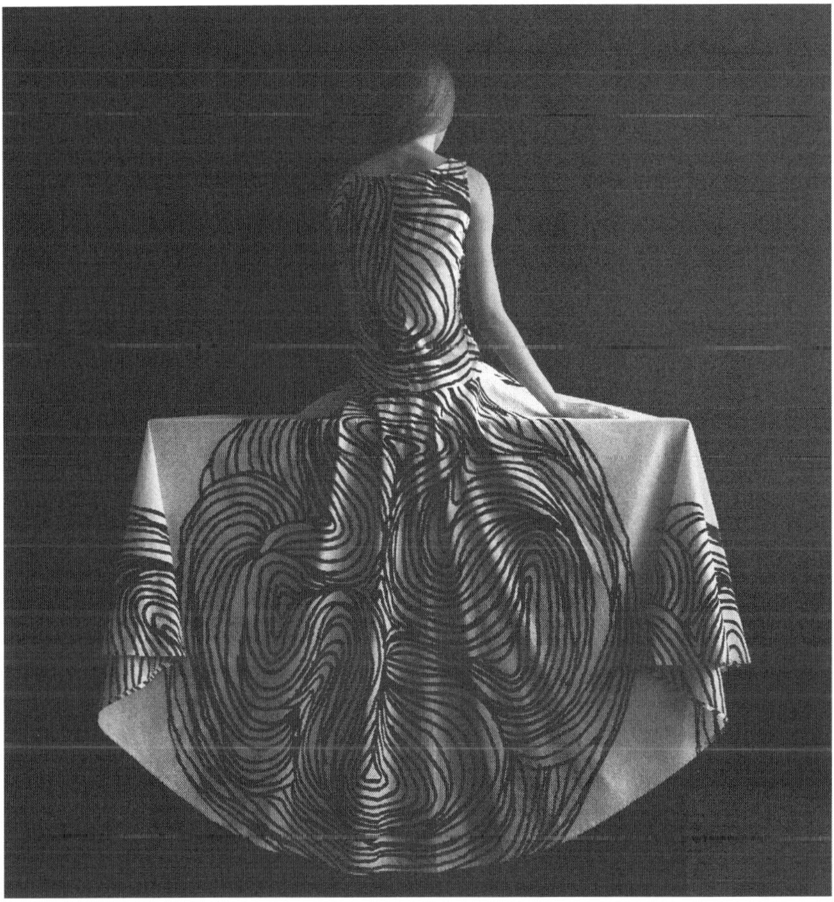

Figure 4.2 Julia Hetta was one of the contemporary photographers represented at Preus museum's exhibition on fashion photography "Motefotografi. Tradisjon og nyskapning" in 2012. This particular image was produced for SSAW Finland 2012. Dress from the Vuokko archive. Photography © Julia Hetta.

Norwegian Photo museum, Preus. Its exhibition "Motefotografi: Tradisjon och nyskapning" (2012) included vintage prints by internationally renowned photographers like Erwin Blumenfeld, Edvard Steichen, and Deborah Turbeville. Simultaneously the exhibition presented images by eight contemporary Nordic fashion photographers such as Julia Hetta, Torkil Gudnason, and Lukas Renlund.[21] In contrast to the vintage prints, the latter were prints produced especially for the exhibition, albeit already published in magazines and journals. They were all large format, approximately 50 × 70 cm, and mounted on the walls with pins. The simple hanging device made the walls reminiscent of mood boards, the standard way of working among fashion designers and magazines in the production of a new collection of fashion editorial. Furthermore, contemporary and historical copies of fashion magazines were on display in the exhibition as well as contact sheets from fashion shoots. Taken together the exhibition brought to the fore the multitude of material appearances that are significant of fashion photography. The context of display is indicative. Preus museum is a museum devoted to all types of photography, whether it is art photography, cultural historical photography, fashion photography, personal photography, or commercial photography. Thus the question of genre, and the circumstances of production and consumption, does not constrain its collecting activities—nor its exhibition practices.

In conclusion

To sum up, it seems that fashion photography is something like a blind spot for the Swedish museum dedicated to fashion and photography. It happens to fall between two stools. One reason for not displaying fashion imagery may be that the format of the genre defies the format of the typical exhibition as indicated above. Another reason might be the connotations attached to the genre. For the cultural historical museums as well as the art museums, fashion photography may appear too banal and commercial and in consequence not culturally significant enough. For the art museum, fashion imagery may also seem too ordinary, being a kind of image that has circulated widely and has been produced for a mass audience. This may explain why some fashion images have made it into the art museums and others have not. Images that have metamorphosed into art, such as the initially commercially produced photographs for fashion magazines like *American Vogue* by Irving Penn, Richard Avedon, Helmut Newton, and Inez van Lamsveerde, have made it into the museums. In common for these photographers are their collaborations with international exclusive fashion magazines, while at the same time producing “personal works,” i.e. not commercially commissioned images. In this context the anonymous fashion images or the work of the national or local, standard commercial photographer, would not fit. For the cultural historical museum on the other hand the main argument against the significance of fashion photography may rather be its artificial, constructed character. Fashion images lack by definition the austerity or authenticity that other kinds of photographs of dress may have, like documentary, amateur, or press photography. Consequently fashion photographs cannot be used in the same way to verify different dress habits historically, staged as they are and tinted with too much periodic or individual style.

What is evident browsing through the collecting and displaying practices of Swedish museums, is the seeming lack of knowledge or interest in the history and aesthetics particular to fashion photography. As argued above, fashion representations are an important factor in fashion history and the fashion industry. In consequence a museum devoted to fashion should acknowledge the fashion system (Kawamura 2005). That does not only include the objects, like dress and accessories, but also the circumstances for production, circulation, and consumption of fashion in society. Important parts of these processes are the representations of fashion, like photographs and drawings. Furthermore, fashion imagery has itself a history of changing aesthetic. The arguments for and against the singling out and articulation of media specificity vis-à-vis photography is still a hot topic in academic, museum, and institutional practices (McCauley 2007; Tellgren 2008). Yet when it comes to collecting and displaying and, by extension, history writing on fashion photography, the case is clear. For photographic images that oscillate between different genres, conceptual and physical loci the need for photo museums, devoted to photography's whole palette, is obvious. It is not a coincidence that the first and major inventory of the history of fashion photography emanated from The International Museum of Photography at the George Eastman House in Rochester (Hall-Duncan 1979). This exhibition and the accompanying catalog showed the important role the museum and collections may play in the production of photo histories.[22]

As this short inventory of fashion photography on the Swedish museum stage has revealed, there is paradoxically a large public interest in fashion photography while at the same time large collections of fashion imagery are neglected, and there are considerable gaps in the preservation of historic fashion photography. To use a theatrical metaphor, one might say that many of the props are there, as well as the audience, yet what is missing is the permanent stage and dedicated actors.

Notes

1 *Vogue* was for example founded in 1892 but did not include photographs until 1914 when the photographer Adolpe de Meyer was taken on by the magazine (Ducros 1998: 536).

2 When this text was written in 2011 Röhsska had not a single fashion photograph in the collection, www.designmuseum.se and telephone interview with Anna Billing-Wetterlundh, curator, Röhsska Museet, April 26, 2011. Since then the museum has acquired some fashion photographs.

3 "Carl Bengtsson—Modefotografier" was on display September 17–October 16, 2011, http://www.designmuseum.se/tillfuts.htm.

4 www.modernamuseet.se.

5 Email to the author from Håkan Petesson at Moderna Museet, November 8, 2011.

6 A catalog for the exhibition was published in 1993 with the title *Beauty box: sju kataloger till utställningen Catwalk på Fotografiska museet i Stockholm den 24 April–31 Maj 1993*.

7 There exist no catalogs from this exhibition and all the information on it comes from Håkan Petersson at Moderna Museet. Email to the author, November 11, 2008.

8 The exhibition contained fifty-three photographs and was open between February 19 and May 29, 2011, http://www.modernamuseet.se/sv/Stockholm/Utstallningar/2011/Jeanloup-Sieff/.

9 The first museum photographer was August Hultgren (1869–1961) who was employed at the museum between 1906 and 1912 (Fataburen 1906: 4, 1909: 4).

10 Fashion dress has been exhibited at Nordiska Museet since at least the early twentieth century. For example, fashion clothes from the nineteenth century (1918) and the new dress gallery that opened in 1934 (*Nordiska Museet Under 125 år* 1998: 287–302).

11 This conclusion is based on an internally used list of all exhibitions held at Nordiska Museet between 1929 and 2007. See Besöksstatistik Museet, revised December 17, 2007.

12 Email to the author from Ludovit Dobrik at Malmö Museer, September 21 and 23, 2011.

13 The first museum exhibition on fashion photography was at George Eastman House, International Museum of Photography, in 1979. Since then fashion photography has been exhibited at several museums in Europe and the USA. See for example the Museum of Modern Art's (MOMA) "Fashioning Fiction in Photography since 1990" (2004) and the National Portrait Gallery, London, "Portraits in Fashion" (2004–2005).

14 Conversation with Lotta Lewenhaupt, May 3, 2011.

15 In the media coverage the comparison between Moderna Museet and Fotografiska is recurrent. The numbers of visitors to the two institutions are almost equal, despite one being a private exhibition hall and the other a state-funded museum with a prominent history. See for example Tove Leffler, "Moderna tar upp kampen med Fotografiska" (2011).

16 See further: http://fotografiska.eu/Museet/Tidigare-utstaellningar/Fashion!-modefotografi-genom-tiderna (13 March 2013).

17 Images by the following photographers were included in the exhibition: Diane and Allen Arbus, Richard Avedon, David Bailey, Lilian Bassman, Brassai, Michel Comte, Anton Corbijn, Michelangelo di Battista and Tina Berning, David Drebin, Frantisek Drtikol, Arthur Elgort, Louis Faurer, Fernand Fonssagrives, Peter H. Fürst, Esther Haase, Horst P. Horst, George Hoyningen-Huene, Russell James, Mikael Jansson, Steven Klein, William Klein, Karl Lagerfeld, Annie Leibovitz, Peter Lindbergh, Charlotte March, Will McBride, Ralph Mecke, Steven Meisel, Sarah Moon, Barbara Morgan, Martin Munkacsi, Robert Nettarp, Helmut Newton, Irving Penn, Rankin, Man Ray, Blaise Reutersward, Bettina Rheims, Herb Ritts, Paolo Roversi, Mark Seliger, Jeanloup Sieff, Vanina Sorrenti, Edward Steichen, Antoine Verglas, Ellen von Unwerth, Albert Watson, Bruce Weber, Pierre Winther, Camilla Åkrans. See: http://fotografiska.eu/Museet/Tidigare-utstaellningar/Fashion!-modefotografi-genom-tiderna (13 March 2013).

18 Whether this is a national tendency or an international phenomenon is outside the scope of this limited survey.

19 The make-up of personal photo albums and their reliance on oral stories is discussed in Martha Langford's *Suspended Conversations* (2001).

20 Two photographs of the exhibition hanging can be seen at the gallery's website: http://fotografiska.eu/Museet/Tidigare-utstaellningar/Fashion!-modefotografi-genom-tiderna.

21 The eight contemporary photographers were Aorta (SE), Julie Hetta (SE), Torkil Gudnason (DE), Mads Teglers (DK), Jorgen Gomnaes (NO), Siren Lauvdal (NO), Benjamin Alexander Huseby (NO), and Lukas Renlund (FI).

22 Another emblematic example of this is of course the first comprehensive history of photography that emerged from MOMA (Newhall 1937).

References

Andersen, Charlotte (2006), *Modefotografi. En genres anatomi*, Copenhagen: Museum Tusculum Press.

Batchen, Geoffrey (2011), *Repetition och skillnad. Fotografins re/produktion*, Stockholm: CO-OP (editions).

Beauty box: sju kataloger till utställningen Catwalk på Fotografiska museet i Stockholm den 24 april–31 maj 1993, Stockholm: Moderna museet, 1993.

Bengtsson, Carl (2011), *Portraits*, Malmö: Arena förlag.

Born, Georgina (1998), "Public Museums, Museum Photography, and the Limits of Reflexivity," in: *Journal of Material Culture*, 3, pp. 223–254.

Breward, Christopher (1995), *The Culture of Fashion: A New History of Fashionable Dress*, Manchester: Manchester University Press.

Dahlgren, Anna (2007), "Commercial Realism: Discourse on Photography in Advertising in the 1930s," in: *Journal of Art History*, 76, pp. 135–146.

Dahlgren, Anna (2009), "Mode+fotografi= Bidrag till den svenska modefotografins tidiga historia," in: Louise Wallenberg and Dirk Gindt (eds), *Mode – en introduktion*, Stockholm: Raster förlag, pp. 152–174.

Ducros, Françoise (1998), "The Dream of Beauty: Fashion and Fantasy," in: Michel Frizot (ed.), *A New History of Photography*, Köln: Könemann, pp. 535–553.

Ekeberg, Jonas and Harald Ostgaard (2008), "Innledning," in: Jonas Ekeberg and Harald Ostgaard (eds), *80 millioner bilder. Norsk kulturhistorisk fotografi 1855–2005*, Oslo: Forlaget Press, pp. 9–13.

Eldvik, Berit (2009), *The Power of Fashion*, Stockholm: Nordiska museets förlag.

Fataburen (1906), Stockholm: Nordiska museets årsbok.

Fataburen (1908), Stockholm: Nordiska museets årsbok.

Hall-Duncan, Nancy (1979), *The History of Fashion Photography,* New York: Alpine Book Company, Inc.

Kawamura, Yuinya (2005), *Fashion-ology: An Introduction to Fashion Studies*, London: Berg.

Langford, Martha (2001), *Suspended Conversations: The Afterlife of Memory in Photographic Albums*, Montreal & Kingston: McGill-Queen's University Press.

Lettler, Love (2011), "Moderna tar upp kampen med Fotografiska," *Dagens Nyheter*, January 21, p. 46.

Lewenhaupt, Lotta and Tonie Lewenhaupt (2009), *Bilden av modet*, Malmö: Arena.

McCauley, Anne (2007), "The Trouble with Photography," in: James Elkins (ed.), *Photography Theory*, New York: Routledge, pp. 403–430.

Newhall, Beaumont (1937), *The History of Photography from 1839 to the Present Day*, New York: Museum of Modern Art.

Nordiska Museet Under 125 år (1998), Hans Medelius, Bengt Nyström, and Elisabet Stavenow-Hidemark (eds), Stockholm: Nordiska Museets förlag.
Rasch, Tone (2012), "Tendenser fra Norsk Motefotografis Historie," in: *Motefotografi. Tradisjon och nyskapning*, Horten: Preus Museum, pp. 21–37.
Schwartz, Joan M. and Terry Cook (2002), "Archives, Records, and Power: The Making of Modern Memory," in: *Archival Science*, 2, pp. 1–19.
Shinkle, Eugénie (2008), "Introduction," in: Eugénie Shinkle (ed.), *Fashion as Photograph: Viewing and Reviewing Images of Fashion*, London: I.B. Tauris, pp. 1–14.
Tellgren, Anna (2008), "Fotografi och konst. Om Moderna Museets samling av fotografi ur ett institutionshistoriskt perspektiv," in: Anna Tellgren, Martin Sundberg and Johan Rosell (eds), *Historieboken: om Moderna museet 1958–2008*, Stockholm: Moderna Museet, pp. 123–152.
Williams, Val (2008), "A Heady Relationship: Fashion Photography and the Museum, 1979 to the Present," in: *Fashion Theory: The Journal of Dress, Body & Culture*, 12, pp. 197–218.

SECTION 2

FASHION CONTROVERSIES: WHEN BODIES BECOME PUBLIC

5
GENDER CONSIDERATIONS IN FASHION HISTORY EXHIBITIONS

Julia Petrov

Although a wardrobe is a gender-non-specific piece of furniture, the public wardrobe of a museum has overwhelmingly been gendered female. Thus, if the public in "public wardrobes" is seen as a representative audience, then museum collections of fashion cannot be public as such. Although many early collections were established and managed by men, the largest proportion of these collections was devoted to the clothing and accessories of women, and was designed to appeal primarily to female audiences. In addition, although the explicitly stated purpose of many early collections in England and North America was to inspire and reflect contemporary industrial production, the material contained within, instead reflected and inspired the consumption of leisured women. This chapter traces the gendered and socioeconomic contradictions inherent in English and North American museum collections of clothing from their beginnings until today. While it is often said that displayed dress is engaging for the public because of the fact that the act of wearing clothing is common to everyone, this chapter challenges this notion by documenting the elite forms of production and consumption displayed in fashion history exhibitions. While the contemporary situation seems to favor fashion exhibitions at all kinds of cultural institutions, this chapter draws on archival sources to investigate whether the gendered history of fashion exhibitions in museums limits its present development.

The gallery of fashion

It was because of the connections between the worlds of economy and history that historical fashion entered and was interpreted in museums. Indeed, one of the first suggestions for a British museum of costume came from a satire on the consumerist tendencies of fashion-mad women. In an 1847 *Punch* article titled "Hints for the British Museum Commission," the anonymous author suggested that rather than natural history specimens, examples of fashion might induce "the softer sex to find attractions in the British Museum" (1847: 59). The article went on:

> Fashion and dress always present points of interest to the sex we are desirous of enticing within the walls of the British Museum; and we propose, therefore, to invest the great national depository with attractions for the female visitor, by commencing a collection of the newest patterns in caps, shawls, bonnets, *visites*, and other articles of attire, which come home to us all—in bandboxes, with tolerably long bills tacked on to them.

Fashion here is portrayed as populist: familiar from its commercial incarnation, and particularly attractive to women, who were throughout the nineteenth century categorized as magpie-like spendthrifts.

While the 1847 *Punch* article reflects the attitude also documented by Klonk (2009) of early museum administrators and commentators that the traditional museum was not of intellectual interest to women, it also suggests that fashion could contribute something new to the museum experience: a connection to the commodified world outside. Whereas capitalism promises consumers that they can buy an identity in the shops, museums show the range of objects that represented and embodied identities bought and sold over time.

Because both fashion and museums are part of the same economic and political processes—western urban (bourgeois) capitalism—their processes overlap, as Alexandra Palmer points out: "In North America in particular, many costume and textile collections stem from the founding links between museums and the fashion world. The fashion industry operates on a seasonal Western fashion system, which has been incorporated into museums' display schedule and is then linked to fundraising openings, the social season, and parties" (Palmer 2008: 54).

Additionally, fashion's adopted museal aspects are reintegrated into the aesthetic cycle—the British fashion designer Vivienne Westwood is well known for using the Victoria and Albert Museum's (V&A) collections as inspiration for her catwalk designs. Equally, museums knowingly cooperate with the fashion industry to promote their own cultural relevance and authority (Silverman 1986)—the 2006 V&A exhibition "Fashion-ology," which celebrated the work of *Vogue* editor Anna Piaggi, demonstrated this particularly well. Piaggi, whose double-page spreads highlight inspirations from catwalks to museums, was herself musealized. While fashion has been accused of blurring the boundaries further in an already confused landscape of museums and the market (Preziosi and Farago 2004: 2), there is no doubt that it would not inspire such strong feelings were it not for its sympathetic reciprocity as a commodity of both economic and cultural value.

Museums, fashion, and gender

While *Punch* had suggested in 1847 that English museums partner with the fashion industry, it took over sixty years for this to actually occur: historical fashion appeared in the galleries of the Museum of London in 1912 and at the V&A in 1913. Both collections were founded from the material given by or purchased from historical genre painters (Edwin Austin Abbey, John Seymour Lucas, and Talbot Hughes; see Petrov 2008) who accumulated antique costumes as props for their studio practice. The clothes were not worn by the donors as fashion, but were instead used for professional or antiquarian purposes.

Maintaining a fashionable identity during this period was a leisure activity, and therefore part of the upper- and middle-class feminine domain. A 1907 etiquette manual instructed aspiring gentlemen that: "Display, in short, is ever to be avoided, especially in matters of dress. The toilette is the domain of the fair sex. Let a wise man leave its graces and luxuries to his wife, daughters, or sisters" (MHE 1907: 52). Contemporary commentators singled out excessive interest in fashion for censure by using insinuations of transgressive effeminacy. Historian Brent Shannon writes of popular morals in this period:

> Men's conduct literature had historically reflected popular middle-class anxieties regarding the effeminacy equated with the dandy's idle status, flamboyant mannerisms, and fastidious attention to the minutiae of dress. Certainly, antagonism toward effeminate behaviour accelerated during an age in which rugged masculinity and athleticism were enthusiastically celebrated by popular culture. Any man who seemed to care too much about his appearance risked accusations that he was weak and womanish, and upper-class dandies and mincing shop clerks were familiar caricatures in popular culture.
>
> Shannon 2004: 612

Shannon suggests that concern over male fashion's connection with transgressive sexuality was transformed into a positive by associating men's healthy interest in dress with a drive for professionalism, decorum, and respectability. Significantly, professionalism was also the key quality that made male interest in dress respectable. The genre painter-collectors mentioned above, for instance, could not have been accused of effeminate interest in fashion because they approached it with a tasteful and educated spirit of historical inquiry (see Petrov 2008). Because of their qualifications as artists and gentlemen, the genre painters were instead seen as experts to help the museum in its aesthetic aims.

Museums, from their inception, were largely male spaces. Established by men who had access to education and wealth, and accessible at least in the beginning only to their peers, museums as cultural institutions have mirrored the social processes of the elite, and have functioned as public monuments to the established order. The art historian Lara Perry asserts that the administrative system of museums largely excluded women, the result being that "museums and galleries in the nineteenth century (and often the twentieth) appear to function as a 'boy's pocket', offering up collections of treasures traded in men's rooms and selected for masculine tastes" (Perry 2006: 2). Yet even her assertion that "the evidence suggests that women had access to such substantial involvement in museums and galleries and suggests that they were a large and significant constituency within the class of nineteenth-century museum makers" (2006: 2), nevertheless does not mean that museums were a space for equality of the genders; indeed, they were instead spaces for the expression and representation of cultural norms, one of which was male gender dominance.

In the case of the V&A, for example, the female amateur was erased completely from the provenance of the collection. Before gifting the whole to the museum, Harrods department store augmented the painter Talbot Hughes' collection with pieces from at least one other, that of a Miss Mallet. Museum director Sir Cecil Smith wrote at the time:

> I called by appointment on Mr. Burbidge today. He showed me the exhibition of costumes a large series which Mssrs. Harrods have acquired since the exhibition was first mooted, and which are independent of the Talbot Hughes collection. I understand from him that a firm in Bond Street formed this series with the intention of having a rival exhibition, and Mssrs. Harrods bought the whole series largely in order to prevent this. [. . .] Mr. Burbidge desired to know whether any or all of these costumes would be acceptable for the Museum, as in that case, Mssrs. Harrods are prepared to present them with the rest of the collection.
>
> Smith 1913

Yet peculiarly, Miss Mallet's name or even the presence of a subsidiary dress collection was never mentioned in the publicity for the exhibition and the donation. The only name consistently mentioned and celebrated in the press was that of Talbot Hughes. It is also noteworthy that there is not one woman mentioned in the published list of people (Anonymous 1913) who attended the exhibition's inaugural luncheon at Harrods; male politicians, artists, businessmen, as well as dignitaries associated with the museum and the theater are listed instead. This does not necessarily mean that women were not present, but rather, it does suggest that those guests who were considered important were all men.

While the late nineteenth-century construction of middle-class masculinity may have been initially threatened by an excessive interest in fashion, its hegemony was actually reinforced through a number of strategies. Rather than being viewed as an aspect of fashionable dress, antique clothing was instead presented as a historical artifact, both requiring and required by the professional expertise accumulated by male leaders in the cultural and industrial spheres.

The V&A, founded as a result of an exhibition of arts and manufactures, continued to have as its guiding principle the education of generations of craftspeople and the promotion of home-grown industry and talent (Baker and Richardson 1997). Eventually, fashion was also included in this remit. The speeches given on the occasion of the Harrods gift reflect the intentions of the museum administrators for it:

> Mr. Pease [President of the Board of Education] said it was no doubt it was a very valuable collection from an educational point of view that was being handed over [to] the Victoria and Albert Museum. Attention to dress was thought by some to be a frivolous occupation, but time worked great changes, and what was once frivolity at another time became an invaluable and concrete reality. [. . .] The collection would stimulate the imagination of the present and the future, and would help in the scheme of colour and design, which was so necessary to the dressmaker.
>
> Anonymous 1913

Historical fashion, no longer a commodity on the open market, could nevertheless influence manufacture through providing inspiration for female dressmakers, if ideal examples were selected with care by aesthetically minded male experts.

The self-styled consumer

Despite the importance of women to the production aspects of the fashion industry, the properties and "furniture" of fashion exhibitions echo the retail environment instead. Retail historian Sara Schneider notes that "the aesthetics of museum display reflects just how similar these have grown to visual-merchandising strategies in the commercial setting [. . .] Many of the audiences or buyers for display are the same as those for museum exhibitions" (Schneider 1995: 36–37). Alongside this perhaps subliminal similarity are more obvious ones, particularly when exhibitions are designed specifically to emulate the environment of the shop or designer salon.

Among the early vignettes featured at the Fashion Museum in Bath was one titled "The Draper's Shop," set in the 1860s, and another titled "A Shawl Shop 1870–80" (Anonymous 1971; Byrde 1980, 1984). On the one hand, this was a practical and convenient conceit by which to display lengths of textiles and sample books of ribbons and fabrics; on the other, it also called to mind in the visitors a lost age of personalized service and design for leisured, wealthy women. This sense of mixed awe and nostalgia is also often present in exhibitions on a form of elite fashion: haute couture.

The 2007 V&A exhibition “The Golden Age of Couture” focused on tailoring and the designer’s presence, albeit in an ambiguous way: Land Design Studio designed the second room with “an open catwalk display of tailored suits and daywear from 1947–1957, a demonstration of highly-skilled cutting and stitching” (Ward 2007: 2). Here, the device of the catwalk, while a practical means of displaying a large quantity of clothing, was also used to visually refer to the purchasing environment for high fashion. Indeed, even the architecture of couture is sometimes used as inspiration for exhibition design. The 2002 show “Elite Elegance: Couture Fashion the 1950s,” curated at the Royal Ontario Museum by Alexandra Palmer, was designed by Yabu Pushelberg to evoke the atmosphere of upscale Toronto mansions (Birchall-Spencer 2003: 20), placing the focus squarely on the consumers of couture. However, the section “Haute Couture Today” featured a mock winding staircase (Moore 2002: 4), a clear reference to the famed staircase at the Chanel salon. In this room, the objects and text combined with the design elements to suggest the continuity of a glamorous tradition.

Nostalgia or awe at a lost and/or unattainable world of shopping experiences are economically unproductive, however. Creativity in industrial production and the economic stimulus provided by consumer shopping behavior, by contrast, are different. The exhibitionary focus on the fashion consumer is not merely a true reflection of the goods cycle: it has important implications for the construction of the subject in museums of historical fashion. Thus, an important genre of historical fashion exhibitions has been that of the “ideal consumer.” Occasionally a generic period clotheshorse, but more frequently a named figure, such persons (most often women) are made iconic. They define style but are also celebrated for their acts of self-definition through consumption.

Collecting clothing actually worn is an important part of the acquisition strategy of most fashion collections. The documentation around each dress (oral history about why the item was purchased, how and when it was worn, as well as photographs of it being worn) is vital for creating social history narratives around fashion consumption. This is not as representative a process as it might ideally be; few people hoard their entire wardrobe and gift it to a museum, and those women who might be approached for donations of their clothing are selected because of personal ideas about taste from curators and individuals affiliated with museum collections. In preparing his 1971 exhibition “Fashion: An Anthology by Cecil Beaton,” the photographer and designer Cecil Beaton approached individuals he considered arbiters of high style (de la Haye 2006), many of whom he knew personally through his work in theater, film, and fashion; these tended to be the upper-class purchasers of couture active after 1920, rather than average consumers of high street fashion, and the museum's collection was subsequently skewed toward that demographic (Mendes 1984: 77). Likewise, the wardrobe of Heather Firbank (acquired and exhibited in 1960) did provide a glimpse into the life and priorities of a fashionable and affluent young woman whose couture outfits had been well preserved; her taste, however, was conservative and English, and so the V&A did not have contemporary outfits by avant-garde French couturiers, for instance (Mendes 1984: 79–80). The documentation around the Firbank collection, however, did allow the curators to reconstruct a picture of the woman through the traces of her consumption.

Even if exhibitions of celebrity wardrobes are excluded (because they include or consist of stage and film costumes), one can trace a rising genre of historical fashion exhibitions that focus on specific female fashion consumers. These may not be conventional shows of historical fashion inasmuch as they may feature living women; however, these women may be portrayed as historically important due to their patronage of and influence on important designers (Lulu Guinness, Museum at FIT 2011) or their use of historical garments to effect in their wardrobes (Iris Apfel, Costume Institute 2005; Lulu Guinness, see above; Anna Piaggi, V&A 2006). These women are iconic not in an aesthetic sense but in an artful sense: they are known for the image they create for themselves. They are highlighted by museums not just because of the importance of individual pieces within their wardrobes, but because of the way they reflect and navigate the consumption side of the fashion system. Not unlike the New York Museum of Modern Art's post-war exhibitions of good design (Staniszewski 1998), where consumers were encouraged under the aegis of "style," such fashion exhibitions feed directly back into the fashion cycle by being featured in the same media outlets and inspiring the same set of creatives and manufacturers as they promote. Neither is this a phenomenon limited to the English-speaking world: the 1999 exhibition at the Musée de la Mode et du Textile in Paris, "Garde-robes: Intimités Devoilées," featured clothing from such individuals as Belle Époque courtesan Cléo de Mérode, the Duchess of Windsor, Denise Poiret (wife of the couturier), and fashion photographer Norman Parkinson (Golbin 1999, Hill 2011).

Likewise, Diana Vreeland's 1975 exhibition "American Women of Style" highlighted the personalities of specific fashionable women through their clothing, as Vreeland wrote in the catalog: "This is not a dress show. This is an exhibition to project, through the beholder's imagination, a vision of ten American women of style" (Vreeland 1975). Stella Blum, the professional curator of the Costume Institute (Vreeland's title was "special consultant") struggled in her foreword in the catalog to find the logic behind the selection of such disparate women: Rita de Acosta Lydig, Josephine Baker, Irene Castle, Isadora Duncan, Mrs. John W. Garrett, Mrs. Charles Dana Gibson, the Duchess of Marlborough, Millicent Rogers, Gertrude Whitney, and Elsie de Wolfe. Indeed, Mrs. Vreeland used a liberal dash of artistic license: as no original clothing belonging to Mrs. Gibson

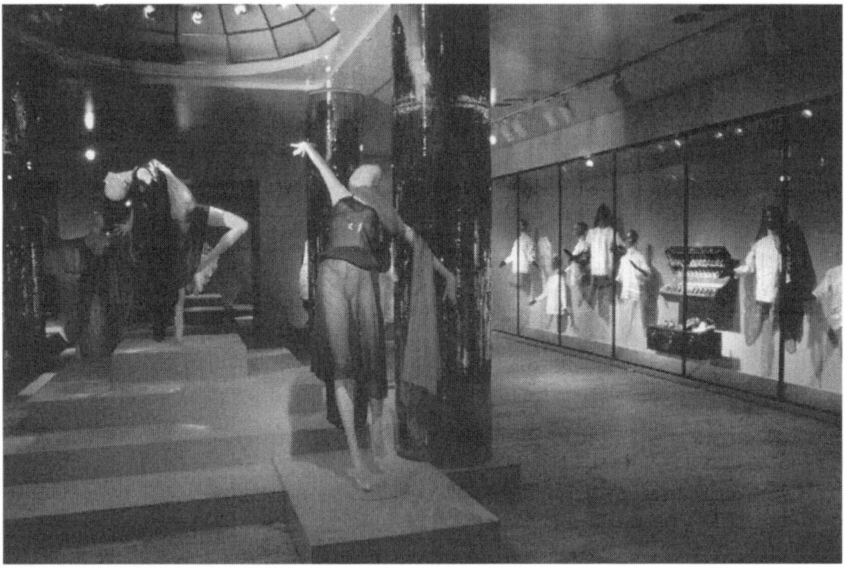

Figure 5.1 Al Mozell, The Metropolitan Museum of Art: "American Women of Style" (December 13, 1975–August 31, 1976), view of Isadora Duncan section at left. © The Metropolitan Museum of Art.

existed, a pastiche of clothing from the period was put together to represent her (Anonymous 1975: 1).

Rita de Acosta Lydig, Mrs. Gibson, and the Duchess of Marlborough were also featured in the Costume Institute's 2010 show, "American Woman: Fashioning a National Identity." Although this exhibition did not primarily celebrate specific women, and rather was organized around stereotyped female roles—Heiress, Gibson Girl, Bohemian, Suffragist, Patriot, Flapper, and Screen Siren—the mannequins were recognizably humanoid, giving the impression of interacting with each other and their backgrounds. In addition, they were styled to represent particular periods, but in some instances embodied the female inspiration for that period: Mrs. Lydig served as the Bohemian archetype, and her characteristic poses, features, and coiffure were reproduced in the mannequins, though they were not all clothed in her surviving outfits. Thus, "American Women of Style," and "American Woman" put specific women on display as subjects, notable for their shopping habits.

Female consumerism is more muted in exhibitions that focus on particular designers, mostly of the late nineteenth and twentieth centuries. The emphasis in such exhibitions was the artistic genius of the creator-designer, able to predict and cater to the tastes of their clientele and society at large. It must be noted, however, that the "genius" celebrated in these exhibitions was usually a male designer producing for a leisured class of women in an industrial culture. High fashion was therefore in this formulation a frivolous and unproductive pursuit, which had to be rehabilitated as being purposeful in another way. The positioning of a rational male overseeing the self-presentation of a female has been noted by feminist art scholars as having an effect on the visuality of art and of galleries (for a useful summary see Richter 2010); it also had an impact on the ways by which exhibitions of historical fashion were constructed as a means of social improvement.

Tasteful consumption: the uses of fashion in art education

Fashion history exhibitions can subvert the commercialism of the fashion system by aestheticizing dress; frequently, this is done with a rationale of promoting "good buying" by educating the consumer into a connoisseur. Here, too, there are important gender ramifications. Art education in museums has had a history of parochial and classist attitudes by experts on the general public's ability to appreciate the aesthetic (Hill 2005; Whitehead 2005; Klonk 2009); fashion has elicited these as well as misogynistic attitudes toward consumers (widely though falsely—see Breward 1999—held to be female). An 1869 article encouraging the establishment of an English museum of costume was published with a decorative element (Anonymous 1869: 373) featuring a nude woman and her children (also in a state of nature) gazing into a mirror (that serves as the article's opening letter "O") that shows them fashionably dressed in a bourgeois interior, with the anti-slavery slogan "Am I not a woman and a sister?" on a banner below, implying that modern women are slaves to fashion and must be freed through the rationalizing influence of aesthetic education about dress.

An early example of the rationale for educating female consumers about fashion history comes from an 1873 article describing the display of antique dress in the Industrial Department of the Third Annual International Exhibition in London. The author writes:

> Ladies, however, are the acknowledged representatives of the art of the toilette. Society would be shorn of more than half its pains and pleasures, if women were to don a universal costume as uninteresting and as unbecoming as that worn by men. Hence the great advantages which a study of the principles of fine art offers to women. And if attention to dress be really one of the penalties they must pay as members of the more angelic half of creation, by all means give them the solace of sound artistic training, with definite aesthetic precepts to go upon, in carrying out the responsibilities and distinctions of their order.
>
> Anonymous 1873: 220

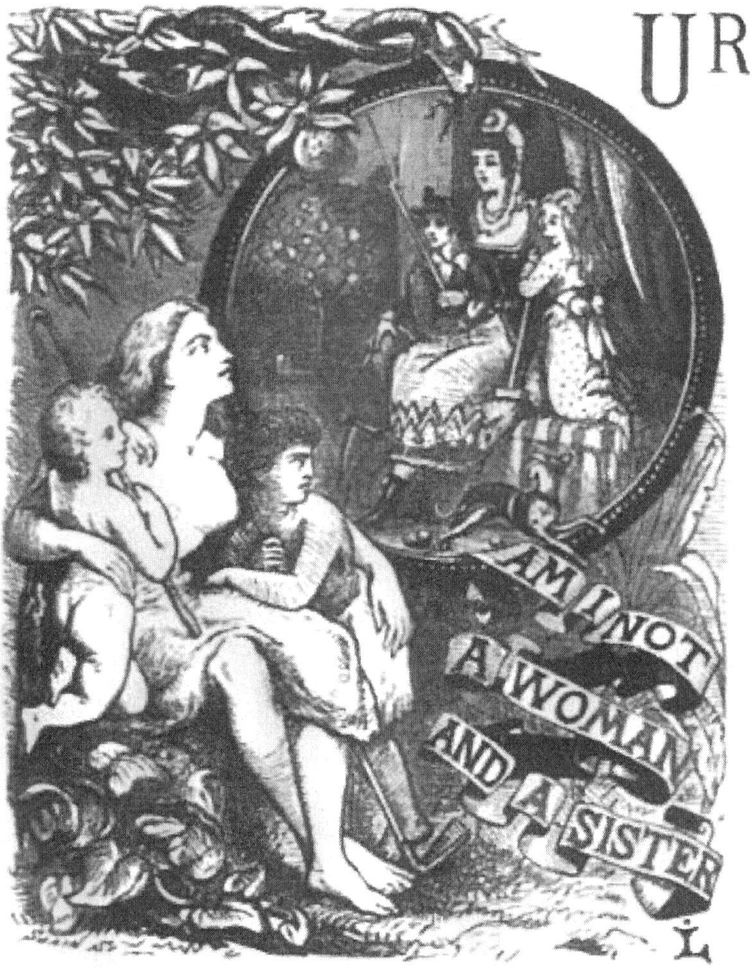

Figure 5.2 I.L. (artist's full name unknown),"Our"; historiated initial in: Anonymous, 1869. "Notes & Incidents," *The Gentleman's Magazine*, 226, pp. 373–374.

In a later installment of the description of these costumes (the space allotted to discussion of this aspect of the exhibition is unprecedented in nineteenth-century descriptions of historical fashion displays), the author concludes that increased exposure to "artistic and well-selected" (1873: 303) examples of timeless good taste has made a difference: "We seem gradually progressing to the adoption of a more sensible and tasteful standard than formerly, and the marked improvement in the costume of the middle and lower classes is strikingly apparent; while there is, happily, less display of violent colour and tawdry finery, there is a decided evidence of increased refinement and judgment" (Anonymous 1873: 51).

It is typical of the cultural commentators of the period that this piece puts the improvement in the material culture of the lower classes down to education, and not to growing economic prosperity. Yet, it also brings up a means by which the exclusive material culture of the upper classes, otherwise unattainable, could be made to have social and cultural value. Disciplining the largely female audience from uneducated consumers into cultured connoisseurs has been one of the social functions of art museums in the modernist period (see for example the discussion of MOMA's "Useful Object" exhibitions in Staniszewski 1998). Navigating brand distinctions for socioeconomic status requires consumer literacy, not indiscriminate hoarding. In this way, representing historical fashion as art both evades and fuels the market forces that drive the fashion system.

Conclusion

As feminist museologist Gaby Porter noted in 1988, women and femininity are all too often encoded in museum displays with the material culture of domestic toil and the textile arts. The decorative arts have traditionally been gendered feminine (Richter 2010: 34), and particular types of viewership have been seen as feminine, also (Rose 2002; Richter 2010: 28–29), and as this chapter has described, fashion history exhibitions often reflect what might be termed a parochial attitude to a predominantly female audience. Although fashion curation is now largely female-dominated, it continues to struggle for equality with more traditionally masculine occupations (Taylor 1998, 2004). Alexandra Palmer writes of the impact of this for professionals:

> The fact that the craft of installing costumes and textiles has been largely performed by female curators and arty window-dressers has, I believe, been an important factor in the low status of these collections within museums. [. . .] Costume and textiles staff within museums have often been marginalized and perceived as a group of style-obsessed ladies and gay men playing dress-up with large dolls.
>
> Palmer 2008: 47–48

Palmer goes on to point out that working with fashion can be perceived as an extension of women's traditional domestic and childcare duties (2008: 54), which is a disturbing application of gender essentialism; it cannot be stated that the museum is an equal opportunity space if women are doing women's work with women's objects. Indeed, the objects of dress in museums do tend to be overwhelmingly female, and donated by women. The preponderance of female items may be because women are seen as keepers of family histories (Hill 2011), but, as Belk and Wallendorf (1994) suggest, this is still a view of females as amateurs—consumers and hoarders, not collectors—something that does not threaten the masculine hegemony of collecting objects of art. The role of the market is important, too, if women are manipulated into participating on an unequal basis (Pearce 1995: 409) and the fashion system, pervading as it does the space of the museum, may preclude curators of fashion from doing intellectual work of a high standard (Palmer 2008: 54), if critique is feared to incite financial reprisals from powerful sponsors in the commercial fashion world.

Thus, we cannot take the contents or the presentation of the public wardrobe for granted. As dress historian Leigh Summers has written, "Costume, when it is authentically and sensitively used to represent women, has the ability to summon up in our imagination an embodiment, rather than an ethereal caricature, of our foremothers" (Summers 2000: 6). The representation of female garments (their quantity and quality) has implications for the history and current status of women and women's work. To characterize women as rabid fashion consumers is to deny the materiality of garments and their wear, as well as the economic history of the clothing industry. Furthermore, it dishonors the diversity of the dressed experience: men, women, children, subcultures, and minorities of all socioeconomic classes have a right to be represented. Curators, whether they are female or male, heterosexual or homosexual, also have a responsibility to be honest about this to their audiences. Fashion history is not frivolous and neither is it solely a feminine affair. It is unfair to categorize it as such, because this allows the binary gender stereotypes of female domesticity and decorativeness to continue, and essentializes and marginalizes women's contributions to the material world. Only thoughtful practice, based in considered critique, can change museum fashion collections into truly public wardrobes.

References

Anonymous (1847), "Hints to the British Museum Committee," in: *Punch*, 13, p. 59.

Anonymous (1869), "Notes & Incidents," in: *The Gentleman's Magazine*, 226, pp. 373–374.

Anonymous (1873), "Antiquities at the International Exhibition – Costumes," in: *The Antiquary*, 3, pp. 219–220, 243–244, 271–272, 303; 4, p. 51.

Anonymous (1913), "Old English Dress; Costume Exhibition at Harrods," in: *The Daily Telegraph*, November 22, 1913, clipping in V&A Harrods donor file MA/1/H926.

Anonymous (1971), *The Museum of Costume Picture Book*, Bath: Assembly Rooms and Museum of Costume.

Anonymous (1975), "American Women of Style, Exhibition Checklist," Metropolitan Museum of Art, records of the Costume Institute: American Women of Style.

Baker, Malcolm and Brenda Richardson (eds) (1997), *A Grand Design: The Art of The Victoria and Albert Museum*, London: V&A Publications.
Belk, Russell W. and Melanie Wallendorf (1994), "Of Mice and Men: Gender Identity in Collecting," in: Susan M. Pearce (ed.), *Interpreting Objects and Collections*, London: Routledge, pp. 240–253.
Birchall-Spencer, Meredith (2003), "Tailor Made," in: *Where Toronto*, February, pp. 20–21.
Breward, Christopher (1999), *The Hidden Consumer: Masculinities, Fashion and City Life 1860–1914*, Manchester: Manchester University Press.
Byrde, Penelope (1980), *Museum of Costume*, Bath: Bath City Council.
Byrde, Penelope (1984), "The Collections and Collecting Policies of the Major British Museums," in: *Textile History*, 15, pp. 147–170.
de la Haye, Amy (2006), "Vogue and the V&A Vitrine," in: *Fashion Theory*, 10, pp. 127–152.
Golbin, Pamela (1999), *Garde-robes*, Paris: Union centrale des arts décoratifs.
Hill, Kate (2005), *Culture and Class in English Public Museums, 1850–1914*, Aldershot: Ashgate.
Hill, Kate (2011), "Collecting Authenticity: Domestic Familial, and Everyday 'Old Things' in English Museums, 1850–1939," in: *Museum History Journal*, 4(2), pp. 203–222.
Klonk, Charlotte (2009), *Spaces of Experience: Art Gallery Interiors from 1800 to 2000*, New Haven, CT: Yale University Press.
Mendes, Valerie D. (1984), "Women's Dress Since 1900," in: Natalie Rothstein (ed.), *Four Hundred Years of Fashion*, London: V&A Publications, pp. 77–100.
MHE (1907), *A Manual of Etiquette for Ladies and Gentlemen; Revised and Rewritten from the Work by the Countess of—*, London: Routledge.
Palmer, Alexandra (2008), "Untouchable: Creating Desire and Knowledge in Museum Costume and Textile Exhibitions," in: *Fashion Theory*, 12, pp. 31–64.
Pearce, Susan (1995), *On Collecting: An Investigation Into Collecting in the European Tradition*, London: Routledge.
Perry, Lara (2006), *History's Beauties: Women and the National Portrait Gallery, 1856–1900*, Aldershot: Ashgate.
Petrov, Julia (2008), "The Habit of their Age": English Genre Painters, Dress Collecting, and Museums, 1910–1914," in: *Journal of the History of Collections*, 20: 237–251.
Preziosi, Donald and Claire Farago (2004), *Grasping the World: The Idea of the Museum*, London: Ashgate.
Richter, Dorothee (2010), "A Brief Outline of the History of Exhibition Making," in: *On Curating*, 6, pp. 28–37.
Rose, Gillian (2002), *Visual Methodologies*, London: Sage.
Schneider, Sara K. (1995), *Vital Mummies: Performance Design for the Show-window Mannequin*, New Haven, CT: Yale University Press.
Shannon, Brent (2004), "ReFashioning Men: Fashion, Masculinity, and the Cultivation of the Male Consumer in Britain, 1860–1914," in: *Victorian Studies*, 46, pp. 597–630.
Silverman, Deborah (1986), *Selling Culture*, New York: Pantheon.
Smith, Sir Cecil (1913), Untitled correspondence, November 27, 1913, Harrods file. MA/1/H926, Victoria and Albert Museum Archives.
Staniszewski, Mary Anne (1998), *The Power of Display: A History of Exhibition Installations at the Museum of Modern Art*, Cambridge, MA: MIT Press.
Summers, Leigh (2000), "Sanitising the Female Body: Costume, Corsetry, and the Case for Corporeal Feminism in Social History Museums," in: *Open Museums Journal*.
Taylor, Lou (1998), "Doing the Laundry? A Reassessment of Object-based Dress History," in: *Fashion Theory*, 2, pp. 337–358.

Taylor, Lou (2004), *Establishing Dress History*, Manchester: Manchester University Press.
Vreeland, Diana (1975), *American Women of Style*, New York: Metropolitan Museum of Art.
Ward, Rebecca (2007), "News Release. The Golden Age of Couture," Victoria and Albert Museum Archives MA/51/3: The Golden Age of Couture.
Whitehead, Christopher (2005), *The Public Art Museum in Nineteenth Century Britain: The Development of the National Gallery*, Aldershot: Ashgate.

6

CLASS AND GENDER IN A MUSEUM COLLECTION: FEMALE SKIWEAR

Marianne Larsson

In 1872, the ethnographer Dr. Artur Hazelius collected a red, green, and dark-blue, striped, half-woolen skirt, which was one of ten garments belonging to a so-called "national" costume or "folk" costume from Stora Tuna in Dalecarlia in northern Sweden. This skirt was the very first number (NM.0000001) in the Nordiska Museet collections.

Dr. Hazelius, the founder of Nordiska Museet and Skansen in Stockholm, continued his collecting of costumes and other belongings of the rural population with help from his so-called "providers." At the time, the decorated and colorful peasant costumes, mostly used for feasts and attendance at church, were called national or folk costumes by the national romantic bourgeoisie. In 1873, Hazelius opened a cultural-historical museum with national costumes dressed on full-scale mannequins in six stipulated "authentic" indoor dioramas. The Scandinavian Ethnographic Collection was planned to be a "folk costume museum" (Nilsson 2005: 20–36). In the national romantic conviction of the time, one of the most important reasons for building up Nordiska Museet was to save the history and artifacts of disappearing nineteenth-century rural life. The castle-like building that now houses Nordiska Museet was completed in 1907.

In the 1880s, Hazelius introduced collecting of urban middle- and upper-class fashionable dress as well, as he saw clothing from all social classes in society as representative of Swedish cultural history. When peasant clothing and lower-class clothing, thought of as local and traditional, were organized in a department for dress and textiles, fashion costumes were organized in a separate department for upper-class collections. As urban fashion costumes were seen as unique pieces of art, the user and local context was not documented in the same way as the individuals and the local traditions behind the national costumes. Since the 1950s, when there were not many individuals left who could tell stories about the rural life of the nineteenth century, Nordiska Museet started to investigate contemporary society. And from that time, all clothing belonged to the same department. Nowadays the conviction is that dressed folk costumes and other peasant clothing have been influenced by contemporary urban fashion as well. Following Hazelius' intentions, dress has always been, and still is, one of the most important parts of the Nordiska Museet collections.

As the dress historian Lou Taylor has pointed out, the separation between peasant clothing and high fashion costumes has dominated in most western countries, but furthermore the collections have been separated in either ethnographic or art and design museums. In addition, Nordiska Museet started to collect clothing in the nineteenth century, while many other museums did not start until the first half of the twentieth. The background was that the male museum curators did not see clothing as an important cultural-historical field (Taylor 2002, 2005: 37–59).

Traditionally, peasant and fashionable dress has been shown in separate exhibitions at Nordiska Museet, but in 2010 the permanent exhibition "Power of Fashion: 300 Years of Clothing" was opened. In this, costumes from different social classes and cultural contexts are mixed in an ambitious way to avoid the strict categorizations of the past (Eldvik and Landin 2010). The display communicates deeper presentations from three decades, the 1780s, the 1860s, and the 1960s—"times when the economy, currents of ideas and technical developments clearly affected clothing and fashion," as the Nordiska Museet website points out. As a cultural-historical museum Nordiska Museet focuses on dress in a broad perspective.

Based on the rich clothing collections, a dress and fashion profile was declared in the 1990s. According to my interpretation, dress is about the materiality of clothing, whereas fashion means the materiality of fashionable dress and the fashion industry, as well as the relatively newborn focus on contemporary fashion designers and "the Swedish fashion-miracle" (Falk 2011). Today, there are international, well-known Swedish designers and brands in the collections, not least since the museum started to collect one outfit a year, produced by the designer or designer group that won the national design award called "Guldknappen" (The Gold Button), established by the Swedish ladies magazine *Damernas Värld* in 1981. Since the launching of the dress and fashion profile, there have been several exhibitions on body and clothing, and several books have been published with clothing in focus. The website archive shows that the museum has organized lots of fashion events, and that the rich and comprehensive library of Nordiska Museet presents in a detailed way fashion literature and magazines, not least as a resource for the Centre for Fashion Studies at Stockholm University, founded in 2006.

In this chapter, my purpose is to use the museum collections—costumes, images, and written documents—as research sources, not to study museological discourses of Nordiska Museet, but to enlighten some cultural history on female open-air life and female skiing costumes in early twentieth-century Sweden. Without knowing almost anything about the female ski outfit collections, I could quite safely choose my topic, as I am familiar with the possibilities of the enormous clothing collections at Nordiska Museet. My aim is to show that skiing, ski clothing, and ski fashion were an important part of women's liberation.

Fieldwork in the past

Urban middle-class women have been active in open-air activities and sports since the end of the nineteenth century. When men could easily wear a used woolen suit, women had to challenge the fashion of corseted waists and full-length skirts, as well as the conventions that excluded them from physical exercise in public and outside. In this study, I want to show how women's desire for outdoor life has influenced their ski clothing according to new social and cultural patterns. With a focus on female ski outfits from the end of the nineteenth century to the 1930s, my aim is to show the transformation in women's clothing, from full-length skirts and strict overcoats to more functional outdoor-life clothing with long trousers, leisure jackets, and warm knitted garments. The research sources consist of ski garments, written documents, photographs, and other images in the museum collections. It should not be very controversial to regard the development of clothing and fashion for sports and outdoor life as an important contribution to women's liberation (cf. Larsson 2012: 113–136). With a focus on ski outfits, this chapter is part of a wider research project on open-air life and female clothing at the beginning of the twentieth century. The wider project, which concluded in an exhibition at Nordiska Museet in 2013, has been possible due to research grants, with the aim of deepening research in the museum collections, from the Swedish Arts Council.

From the period covered by this study the costume collections are quite extensive, while there are gaps from the late twentieth century. Even so, the contemporary policy governing the collecting of clothing and other objects is rather restrictive. Whether the collecting is active or about accepting donations, new objects should be included in a wider context, ideally linked to a particular individual. The ideal is that the museum pieces, and the individuals linked to them, tell a story that is as rich as possible. To deepen the context of the museum pieces, written documents and photos are provided. Another part of the acquisitions is the conservators' opinion on the quality of the objects and their ability to be saved for the future. According to the museum's profile areas, based on the contents of the collections, the general policy is to ensure and communicate source material through which people, now and in the future, can come to know something about their age and history. The museum's purpose is that the collections and their documentation create contexts and perspectives across time and space, and put the individual in a social and historical context. It must also be imbued with diversity, and as comprehensively as possible reflect the diverse social and cultural identities regarding gender, sexuality, class, age, ethnicity, and religious belief for various times. The ambition is that the museum collections will remain as interesting and relevant as possible for future visitors and researchers.

This study places garments at the center, but linked to each garment there are facts that you cannot find in a museum store. Important details are enrolled in a master ledger, listed on catalog cards, and posted in the museum's database, Primus. Besides the database, I have frequently used the old catalog cards, where I have been able to find descriptions of each garment and an indication of when, how, and from whom the garment arrived at the museum. Ideally there is a photo and at best there is information about the garments added by the carrier or the donor. As there are about 1.5 million objects in the collections, the database is not absolutely complete. In this chapter I want to tell the cultural history of female skiing and skiwear, as far as it is possible to achieve based on the collections of documents, images, and skiwear.

Outdoor life on skis

According to the American author and ski enthusiast Roland Huntford, Norway was the forerunner of the "sportified" ski interest, meaning skiing for pleasure and not for necessary transport. The first modern ski competition took place in Norway in 1843, and in 1870, in Norway as well, the world's first ski race officially open to women was organized (Blom and Lindroth 1995; Huntford 2008). The first ski races in Sweden were held in 1879 in Bellevueparken close to Stockholm (*På Skidor* 1900/1901, 1901/1902; Lindhagen 1959: 3–7). In 1892, The Association for Ski Promotion in Sweden, "Skidfrämjandet," was founded, inspired by the growing sports activities in England, and those of the Swedish Tourist Association, formed in 1885. Skidfrämjandet immediately began organizing competitions in order to popularize skiing as a leisure activity (Yttergren 1992). The initiators were high-ranking military men, i.e. urban bourgeois men who mainly had other men in sight, but in 1894/1895, cross-country skiing, at distances of two and five kilometers, was planned for women and girls as well (*Skidfrämjandet* 1894/1895).

Essays and photos in Skidfrämjandet's yearbook *På Skidor* (On Skis) show that women were relatively frequently connected to ski clubs and took part in ski tours. The yearbook also shows that women took part to some extent in ski competitions and contributed as writers (*På Skidor* 1900/1901, 1901/1902). In the 1910 issue of *Vinterboken* (The Winter Book), the editor was promoting sports and outdoor activities for everyone, even for women, but in contrast to men's desire to conquer nature, the purpose was to train healthy and good mothers. There are several guides that provide advice on appropriate equipment. It was generally male experts who wrote manuals and essays on skiing, and in cases where women are the focus, often in a separate section, their impractical clothing was almost always commented upon, with supporting advice—a great benefit to this study. Given the male perspectives of the early 1900s, good motherhood and physical beauty were regarded as motives for female outdoor activities.

Winter sports and bourgeois fashion apparel

For the benefit of women's independence the American woman Amelia Bloomer, in the 1850s, launched a dress with a knee-length skirt over long, wide trousers. The Bloomer costume was severely criticized in its time, but still the style was important in the development of sportswear and swimwear during the second half of the 1800s. Inspired by the Anglo-Saxon countries, a dress reform movement started in Sweden as well. In 1886, some intellectual women in Stockholm formed the Swedish Dress Reform Association, in order to actively work to reform the impractical ankle-length skirts and laced waists (Hazelius-Berg 1949: 127–156; Bergman 1988: 32–55).

At the end of the 1800s, bourgeois women were still tied to the home, marriage, and motherhood. As skiers, women broke the power structures of society. It was not feminine to indulge in athletic activities in the countryside, and the traditional dress was extremely impractical for this purpose. However, this did not prevent women from climbing mountains, hiking, or skiing, but they sometimes had to endure their so-called "tourist costumes" being referred to as "hermaphrodite costumes" by some men (Arenhill 2005: 108–113; Eskilsson 2008: 362–391).

Regarding women's clothing for winter activities, ice-skating costumes first appeared in the fashion magazines. Skating for pleasure appeared much earlier than skiing. The "skate suits" on display in the exclusive magazine *Freja*, first issued in 1873, did not differ significantly from other fashion apparel for outdoor use at the time. Perhaps the skirt was a little shorter; in the fashion plates you can see the boot with its blade (*Freja* 1873–1900). In the museum there is a very slender, dark-blue woolen skate suit with a fur collar and a fur hat (NM.0258121–24). In this outfit, in the 1880s, the user Hanna Palme was ice-skating to live music on an ice rink decorated with electric lamps. On the sea ice in the city of Stockholm, ice-skating was a social activity where young men and women met. A *carte-de-visite* portrait from the 1890s shows Mrs. Amelie Pettersson in a ski suit that in elegance matches the elegant skate suits in *Freja*. In her right hand she is holding a pair of skis and in the left hand a long ski pole, but it is impossible to know whether she ever skied in this seemingly urban clothing. Although not dressed as elegantly as the lady in the photo, many women were skiing in ordinary winter clothes. Old photographs of women on skis dressed in long woolen skirts are common, but it is not always clear if the skis were used for necessary transport or if the women were skiing for pleasure.

Female ski runners in "Lapp costumes"

A women's ski costume that emerged with particular prominence around 1900 was the "Lapp costume," a Sami-inspired outfit consisting of a full-length frock of cloth, worn with a bodice or chest cloth, a belt, and a cap. Photos, costumes, and written documents tell the same facts. In an exhibition in 1953, the museum highlighted that a female skier in a "Lapp costume" was an urban phenomenon. A mannequin dressed in a Lapp costume of dark-blue cloth was completed with skis and ski poles. The costume was made for and used by Miss Eva Strindberg from Stockholm (NM.0229375). In all, there are four Lapp costumes in the collections, described as "ski suits" or "sports suits" (NM.0221161, NM.0267511, NM.0331638). Three of them are made of dark-blue cloth and one is dark green. All the costumes use the characteristic colors of the Sami costume, blue, green, red and yellow, but in somewhat obscure nuances, and they are all decorated with Sami-inspired jewelry. A visit to the museum store shows that the costumes are quite voluminous. The straight cut is similar to the cut of the reform dresses in the Old Norse style, launched by the Dress Reform Association in the late 1800s. Even though a belt would tighten the dress at the waist, it would obviously be possible to wear it without a laced waist. Perhaps the Lapp costume was launched as appropriate sports clothing for radical women in the spirit of the reform movement's everyday clothing.

Female skiers in Lapp costumes are also shown in expressive staging on the very popular *carte-de-visite* portraits. Several studio portraits show young women, one or more in an ankle-length "Lapp costume." Skis and ski poles are used as props, sometimes against a background of a winter landscape. It is easy to imagine that the women were involved in the staging themselves, as healthy, sporty, independent, and modern. As an example, three young women, Elsa, Dollan, and Joy, were photographed in a studio in 1901. They are posing with skis and ski poles in front of a snow-covered spruce fir, and are all wearing ankle-length skirts. At least one of them is wearing a Sami-inspired ski outfit.

In the absence of a given winter costume, the bourgeois woman's ski suit got inspiration from Sami costume. One reason may be that the Norwegian female skier Eva Nansen, wife of the Norwegian explorer Fridtjof Nansen,

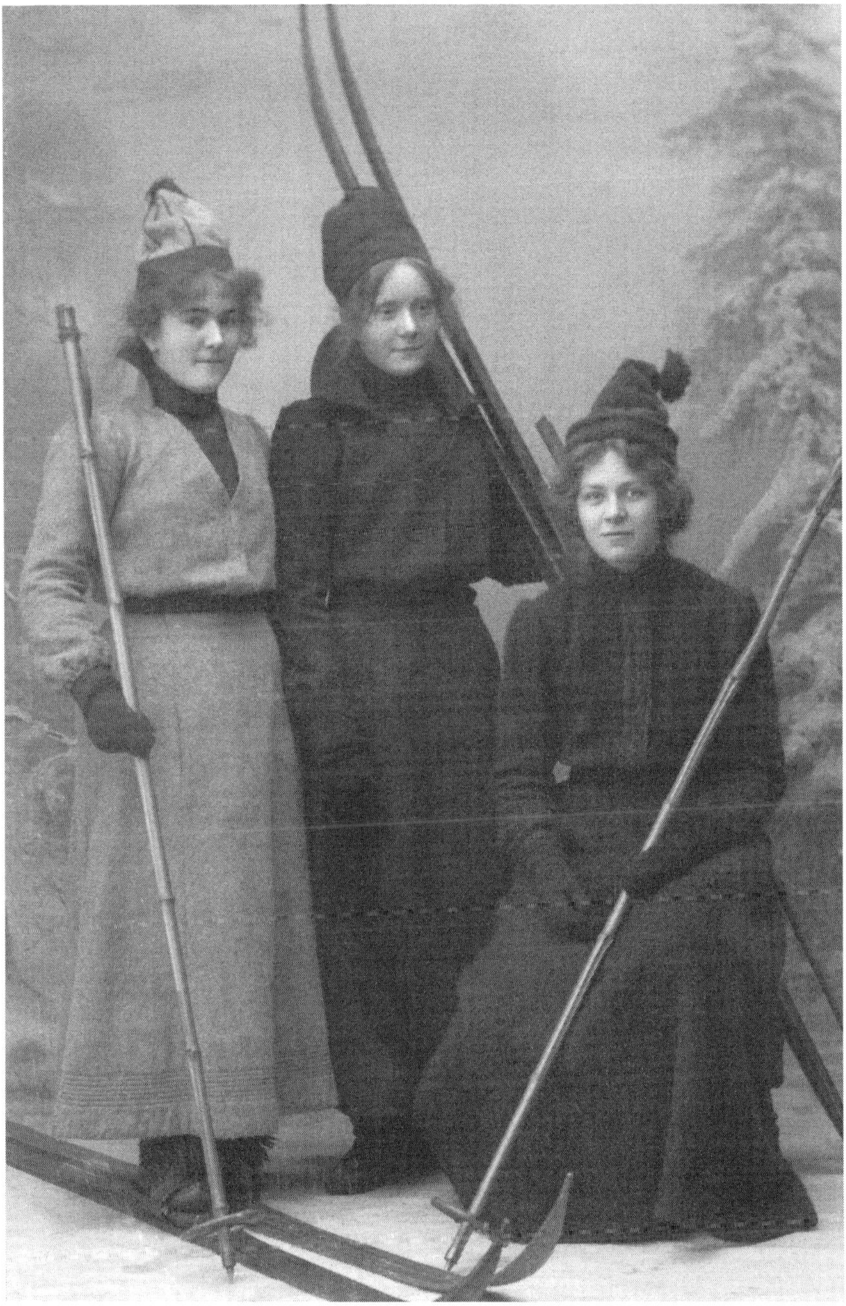

Figure 6.1 The sporty and modern ladies, Elsa, Dollan, and Joy, are posing on a *carte-de-visite* portrait photographed in 1901 in Maria Kihlbaum's studio in Sundsvall. The women are wearing less decorated versions of the Sami-inspired "Lapp costume." Photograph by Maria Kihlbaum, © Nordiska Museet.

wore “a revolutionary skiing outfit” made of thick, gray wadmal when the couple crossed Hardangervidda on skis in 1892. “It consisted of a pair of loose trousers, worn under a kind of doublet, like a Lapp woman’s garment, with a short skirt reaching below the knee. It made skiing easier. Its real defiance was to expose a recognizable portion of the legs,” according to Robert Huntford (2008: 174). Fridtjof Nansen designed the costume, and Eva Nansen sewed it.

Not surprisingly, skiing associates with the Sami way of life in wintertime. For centuries, the Sami have used skis for transportation. Skidfrämjandet showed Sami men on the yearbook cover as early as the 1890s (Yttergren 1992). Even today, a ski-running Sami is included in the logo of what is now called “Friluftsfrämjandet” (The Association of Open Air Promotion). The use of the “Lapp costume” was well in line with the national romantic flirtations of the 1800s. With inspiration from the costume collections of Artur Hazelius and the growing interest in the national folklore, bourgeois youth made free interpretations of folk costumes, which were used when they were practicing folk dances at parties in a national romantic spirit. Usually the Sami costumes, which are still used, are not discussed in connection with folk costume. Around 1900, however, the “Lapp costumes” were probably perceived in the same way.

While I was writing this study, Nordiska Museet was offered a further Sami-inspired ski or sports outfit from around 1903/1904. This one was used by “Benny” Lindgren, born in 1883 on the Swedish west coast. The question was whether it was justified to add another Lapp costume to the collections when there were already three. What made this outfit interesting, however, was that the possible donator reported a rich context. The Lapp costume was mentioned by the user in a letter, and the user wore it in a photo. Unfortunately, the user was not on skis, instead she was posing with a group of people linked to the crafts college of Nääs which she visited several times between 1902 and 1904. A couple of documents introduce “Benny” Lindgren to the crafts college. One of them states that she was welcome to bring a national costume if she had one. It also stipulated that corsets should not be used during lessons, and that skirts were preferred to end 10 centimeters (4 inches) above the ground. The context was crucial for the final decision, and in the end Benny Lindgren’s Sami-inspired Lapp costume (NM.0331638) contributed interesting cultural history to this female outdoor clothing project.

Twin sisters Wiking ahead of their time

The daughter of Sigrid Wiking has donated costume pieces as well as photos and archival documents to the Nordiska Museet collections. Some costume images and press cuttings are mounted on catalog cards. The photos, dated to 1909 and 1910, show the women’s line-up at ski races in Saltsjöbaden, a residential district south of Stockholm. The 16-year-old twin sisters Sigrid and Tora Wiking from Djursholm, a residential district north of Stockholm, are highlighted as pioneers. In a press cutting that pays attention to the ski races of 1909, the twin sisters are described as the first female skiers in Sweden to compete in trousers.

In an incomplete press cutting from an unknown Stockholm journal (March 14, 1909), the writing seems to be about the female skier's impractical, long, woolen skirts, which had become wet and heavy from the snow: "And yet our female skiers, cheeky and healthy young women, have not thought of getting rid of this garment. Not until they via Skidfrämjandet's yearbook *På Skidor* got to know that in other countries, especially in Switzerland, ladies used to go skiing in trousers." The author assumes that the young women who appeared in breeches at the ski races were inspired by the article in *På Skidor* and that "this without, they hardly had the moral courage to act practically dressed for skiing." The first shock of women wearing trousers or divided skirts concerned female cyclists a decade earlier, but the author believes that the trousers were not absolutely necessary when riding a bicycle as they were when skiing, because in skiing:

> [. . .] you have to take the plunge and move from the skirt directly to the breeches. And now that our young girls in our country have begun, it will surely not be long before we take final leave of "Lapp costumes" and all other variants of ski apparel. You can be assured that breeches and the sweater are coming, eventually to become supreme in the realm of skiing. The sweater is a garment that is gaining ground more and more [. . .] every year.
>
> Unknown press cutting, 14 March 1909

The article is illustrated with one of the Wiking sisters wearing wide, knee-length trousers. Unfortunately, the sisters left no breeches to the collection. However, the museum received Sigrid Wiking's white, machine-knitted woolen sweater and a woolen cap. Photos show that female skiers wore bright woolen sweaters frequently. It was often, but not always, young women who went skiing, and the Wiking sisters show that the first ski breeches appeared among young wealthy women.

Sigrid Wiking was not only a pioneer in ski breeches; she was also the first female ski-jumper in Sweden. A press cutting from the German magazine *Sport im Bild* shows the 15-year-old Sigrid at a jump in Fiskartorpsbacken during the winter of 1908. She is wearing two braids with big bows in her hair, a light sweater, and a skirt that wraps her legs for the jump (*Sport im Bild*, 1909). The land at Fiskartorpet near Stockholm has been used for skiing and other outdoor recreation since 1870. The annual Fiskartorpet Day with ski races and ski-jumping was a big attraction (Schantz 2008: 238–257). Several standing tickets for the ice on the lake below the ski jump show that Sigrid Wiking was a frequent visitor at the ski races at Fiskartorpet. Together with lots of other documents that create an impressive context, these simple paper tickets are saved in the Sigrid Wiking-Olsson archive (NMA 46/1981).

Several ski racing guides from 1909 show that the twin sisters were very active skiers, and in the paper *Stockholms Dagblad* (March 15, 1909) they were dubbed "our best female skiers," when they had reached first and second place in ski races in Djursholm. Badges from the Olympics in Stockholm in 1912, and from the Baltic Games in 1914, confirm Sigrid Wiking's continuing interest in sports, but she had other interests as well. In her personal archive, there is a statute from 1911 for the woman's political right to vote (NMA 46/1981). If her active skiing and commitment to the suffrage movement went hand in hand with sympathy for the dress reform movement, she worked for women's emancipation in many ways.

Sigrid Wiking finally appears in the handbook *Skidlöpning för kvinnor och ungdom* (Skiing for Women and Youth) written by the sports editor, Erik Pallin (1919). An image shows a smiling Sigrid on skis in remarkably thin clothing. She is wearing a blouse with an open collar and quite short sleeves, combined with wide breeches, stockings, socks, and boots. In the book, a piece of a brown envelope glued to the inside of the cover shows that the copy in Nordiska Museet library belonged to Sigrid Wiking-Olsson. This entire valuable context implies that it should be possible to write exciting cultural history, especially about Sigrid Wiking and her twin sister.

Short skirts hide the breeches

In the 1910s, the skirt began to become shorter for women who were engaged in skiing for recreation. Soft, knitted scarves, caps, gloves, and sweaters replaced the tight woolen suit with ankle-length skirt and form-fitting jacket. Women could show the lower part of the leg in a pair of thick tights, with feet in boots and socks. The female skier became increasingly visible in newspapers and fashion magazines.

While the Wiking sisters were skiing in breeches, *Vinterboken* was published. In a chapter about women's ski apparel the author speaks in favor of wide, knee-length, ski breeches, as opposed to heavy and hindering full-length skirts and stiff jackets. Combined with breeches, he suggests a sweater, and, if necessary, a long and not tight-fitting jacket of light, thin, soft material. One advantage of rather short and close-fitting breeches was that, when traveling by rail or walking through the city, they could be hidden by a thin skirt, which when not used could be carried in a backpack (*Vinterboken* 1910: 256). A drawing in the magazine *Nyaste Pariser Mode* (Newest Paris Fashion) shows a woman in a ski suit consisting of a long jacket and breeches worn clearly visible under an unbuttoned calf-length skirt with full button closure. The following issue claims that Scandinavia was the forerunner of modern skiwear, and that it was called "*à la suedois*" by women on the European continent (*Nyaste Pariser Mode* 1913). Nevertheless is was not yet the time for a woman to be able to appear in general public life wearing trousers.

In the collections, there is what I first thought and hoped would be an example of breeches and skirt in combination. Knee-length "ski trousers" and a "sports skirt," both of beige ribbed velvet, suggested that it was a combination. The garments were briefly described on the catalog cards but there were no pictures. However, they told that the brand of the breeches was Fritz Schultze, München, and that Mrs. Bib Adelsköld from Stockholm had used the garments in St. Moritz in Switzerland (NM.0248292–93). To find out if the skirt could have been used to hide the ski trousers, I had to study the garments themselves. I found that the breeches looked like what in English used to be called "elephant-ear" breeches, a garment taken from the male wardrobe. The rather thick fabric, and the narrow waist of the skirt, told me that it could hardly have been worn on top of the breeches. And the skirt was too voluminous to be carried in a small backpack. Despite this, even if the age is rather uncertain, these breeches are likely to be the oldest female ski trousers in the Nordiska Museet collections. In the 1910s, Bib Adelsköld was about 20–25 years old. Ski trousers were already used abroad, especially in Switzerland. At that time, St. Moritz was an elegant winter sports tourist resort that attracted Europe's upper social strata. Ski clothing made of ribbed velvet, with buttons of mother-of-pearl, would fit in quite well with that context.

Erik Pallin would not discuss the issue of skiing in trousers or skirts; women were free to decide, but one can conclude that he preferred the knee-length skirt, even if trousers were "introduced everywhere abroad, not the least at the big fashionable winter sports sites" (Pallin 1919: 15). He suggests, for example, a white cap, a rather long, wine-colored sweater, a white woolen skirt ending just below the knees, and high, thick, knitted gray socks. He thought that a white sweater, white skirt, and green cap could be beautiful. Was there in reality such a display of colors behind the black and white photos in the collections? As in *Vinterboken*, Pallin points out that it attracted attention if a woman walked through the town in trousers.

Ready-made clothing was still fairly scarce, but was available by mail order. Mail order catalogs are wonderful source material as the garments for sale are accompanied by accurate descriptions. In the Åhlén & Holm mail order winter catalog from 1915/1916, there are two sports sweaters for women, equipped with a high collar, but no sports skirts or trousers. The words "skiing" or "skiwear" do not occur at all. Mail order catalogs reflect quite well the current fashion, without being at the forefront, but the intended customer was primarily not the social group devoted to skiing for pleasure.

Sports and skiwear in vogue

In the 1920s, female fashion underwent a radical change. A common interpretation is that many women in Europe were forced to contribute to production when men were drafted to fight in the First World War. Long skirts disappeared along with the corset when women had to perform tasks that required a strong and agile body. In addition, the growing interest in sports and outdoor recreation had a major influence on fashion. When sportswear and fashion history meet, "Coco" Chanel used to be mentioned. She is considered the designer who introduced casual and comfortable clothing for the modern woman. Chanel created soft, pliable garments, with skirts that ended just below the knee. The stiff corset was gone. Oddly enough, I found just a few traces of ski suits clearly dated to the 1920s. They are absent in the costume collections, they occur rarely in photos, and they still do not appear in Åhlén & Holm's catalog. Yet, there are a couple of photos in the collections. One shows five women on skis in 1924 in the Swedish mountains and demonstrates clear signs of transition. Two women are dressed in calf-length skirts, while the others seem to be wearing full-length trousers with a large expanse of fabric over the thighs, like the elephant-ear breeches, but laced over the calves. They are all wearing knee-length jackets, and one of them wears a scarf, a cap, and gloves of knitted wool. Another photo, dated to 1925, shows a mother and her daughter on skis. The mother is wearing a long jacket with a slim waist and a calf-length skirt, plus a hat with a narrow brim. The daughter, and donor, explains that it was her first ski trip with her mother, and she compares her knee-length coat with the 1950s, practical children's overalls.

While the first photo seems to show a group of modern middle-class women on a mountain holiday, the other gives the impression of skiing in the neighborhood. My reading is that mother and daughter are skiing in ordinary winter clothes instead of ski suits dictated by sportswear fashion. The opportunity to go on a mountain vacation and to be dressed in modern skiwear was a matter of urbanity, class, and economic assets. However, during the 1920s, the view of the female skier was normalized, as sports and physical exercise were given elements in the society. Female skiers were no longer perceived as unique, even if skiing was still a pursuit mostly reserved for the upper or middle classes.

Skiwear for everybody

In the 1930s, however, opportunities for leisure and holidays spread to all major segments of the population. In 1938 most employees in Sweden were entitled to a two-week vacation. Outdoor activities and sports involved new social classes and people in rural areas as well. Inspired by the German doctrine of physical culture and strengthening outdoor exercise, healthy and strong bodies were the height of fashion. Men should be strong and muscular, while women should be curvy and healthy, all in contrast to the 1920s skinny and boyish-like body fashion. The modern human should radiate energy and health. Outdoor activities expanded considerably. In summer it was fashionable to go hiking, biking, and camping, and in winter the interest in skiing was growing. The Swedish welfare state was under construction, and according to its ideas about how people should live in the best way, people were expected to learn how to take advantage of their non-working time. It must not be wasted (Frykman 1992; Eskilsson 2008). New needs created ready-made sportswear and outdoor clothing. The assortment of ski clothing grew in shops and department stores.

In contrast to the 1920s, the 1930s add a richness of ski clothing and pictures with different representations of the female skier. In the winter of 1930/1931, Åhlén & Holm for the first time launched female sports trousers, in a "balloon model with lacing on the shin." The trousers were worn with a wind jacket in "modern sports model of ordinary length," already recognized in the photo from 1924. The following winter, a women's "ski suit" of "dark-blue, extra strong, thick and heavy woolen cloth" was launched. It was emphasized that it was a novelty. A short jacket with a short zipper in front and a collar, waistband, and cuffs knitted in red, blue, and white, was combined with a pair of wide, full-length trousers with a piece of elastic under the foot (Åhlén & Holm 1930/1931; 1931/1932).

It did not take very long before the male "balloon model" was replaced by wide, woolen, full-length ski trousers. Soon, the elegant cut and the design of the pockets and the buttons showed that skiwear was fashionable. With very modern and sophisticated details and decorations, the same style appears in the fashion photographer Erik Holmén's collections for the department store NK in Stockholm. From the period 1929 to 1939 there are at least eight black and white studio photos, showing models with skis and/or pole sticks. Knitted sweaters or short jackets with narrow waists are worn together with baggy ski trousers tucked into thick socks. The socks are elegantly folded over the skiing boots.

In the costume collections, an elegant ski suit is made up of a waist-length jacket and baggy trousers of dark-blue woolen cloth. It was used by Kerstin Gyllensvärd from Lidingö, born in 1917, when she was young and did a lot of skiing (NM.0313648). She relates that the outfit was bought in the late 1930s and that it was used for a number of years. In the back of the jacket there is a label of woven textiles. The brand Collijn's Sport crowns the logo of Skidfrämjandet, and under the logo the text reads "Approved by Skidfrämjandet." It seems amazing that Skidfrämjandet should have the mandate to approve ski clothes. The dark-blue woolen ski outfit is as modern and elegant as the outfits on the fashion plates. When used, however, there might easily be a gap between the

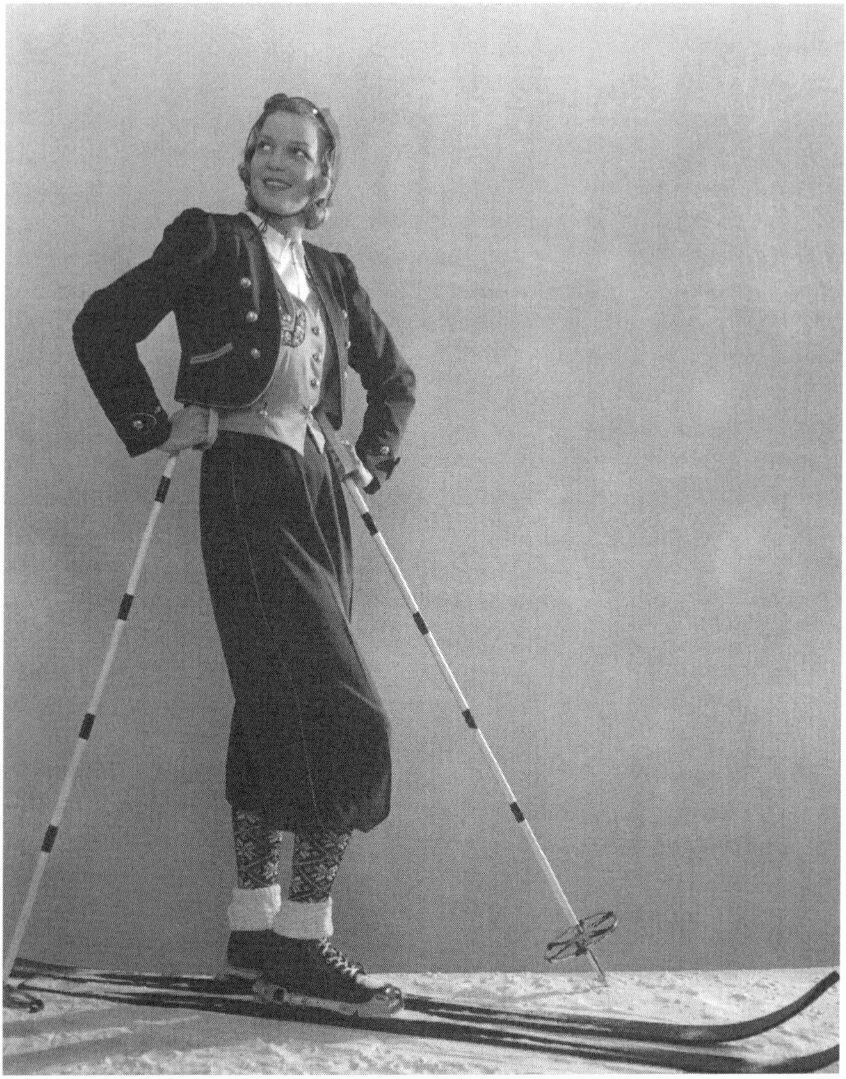

Figure 6.2 Ski outfit from 1938 in a fashion plate for the department store NK in Stockholm. Calf-length woolen trousers with exclusive patterned woolen socks were as modern as full-length trousers. Photograph by Erik Holmén, © Nordiska Museet (NK Archive).

short jacket and the trousers, something that likely made the suit rather impractical in the winter. But in the back of the jacket there are some straps, which made it possible to button together the jacket with the trousers. There is no doubt that this smart ski suit was very modern.

Full-length, wide trousers

While outdoor activities spread to wider sections of the population, it remained the case that the upper stratas of society were those contributing gifts to museum collections. Family names and domiciles connected to the ski garments mentioned in this chapter are clear examples. In the early 1990s a large collection of objects and photos was donated by the daughter of Nanna Svartz, a well-known medical doctor in Stockholm, and a researcher in internal medicine. When Dr. Svartz, in 1938, was appointed a professor in medicine, she was the first female professor of the government service in Sweden.

The Svartz-Malmberg family spent one week a year at the well-known ski resort Åre in the Swedish mountains. A photo from 1935 shows Nanna Svartz and her daughter on skis. Both are wearing dark, wide ski trousers that are constricted at the ankle and tucked into socks. The mother is wearing a sweater, ski boots, a blue cap, and a striped scarf. In a photo from 1937, she is wearing wide woolen trousers together with a grayish-white windbreaker with a belt in the waist, combined with a cap made of off-white poplin, with screen, ear, and neck protection of the same fabric. A label in the cap says "the genuine Dyhlén-cap, sole concessionaire NK's sports department" (NM.0318544). The squadron leader and outdoor authority Gunnar Dyhlén was a good friend of the Svartz-Malmberg family, and a prominent member of Skidfrämjandet, and he was the missing link to Collijn's Sport (*Collijns sportdräkter* 1936). This makes clear an interesting relationship between retailers of modern skiwear and Skidfrämjandet. Most of the Nanna Svartz garments mentioned above are now in the museum collections.

The cover of the Åhlén & Holm winter catalog from 1937/1938 shows a stylish color photo of a man and a woman enjoying a break from skiing. In the same catalog, there are several black and white photos of female models in elegant and modern ski outfits consisting of jackets with belts at the waist and full-length, wide ski trousers. Both trousers and jackets are made of thick, dark-blue woolen cloth—with the exception of a beige jacket made of windproof poplin worn with a "ski and sports hood" of the same fabric. At the end of the 1930s, women of different social groups were able to ski in functional ski suits that did not stop them from moving their legs, although it would take another thirty years before female trousers were accepted except for free time and recreation.

Conclusion

As an ethnologist I am not primarily interested in fashion systems, brands, or tailoring, but in how people wear everyday clothing and how they perform. In the Nordiska Museet collections I have found about seven nearly complete female ski outfits and several odd items. The outfits were all collected in the second half of the twentieth century, when the museum was building up its documentation on contemporary society. On some occasions the donor has completed the documentation with a short story. Together with images and written documents, and with fashion magazines, a story of female skiing has been produced. It is not the fact that clothing and fashion is a profile area that is extraordinary, but the rich costume collections themselves.

A longing for freedom and fresh air, and a desire to move the body, have attracted women to nature since the late nineteenth century. Thanks to the expansion of the railways, and the legal right of access to open country, it was easy to go touring in Sweden—at least for the social class with the money and free time to do so. In the struggle for emancipation, an important question was about the length of the skirt. The restrictive corsets and full-length skirts were gradually superseded by breeches and long trousers. In the 1930s, when most employees got two weeks free a year, there was an explosion in interest in open-air life. The new social-democratic government wanted to create "a good home" for everybody, and people had to learn how to use their free time in a good and healthy way. When skiing became popular among wider social classes, skiwear, fashion, and ready-made clothing went hand in hand. The growing industrial society, labor movement, women's liberation, the war, and the new welfare state ideal all contributed to the change—as did sports and outdoor life.

Nordiska Museet has never been actively involved in collecting of female skiwear or outdoor clothing. More often, skiwear has been collected spontaneously, donated by someone who thought it was worth preserving. It is not difficult to see that the ski outfits on several occasions were related to women in the upper classes, primarily in or outside Stockholm, but it is impossible to say, given the limitations that exist in museum collections, to what extent skiing was a regular activity for this group. Maybe the conclusion should be that it was people from the upper social classes who were comfortable with the idea that you can donate your personal items and history to a well-known national cultural historical museum, such as Nordiska Museet.

References

Arenhill, E. (2005), "Fruntimmer på fjällets topp: En forskningsresa i Svenska Turistföreningens arkiv," in: B. Svensson (ed.), *Föremål för forskning: Trettio forskare om det kulturhistoriska materialets möjligheter*, Stockholm: Nordiska Museet.

Bergman, I. (1988), "Kvinnorna och byxorna," in: I. Bergman (ed.), *Kläder, Fataburen 1988*, Stockholm: Nordiska Museet.

Blom, K.A. and J. Lindroth (1995), *Idrottens historia: Från antika arenor till modern massrörelse*, Farsta: SISU idrottsböcker.

Collijns sportdräkter för damer och herrar (1936).

Eldvik, B. and M. Landin (2010), *Power of Fashion: 300 Years of Clothing*, Stockholm: Nordiska Museet.
Eskilsson, L. (2008), "Friluftsliv," in J. Christensson (ed.), *Signums svenska kulturhistoria: Det moderna genombrottet*, Stockholm: Signum.
Falk, K. (2011), *Det svenska modeundret*, Stockholm: Norstedts.
Freja: Illustrerad Skandinavisk Modetidning (1873–1900).
Frykman, J. (1992), "I rörelse: Kropp och modernitet i mellankrigstidens Sverige," *Kulturella perspektiv*, 1, pp. 30–42.
Hazelius-Berg, G. (1949), "Dräktreformer under 1800-talet," in: *Fataburen* 1949, Stockholm: Nordiska Museet.
Huntford, R. (2008), *Two Planks and a Passion: The Dramatic History of Skiing*, London: Continuum.
Larsson, M. (2012), " 'Huru skidåkerskan fick ta steget fullt ut: Skidkläder, kroppsrörelse och kvinnlig frigörelse," in R. Qvarsell and B. Svensson (eds), *Markeringar och maskeringar: Att visa eller dölja sin kropp*, Stockholm: Nordiska Museet.
Lindhagen, S. (1959), "Skidsporten växer ur lapptossorna," in *Följ spåret. Svensk skidsport genom tiderna*, Stockholm: Framtiden, ungdomstjänsten.
Nilsson, B.G. (2005), "Att förkroppsliga nationen: Om folkdräkternas betydelse när museimän och folklivsforskare upptäckte folket," in B.G. Nilsson (ed.), *Påklädd, uppklädd, avklädd: Om kläder, kropp och identitet*, Stockholm: Norstedts akademiska.
Nyaste Pariser Mode (1913), January and February volumes.
På skidor: Skid- och friluftsfrämjandets årsbok (1900/1901, 1901/1902), Stockholm: *Skid- och friluftsfrämjandet*.
Pallin, E. (1919), *Skidlöpning för kvinnor och ungdom* (On the cover, the book has the title *Skidlöperskan: Ungdomen på skidor*), Stockholm: Björck & Börjesson.
Schantz, P. (2008), "Det tätortsnära naturmötet," in K. Sandell and S. Sörlin (eds), *Friluftshistoria: Från 'härdande friluftslif' till ekoturism och miljöpedagogik. Teman i det svenska friluftslivets historia*, Stockholm: Carlsson.
Skidfrämjandet, program (1894/1895).
Taylor, L. (2002), *The Study of Dress History*, Manchester: Manchester University Press.
Taylor, L. (2005), "Föremålsbaserade perspektiv på dräkt- och textilhistoria," in B.G. Nilsson (ed.), *Påklädd, uppklädd, avklädd: Om kläder, kropp och identitet*, Stockholm: Norstedts akademiska.
Vinterboken (1910), *En vägledning för ung och gammal: Med biträde af fackmän utg. af Gustaf Stjernström*, Uppsala and Stockholm.
Yttergren, L. (1992), *Friluftsfrämjandet 1892–1992: Från skidsport till skogsmulle*, Stockholm: Friluftsfrämjandet.

Nordiska Museet collections can be viewed at http://digitaltmuseum.se/info/owners/S-NM.

7

EXHIBITING THE BODY, DRESS, AND TIME IN MUSEUMS: A HISTORICAL PERSPECTIVE

Anne-Sofie Hjemdahl

The headless mannequins are so filled with character that one can easily imagine the missing faces with their hairstyles and hats.

Dagbladet, October 17, 1952

Fashion journalist of the Norwegian newspaper *Dagbladet*, Love Yngve Anderson, was in 1952 exuberant in her praise of the first dress exhibition showing fashionable dress[1] mounted on headless mannequins at the Museum of Decorative Arts and Design in Oslo (Kunstindustrimuseet). She especially praised the mounting work done by the museum's head of textile conservation, Mrs. Kielland. Andersen's description suggested that if the exhibition mannequins are designed in a lifelike manner, the absent heads as well as the character of the people once inhabiting the dress will nevertheless appear.

This glimpse into the dress exhibition at the Museum of Decorative Arts and Design shows us that it was then an important objective to give the displayed dress a bodily form so that it would appear as more than just clothing. It was important to create illusions of human bodies and lived lives. What was, however, seen as the correct body for the different types of dress?

The relationship between the body, dress, and fashion has become a field of interest within contemporary fashion and dress research over the last twenty-five years. The dominant view presented by this research is that the body and how it is dressed, in accordance with certain fashions, must be seen as a mutual relationship where these factors constitute and create each other (e.g. Wilson 1985; Steele 1999; Entwistle 2000; Graden and McIntyre Petersson 2009).

I would like to employ this perspective when analyzing museums and their display practices. I would also like to explore how specific bodies produced by museum staff may influence the public's reception of dress and time. Apart from the work of Taylor and Palmer (Taylor 2002; Palmer 2008), museological research on dress as museum objects seems not to have been particularly concerned with the historical practice of displaying dress. It is, however, interesting to ask how different exhibition practices have produced specific bodies and to explore how museums have related to bodies and to human life itself in exhibitions of dress and fashion. I believe this perspective will establish an understanding of how museum objects are entangled into their surroundings and how these surroundings both affect and become part of the objects. Within actor-network theory such a perspective is called "co-production" and underlines the way things come into being with other things, with people, practices, institutions, etc. (e.g. Mol 2002; Law 2004; Latour 2005). Donna Haraway talks about this as "becoming with" (Haraway 2008). This perspective will help situate the museum object and create an understanding of dress and bodies as enacted artifacts.

In this chapter[2] I concentrate on museum display methods and how curatorial practices produce museum displayed dress, exhibition techniques, and ultimately knowledge. My analysis is based on case studies of two Scandinavian museums: Nordiska Museet, a cultural history museum in Stockholm, and the Museum of Decorative Arts and Design in Oslo. Both were pioneers in developing new ways of displaying dress and fashion from the early 1930s to the 1950s. Nordiska Museet even developed a new flexible mannequin named the Swedish System[3] that could be adapted in many ways to individual garments. I will explain this further in this chapter. I will also demonstrate and discuss the different versions of bodies which the Swedish System produced in these Scandinavian museums. Through the analysis of changing display practices I will discuss how these are connected to different sets of knowledge-based traditions, i.e. academic disciplines, and also to changing perceptions of time and bodies.

In my analysis the term *dressed figure* is central. It denotes the dressed mannequin as a configuration and entangled embodiment of several factors, such as: museum practices, technical display solutions, type of dress, people-object owners, and knowledge traditions among curators.

Dress, body, and time

At the beginning of this chapter I asked: What is seen as the correct body for different types of dress within museums? I will argue that a museum-dressed figure captures the relationship between dress, body, and time. The question thus becomes: What kind of dress, what kind of body, and what concept of time is produced?

Fashionable dress, which is my focus, often belonged to the well-to-do classes[3] and embodied the latest aesthetic. It was dress defined at a given moment as desirable, beautiful, and popular (Entwistle 2000: 1). These kinds of garments were for the most part tailor-made, made to measure, and were worn before ready-to-wear fashion became available. However, I will also draw attention to the display of pre-twentieth-century folk dress and draw attention to the differences in display strategies.

When using the term "body" I am obviously not talking about biological or human bodies. I am talking about various bodily representations, such as exhibition dummies, dressed mannequins, and also dress racks used to display dress which to a greater or lesser extent give them the appearance of the human form. At the same time the body is also present as references to the human living bodies that once perhaps owned, wore, or were by the designer imagined to wear, these garments. The body, it could be argued, is thus present in the concrete and tangible materiality the dressed figure presents. In this context, the body is also a reference to something outside and beyond.

In the book *Living Pictures, Missing Persons* (2003) by media theorist Mark Sandberg, the presence or absence of bodily representations is argued to play a distinct role in relation to museum visitors. The audience is given an interactive role, they are expected to fill in the missing picture, just as a radio listener or a book reader will create their own image when listening or reading. Sandberg has studied wax cabinets and exhibitions in Scandinavian cultural history museums and their work on recreating the dress owners' bodies at the turn of the nineteenth century. He points to how museums have played with both presence and absence of bodily representations in their exhibitions. One of his claims is that the absence of bodily representation creates a missing person effect that affects the visitor's role. The absence of a physical body makes room for the visitors' potential presence in that they can fill in the picture in their own minds. The viewer must distance themselves from their own bodies in order to participate in this game. As Sandberg points out: "The display [method] creates missing persons on both sides of an imaginary divide; it encourages spectators to be border dwellers, both inside and outside the display" (Sandberg 2003: 1).

Sandberg's work is interesting as it is particularly concerned with the relationship between body and place. But he is not concerned with to what extent an embodiment or how any degree of embodiment affects a meeting between the public and the dressed figures. He discusses either the presence or the absence of bodies, not the in-between positions. Nor does he ask what the absence or presence of people and bodies might consist of. The point I would like to make in this chapter is that the distinction between absence and presence of body is not clear-cut and needs to be nuanced and explored. This is especially the case for dress exhibitions where bodies are absent but also present albeit in different ways and in different configurations.

As mentioned above, the body is also present as a reference to the specific human body that once owned and wore the dress. The general situation in museum exhibitions is the broken relationships between dress and its previous owner or user. Dress in museum collections is often, if not collected brand-new directly from a fashion house or production site, separated from the body who once wore it and gave it a certain expression and life. As such, museums may be viewed as cemeteries for "dead" clothes (Steele 1998: 334). However, the physical absence of the human bodies that once inhabited them does have the capacity to open up spaces for reflection and loss. British fashion and dress researcher Elizabeth Wilson (1985) reflects upon this aspect. In the initial passage of her book *Adorned in Dreams* she comments on both the physical loss that characterizes the dress museum and emphasizes the obscure, even secretive relationships of dress with former bodies and lives. She points to how dress allows us to reflect on the body's shortcomings and corruption: bodies stop living; they have their own temporality because they die. Wilson also creates a sense of wonder as to why museums do not allow clothes to die with their bodies, but instead keep them artificially alive almost like ghosts. Dress detached from its bodies becomes alienated, she says. Joanne Entwistle expands on this by claiming that this type of bodily alienation may go even deeper as dress and shoes tend to bear clear traces of a body when the shape of an arm or the print of a foot in a shoe is clear and visible (Entwistle 2000: 10). In such situations, the absence of the owner's body in fact becomes extremely present. With these reflections about how dress is present in museums, I will now take a look at the Scandinavian museums at the first half of the twentieth century.

Dress collections and exhibitions in Scandinavian museums

At the beginning of the twentieth century, Scandinavian cultural history museums and especially the open-air museums had a tradition of collecting both pre-industrial folk dress and fashionable dress as part of a national identity-building project (Taylor 2002). Culture was perceived as a connected whole and in cultural history museum collections and exhibitions the ambition was that all social groups should be represented (Aall 1916). At Nordiska Museet in Stockholm, there was a strong tradition of displaying folk dress mounted on realistic wax figures, while the display of fashionable dress had not yet assumed a particular display standard. Several exhibition techniques had been explored, among them commercial mannequins used in shop windows at the time (Hazelius-Berg 1934). In 1907, when Nordiska Museet reopened in its new museum building at Djurgården, folk dress was displayed on wax figures in panoramic landscape rooms together with artifacts from specific geographical regions, while fashionable dress was displayed in period rooms with furniture, paintings, and other examples of the decorative arts to exhibit the style of a given period of time (Nylen 1957).

In the period between 1900 and the Second World War, many changes took place within the field of dress in Scandinavian museums. New knowledge ideals now centered on the singular museum object as a historical document and an entrance to a historical past (Edman 2008: 34). Collecting and display practices also changed.

Historical fashionable dress seemed here to present a new display challenge. These clothes had their own silhouette as well as a distinct embodiment. It was therefore important to reconstruct the correct silhouettes while at the same time, given these garments were often heavy, provide the necessary support when put on display. In 1933 and 1934, Nordiska Museet opened an entirely new dress gallery where historical dress was mounted on specially designed headless mannequins and presented in groups to the public inside big glass cases. For the first time exhibited dress was illuminated by electric light while the public's area was left in the dark. The new gallery received a lot of attention, mainly because of its modern new exhibition design where a new type of mannequin, later named the Swedish System, was among the inventions. This mannequin became the common solution in many museums in Scandinavia and was used to display fashionable dress as well as folk dress.

The Swedish System

The new mannequin developed by Nordiska Museet was a piece of mechanical technology consisting of modules of iron and wood. It was mounted on an adjustable skeleton, a framework with a footplate of iron and an adjustable reed with a special screw. The reed was fastened to a disc for the shoulders. Two iron poles were attached to that same disc, and three oval and movable wooden discs—a breast disc, a waist disc, and a hip disc, were mounted on the poles. The wooden discs could be raised or lowered and generally regulated according to the dress measurements. For male dress the shape of the wooden blocks and the position of the holes were different to allow for the fixing of trousers (Buck 1940: 35). The upper body would be covered with canvas and a padding process gave the mannequin its final shape. To sum up, the principle was based on mechanical flexibility to fit different kinds of dress and especially tailor-made dress.

Compared to the wax dummies and mannequins made of hessian and straw that earlier had been used to exhibit folk dress, the Swedish System represented a shift in the display of dress. The older mannequin technology produced extremely realistic and individual dressed figures whose bodies were given

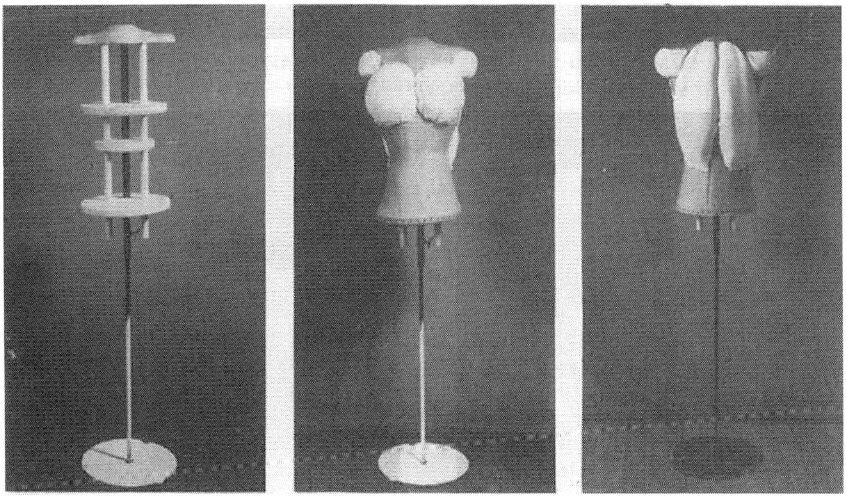

Figure 7.1 The Swedish System mannequin was developed at Nordiska Museet in 1933. Soon it became the most common solution when displaying both fashion and peasant dress in many Scandinavian museums. This is how it was represented in the Norwegian museums journal *Museumsnytt* in 1955. With permission from the Museum of Decorative Arts and Design in Oslo. © Teknisk Museum.

individuality every time by using hessian and straw stuffed into the right body shape. They also had realistic wax heads and hands. The wax figures were also made by artists. The new mechanical mannequins on the other hand produced abstract and anonymous bodies made by the museum's carpenters and dress curators. While the carpenter made the skeleton, the dress curator did the measuring, the padding, and dressed the figure and gave it its final form. These exhibition bodies were individually adjusted to each dress for display. The Swedish System mannequin was firmly placed within a knowledge-based tradition where the bodies were made anonymous. I will argue that these new constructed bodies were the integral result of the professionalization of museum staff working with dress and dress display.

In other words, this new technology was influenced by that age's functionalistic aesthetics and its emphasis on a simple and mass-produced bodily presentation. The functionalistic idea was based on the collective and the mass produced. From 1930 onwards, functionalism and Swedish modernism made a big impact on both exhibitions and display technique at Nordiska Museet and led to the embracing of new pedagogical ideas (Edman and Bergström 2005; Arrhenius 1998; Hjemdahl 2013).

The Swedish System mannequin could be compared with what the French critical theorist Bruno Latour (1987) has named as an "immutable mobile." The System's denotation of the body remained stable and unchanged as it was transported to and used by Nordiska Museet's network of dress curators at the other museums in Scandinavia. The British Museum worker Anne Buck (1940) visited Scandinavian museums in 1939 and noticed how quickly the mannequin was adopted by other important Scandinavian museums such as at the National Museum in Copenhagen, the Museum of Applied Arts in Copenhagen (since 2011, Designmuseum Danmark) and The Old Town in Aarhus, to display both fashionable and folk dress. By developing this new display technology, Nordiska Museet included other important Scandinavian museums in its network. The flexibility of this technology produced bodies that were both mobile and stable at the same time and therefore enabled knowledge to be moved throughout the scientific (museum) network without being disturbed, destructed, or dissolved (Latour 1987: 223).

There was, however, one tiny but significant difference in the way the different categories of dress were displayed. Buck writes: "In all the museums displaying costume,[5] the figures used for upper-class costume are headless, while peasant figures have heads" (Buck 1940: 34). In many cases the museums used the new modern display technology in combination with the old wax technique by placing realistic wax heads on the top of the Swedish System mannequins and giving them wax hands (Buck 1940).[6] The various practices Buck refers to are also indications of the mannequin's flexibility. This offered museum staff the possibility to customize its shape whether it was used to display fashionable dress or to show folk dress. As such the mannequin itself produced body versions in different stages of abstraction depending on what kind of knowledge category, i.e. academic discipline, the dress was seen as belonging to.

The dressed figure: a mounted mannequin inscribed with class, gender, and the history of style

The French researcher Madeleine Akrich has studied how designers of new technologies inscribe a set of visions of the world into a new technical object (1992). The technical object will have a "script" or "scenario" which defines its identity, interest, goal, type of use, and the space for action as the involved actors are given. In other words, it could be argued that the bodily origin of the mannequin and the relation between bodies and dress intended by the technology are embedded in the display technology itself. This means that there is a certain understanding of the body that is the basis for this mannequin and an understanding grounded within the technology itself. I would also argue that knowledge, for example how objects, time, space, and history are understood, is inscribed in this display technology.

The Swedish System mannequin is extremely straight and rigid, caused by the iron pole that runs straight through the figure. The dress curators at Nordiska Museet do not in particular mention this aspect in their writings. However, it might be relevant to see the straight posture in relation to the historical and bodily practices in a class perspective where good posture, i.e. a straight back, was seen as an expression of moral justice and inner strength among the bourgeois (Ekenstam 1993). At a time when the human body was seen as connected to social position and therefore to manners and how to behave, it was also seen as an expression of a person's character. A person's character was considered hidden inside his or her body. This way of thinking was rooted in the academic writings of the late nineteenth and early twentieth centuries where humans were described and perceived in terms of identifiable categories such as class, nation, and race and where physical characteristics were believed to explain a person's inner qualities (Arrhenius 1998). Later on, in the 1950s, dress curators who worked with folk dress, both at Nordiska Museet as well as at other museums, started to criticize the exhibition mannequin for its straightness. They wanted figures with a more flexible posture.

The Swedish System display technology can also be claimed to produce gender. The absent legs and the many possibilities to adjust the torso according to the measurement of the hips, breast, and waist point back to its origin: the female body and its changing silhouettes.[7] Female dress is represented in museum collections in far larger numbers than male dress. In fact, when male dress was mounted for display, it was done with the same technology and using the female body shape as the point of departure. The female body was the norm. This made the male body a deviation which dress curators had to construct special solutions for. The dress curators discussed these challenges in writing: how could they for instance construct proper legs with a trustworthy corporeality? How could they clothe pants when they faced a mannequin with a supporting iron pole in the middle?

Moreover, the display technology also produced a sense of time and a certain understanding of history. The adjustable discs made bodies that could be adapted to eighteenth-, nineteenth- and twentieth-century women's outfits with their changing silhouettes and all the underwear that was required to get the right posture. Sometimes clothes, and especially underwear, were such a significant factor in giving the human body a particular shape that they in fact have been characterized as display technology in their own right or even as body architecture.[8] The museum display mannequin replaced this type of fashion-based and wearable technology and helped give the same dress, now separated from its live inhabitant, the right expression or style. Dress curator at Nordiska Museet, Mrs Hazelius-Berg, explained the mannequin in an article from 1934:

> The plates are adjusted according to the desired height and then nailed to the staves. Consideration is as such given to the dress style, the plates are to replace the corset's sturdy base, the hip discs can replace the 18th century Pocher, to some extent even the turnyren, the Empire style will get its high waist by the raising of the waist disc, etc.
>
> Hazeluis-Berg 1934: 72–74

The central issue was the mannequin's ability to create bodies with appropriate and authentic historical styles. By giving the dress an approximately correct shape in relation to its time, fashion, and style, the technology also produced time—albeit a particular understanding of time and past.

As the quote from Hazelius-Berg illustrates, dress was interpreted in terms of style epochs such as the Rococo, Louis-Seize, Empire, Late-Empire, etc. This compartmentalizing of dress into style epochs was based on a view of time as clearly defined individual periods. This view was rooted in the eighteenth-century's zeitgeist-thinking where, among others, the German philosopher Johan Gottfried Herder was pivotal. The zeitgeist way of thinking sees every era as having its own unique character that affects all thinking and all actions in that particular period. The style therefore becomes the signature of the zeitgeist and the outer manifestation which gives the era a unifying all-encompassing expression (Herder [1774] 1990; Hvattum 2006).

This way of thinking was echoed in nineteenth-century art history studies where history was seen as a succession of identifiable periods, each expressed through a separate style. History was seen as an evolutionary process where styles were placed in a chronological and linear order. As a subdiscipline of art history, fashion and dress history have traditionally subscribed to this view of history and time (Palmer 2008).

It is within this set of knowledge-based traditions that the Swedish System mannequin should be understood. Dress of the well-to-do was evaluated and exhibited in relation to a changing fashionable silhouette. This understanding also facilitated the exhibition of relatively new dress, because new outfits could be said to belong to a newer style or a later epoch. New outfits were easy to fit into a simplified chronology—as opposed to folk dress that was invariably presented in terms of geography, and not in terms of any fashion style it may have represented.

Compared to the period rooms where fashionable dress had previously been presented as a part of a larger whole and where these museum objects retrieved their stylistic identity in relation to each other, that same dress was now exhibited on a stylistically appropriate body. History of style was now incorporated into the mannequin and became a central and significant part of the display technology itself. This subsequent correct physical representation of style did in turn enact art history.

The ideal of the discrete dressed figure

In an article about the new mannequin in the museum journal *Svenska Museer*, Hazelius-Berg characterized the headless female dressed figures used in Nordiska Museet's Costume Gallery as "discretely dressed figures." In the following analysis I will concentrate on the way the flexible mannequin was used to display fashionable dress at Nordiska Museet and later on at the Museum of Decorative Arts and Design in Oslo which adopted the technology from Nordiska Museet. Both Hazelius-Berg and dress curator Miss Edle Due Kielland at the Museum of Decorative Arts wrote articles about this mannequin technology in contemporary museum journals. The articles were primarily written as instructions on how to use the mannequin in order to build dressed figures, and then they reflected on costume display. Hazelius-Berg (1934: 72) started her article: "Over the past few years, a wish for an aesthetically pleasing way to exhibit the museum's costume collection has developed. The garments are no longer just hung out, one wants to see them sit well and correctly on discrete figures."

The element of discreteness which Hazelius-Berg wants is in other words also related to an aesthetically pleasing form at a time where the simple and functional form was seen as an aesthetic ideal. Nordiska Museet wanted to open up and communicate knowledge to a wider audience in its new exhibitions (Edman and Bergström 2005: 49). The new Costume Gallery was part of this pedagogical effort where the display techniques, the mannequin, the glass cases, as well as the electric light were all expressions of a new attitude towards museum exhibition. It is also worth noting that the museum at the time borrowed well-known elements from both advertising and commercial window displays in Stockholm (Axel-Nilsson 1934; Edman and Bergström 2005; Dahlgren 2010).[9]

But what does it mean that figures are discrete, as coined by Hazelius-Berg? In this case it had to do with not trying to reproduce the actual human body. The mannequin was first and foremost a technology with the purpose to support the displayed dress, give the garments body, and accentuate the displayed dress. It seemed important to keep the technology hidden from the public gaze, illustrated by the way several museums painted the exposed lower part of the iron rod in the same color as the exhibition floor just to make the technology even more discrete (Buck 1940). In its simplest form, this technology produced a torso. Apart from the chest that often shows on low-cut female costumes, virtually all mannequin parts outside the physical limits of the garments were invisible.

The element of discreteness was part of the knowledge tradition that governed fashionable dress exhibition practices. This approach advocated the presentation of dress as singular museum objects in their own right (Taylor 2002). The first question Kielland discussed in her presentation of the Swedish mannequin in 1952 was: "Should mannequins be naturalistic with head, hands and legs or should they be without?" In other words, to Kielland a mannequin with a head

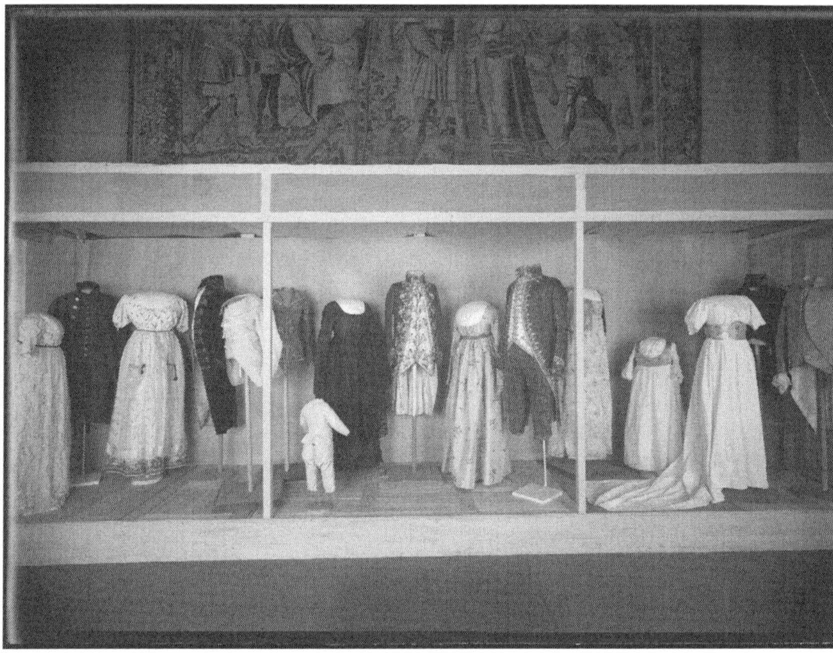

Figure 7.2 In 1933 and 1934, Nordiska Museet opened a new dress gallery. It received a lot of attention, mainly because of its modern new exhibition design where the Swedish System mannequin was among the new inventions. The photos show the gallery during the installation process. With permission from Nordiska Museet.

was a naturalistic figure with a complete set of limbs. She goes on to link this question to various sets of knowledge-based traditions:

> In cases where the headwear is a permanent part of the suit, i.e. a farmer's dress or uniforms, it will be difficult not to use heads [. . .]. When it comes to the civil costumes, hats do not have a permanent relationship with these costumes—wigs on the other hand have had similar decisive importance for the older civil costumes, but the wig material kept is so minimal that a reconstruction of hairstyles and wigs, in my opinion, will lead far beyond what is scientifically reliable. We have therefore [. . .] started to use headless mannequins to display civil suits.
>
> Kielland 1952a

Kielland presents her professional perspective on the display of fashionable and folk dress. The issue of heads is based on a constructed relationship between various dress parts. While headwear was seen as an essential part of farmers' dress when it was put on display, this was not the situation for civil dress, i.e.

non-folk dress. Kielland's argument might, however, be understood in relation to that specific exhibition situation. In the catalogs published as part of the 1952 exhibition at the Museum of Decorative Arts and Design in Oslo, wigs as well as hats were referred to both in texts and pictures.

This difference between the display of fashionable dress and folk dress was directly linked to two different academic disciplines within the field; folk dress was considered to belong to the field of ethnology and ethnography whereas fashionable dress of the well-to-do was seen as an expression of art history (Edman and Bergström 2005). These distinctly different attitudes have to this day affected our understanding of what has led to different cultural expressions. While the culture of the well-to-do has been seen as governed by time and the changes in fashion and by socioeconomic structures, folk dress has been seen as an expression of geographical places and social structures, and has been placed outside the world of fashion. A main task within folk dress research has been to clarify the way dress, and especially headwear, mirror local belonging, social status, and symbolic values (Noss 2004).

In the context of exhibiting fashionable dress, hats were in Kielland's point of view a separate fashion element. Hair and wigs were more important as they were considered to have a closer connection to dress; they were seen as part of the fashioned body. Hair was interpreted in the light of fashion, style periods, and silhouettes.[10] Kielland's perspective was object-oriented and seen from the point of view of style history. She was open to the possibility of reconstructing hair even though she was quick to point out the problem of scientific reliability: display wigs had to be reconstructed from preserved original wigs and have a material authenticity, not just a visual authenticity as paintings of wigs would give: "[. . .] but when the preserved wig material is so minimal, a reconstruction of hairstyles and wigs will, in my opinion, lead far beyond scientific reliability" (Kielland 1952a). This material-oriented approach is interesting. When the museum did not have hats or wigs in its collections, choosing an abstract display technique seemed to be the solution. This was not the case for trousers or shirts, however, which were often copied (Kunstindustrimuseet 1952a). How can we understand this? It might express a need for museums to distance themselves from other actors within the field of older or historical dress, for instance the theater world, where dress is seen as props to support a play's character. In a decorative arts museum, however, dress is regarded as individual and historical.

Although it seemed important to complete the visual and physical impression of the body and display a kind of totality within an art history perspective, the exhibition of fashionable dress was firmly rooted within the art historical view of styles. Even though Kielland did not want to reconstruct wigs, the museum published a separate catalog with portraits just to show historical costumes and wigs (Kunstindustrimuseet 1952b). Nordiska Museet in Stockholm used a similar method when it exhibited hats by replacing the missing heads with paintings.

They employed brushes, paint, and canvases to suggest heads, hairstyles, and hats, and it was with the art historian's eye for each unique costume that these bodies were materialized.

In conclusion

The Swedish System mannequin represented a new and modern solution to the question: how to exhibit dress correctly in museums? This technology was based on the assumption that the mannequin should be tailored to the individual dress and it therefore represented a kind of reverse tailoring (Kildegaard 1993). However, my analysis suggests that the two sets of knowledge-based traditions that ruled the study of fashion dress and folk dress in the 1930s to the mid-1950s led to different uses of the same mannequin which in turn produced two distinctly different types of dressed figure.

In its simplest form, the Swedish System mannequin gave the exhibited dress support and shape without making any attempt at creating a complete body with head and limbs. It produced a bodily abstraction where the dressed figure appeared as a metonymic representation of the wearer of the dress. Fashionable dress was exhibited by presenting the wearers of these in such an abstract way that it was the fashionable dress itself that became the symbol of the human body.

When folk dress was exhibited using the same system, however, mimetic representations of the human body dominated. The wearers of these types of dress were represented as complete dummies with heads and limbs. The Swedish System mannequin was in this respect merely a modernization of the older and naturalistic exhibition practice.

As my analysis suggests, this distinct difference between how fashionable dress and folk dress were displayed also created time in different ways. The metonymic representation, with its lack of a materially visible body, created a kind of missing-person's effect: the specific person and body that once wore the dress is no longer here but belongs to the past. The absolute transience of the body thus communicated and highlighted the human body's temporality. In this sense, time was thematized as an absolute distinction between the dead and the living, between then and now. At the same time, time is perishable; time passes, disappears, and never comes back.

Mimetic reproductions of a present and material body did not examine the body's temporality but were instead a part of our common here and now—our time. A special form of presence occurred and the bodily presence created a sense of timelessness, almost like a religious timelessness—an eternity where time did not exist.

My analysis has also suggested that the distinction between absent and present bodies is not clear-cut but needs to be nuanced. I propose that there is reason to question the exhibited corporeality. Whereas Mark Sandberg discusses either the presence or the absence of bodies, I have chosen to focus on the in-between positions and ask what the absence or presence of people and bodies consists of or what they might consist of.[11] Metonymic representations present a complex picture. In one sense missing bodies create a situation where the audience is free to fill in the picture, to interact, but always within the framework of an already existing and present corporeality. These fashionable, dressed figures have a sense of individuality and character where the corporeality of the dress contributes to create a shadow of the person who once wore the garments. The remaining imprint of a human body in the dress also provides the visitors with a possibility to interact and also gives them impulses when filling in the missing pictures. The previous owners almost come alive, become present, and as such the mannequins are filled with character.

To sum up, the art historical approach to fashionable dress in Scandinavian museums in the period between 1930 and the 1950s did not give much room for mimetic reproductions of the body. Exhibited dress appeared as singular museum objects in their own right and were used as a positivistic proof of how something really was in a historical past. This led to abstraction and an absence of mimetic reproductions of the body. At the same time it also led to a demand for a correct and individual corporeality based on the measurements of the dress.

The Swedish System mannequin materialized this set of knowledge-based traditions. Using this display technology, the dress curators could create bodies that would place the dress in the correct art historical period while still exhibiting dress as singular museum objects. The raising of a garment to the status of museum object and the simultaneously cleansing of any physical context led to fashionable dress being presented as timeless, as dress devoid of time and space. They not only became filled with character but were also presented as eternal and true.

Notes

1 In this chapter, I will use the term “fashionable dress” when referring to a specific category of garments, i.e. clothing in museum collections. The term fashionable dress denotes here primarily made-to-measure clothing belonging to the social elite in pre-industrial Scandinavia. The social elite at the time included members of the upper class, the bourgeois, the merchant class, and civil servants. The term “folk dress,” on the other hand, denotes clothes worn primarily by peasants and their families in pre-industrial Scandinavian farming communities.

2 I would like to thank the editors Marie Riegels Melchior and Birgitta Svensson, as well as the Wardrobe-group for all their comments, enthusiasm and input with this chapter. Also thanks to Mette Irene Dahl for helping me with the English language.

3 It is the art historian Borghild Frimannslund who refers to the mannequin as the Swedish System in her article "Nye draktmannekenger på historisk museum i Bergen" published in *Museumsnytt* (1955, p. 4).

4 I have chosen to use the term "well-to-do classes" and not the more common term "upper-class" in this chapter as the social group I refer to in Scandinavia consisted of a mix of the bourgeois, the merchant class, and civil servants. Scandinavia and especially Norway had at the time a different social structure than other European countries and their upper-class was small if existing at all.

5 E.g. meaning dress.

6 Indeed, at the new Costume Gallery for peasant dress in 1938 and 1939 at Nordiska Museet, peasant bodies were presented in a more abstract and modernistic way by giving the figures schematic or simplistic heads which made them more anonymous.

7 This can be seen in relation to the fact that women's dresses were in a clear majority in museum collections and the museums needed a suitable technology to display them. Besides, contemporary dress research was much more focused on female dress (Hazelius-Berg 1952; Kielland 1952a, 1952b).

8 The director at the Museum of Decorative Arts and Design in Oslo, Thor Kielland, named it as body architecture in 1933. This was related to a dress parade at the museum.

9 In this period central people within the Swedish cultural heritage field argued that museums should be like modern department stores, for example the Swedish Sigurd Curman (Edman and Bjurstöm 2005: 49).

10 While researchers within folk dress research have focused on the relationship between hair and headwear. See Noss (2004).

11 For example, there was a distinct difference between the various mimetic representations as to what extent they were realistic or more abstract. The doll-like figures also contribute to thematizing the distinction between life and death. They mimic life but they also confuse the public with their aliveness (Sandberg 2003). As such the naturalistic wax dolls might contribute to the discussion on the relationship between imitated life and abstracted life.

References

Aall, H. (1916), *Om store og smaa kulturhistoriske museer*, Kristiania.

Akrich, M. (1992), "The De-Scription of Technical Objects," in: Weibe Bijker and John Law (eds), *Shaping Technology*, Cambridge, MA: MIT Press, pp. 205–224.

Arrhenius, S. (1998), "Se skillnaden! Om fotografi och klassifikation," in: David Elliot (ed.), *Skuggan av Ljuset – fotografi och systematikk i konst, vetenskap och vardagsliv*, Stockholm: Moderna Museet, pp. 9–20.

Axel-Nilsson, G. (1934), "Nordiska museets nyöppnade dräktgalleri," in: *Svenska Museer*, pp. 16–19.

Buck, A. (1940), "Textiles in Scandinavian Museums, their Treatment and Methods of Display," in: *Museums Journal*, pp. 25–44.

Buck, A. (1958), *Costume – A Handbook for Textile Curators*, London: The Museum Association.

Dahlgren, A. (2010) "The Art of Display," in *Konsthistorisk tidsskrift/journal of Art History*, pp. 160–173.
Edman, V. (2008), *Sjuttonhundratalet som svenskt ideal: moderna rekonstruktioner av historiska miljöer*, Stockholm: Nordiska Museets förlag.
Edman, V. and A. Bergström (2005), *Folkhemmets museum: byggnader och rum för kulturhistoriska samlingar*, Stockholm: Byggforläget.
Ekenstam, C. (1993), *Kroppens idéhistoria: disciplinering och karaktärsdaning i Sverige 1700–1950*, Hedemora: Gidlunds bokförlag.
Entwistle, J. (2000), *The Fashioned Body: Fashion, Dress, and Modern Social Theory*, Cambridge: Polity Press.
Graden, L. and. McIntyre Petersson (2009), "Innledning," in *Modets Metamofoser*, Stockholm: Carlssons, pp. 9–28.
Haraway, D. (2008), *When Species Meet*, Minneapolis, MN: University of Minnesota Press.
Hazelius-Berg, G. (1934), "Nordiska museets dräktfigurer," in: *Svenska Museer*, pp. 72–75.
Hazelius-Berg, G. (1952), *Modedräkter från 1600–1900*, Stockholm: Nordiska Museet exhibition catalog.
Herder, J.G. ([1774] 1990), *Auch eine Philosphie der Geschichte zur Bildung der Menscheit*, Stuttgart: Reclam.
Hjemdahl, A. (2013), *Liv i museet – Kunstindustrimuseet i Oslo gjør kropp med moteklær, 1928–1960*, PhD thesis, University of Oslo.
Hvattum, M. (2006), "Historisme og modernisme i moderne arkitekturhistorieskriving," in: *Nordisk arkitekturforskning*, 1, pp. 85–90.
Kielland, E.D. (1952a), "Methode de presentation des costumes adoptee par les musees Scandinaves," in: *Congrès International D'historie du Costume – Venise, 31 Aout – 7 Septembre 1952*, Venezia: Centro Internazionale Delle arti E del Costume, pp. 220–226.
Kielland, E.D. (1952b), *Vi kan – og kunne kle oss: drakt og mote i Norge 1700–1950*, Oslo: The Museum of Decorative Arts and Design in Oslo, exhibition catalog.
Kielland, E.D. (1955), 'Montering av drakter', in: *Museumsnytt*, 3:.8–11.
Kildegaard, B. (1993), *Klædt på til tiden*, Copenhagen: Nationalmuseet & Tiderne Skifter.
Kunstindustrimuseet (1952a), *Vi kan og kunne kle oss – drakt og mote i Norge 1700–1950*, Oslo: Kunstindustrimuseet i Oslo.
Kunstindustrimuseet (1952b), *Museets draktbilder: femti portretter fra renessanse til nutid*, Oslo: Kunstindustrimuseet i Oslo.
Latour, B. (1987), *Science in Action*, Cambridge, MA: Harvard University Press.
Latour, B. (2005), *Reassembling the Social: An Introduction to Actor-network Theory*, New York: Oxford University Press.
Law, J. (2004), *After Method: Mess in Social Science Research*, London: Routledge.
Mol, A. (2002), *The Body Multiple: Ontology in Medical Practice*, Durham, NC: Duke University Press.
Noss, A. (2004), "Hovudbunad og norsk drakttradisjon," in: Njål Høstmælingen (ed.), *Hijab i Norge*, Oslo: Abstrakt, pp. 72–94.
Nylen, A. (1957), "Permanent utställning av folkdräkter på Nordiska Museet," in: *Svenska Museer*, 3, pp. 9–13.
Palmer, A. (2008), "Untouchable: Creating Desire and Knowledge in Museum Costume and Textile Exhibitions," in: *Fashion Theory: The Journal of Dress, Body & Culture*, 12, pp. 31–63.

Sandberg, M. (2003), *Living Pictures, Missing Persons: Mannequins, Museums and Modernity*, Princeton, NJ: Princeton University Press.

Steele, V. (1998), "A Museum of Fashion is More than a Clothes-bag," in: *Fashion Theory: The Journal of Dress, Body & Culture*, 2, pp. 327–336.

Steele, V. (1999), "The Corset: Fashion and Eroticism," in: *Fashion Theory: The Journal of Dress, Body & Culture*, 3, pp. 449–473.

Taylor, L. (2002), *The Study of Dress History*, Manchester: Manchester University Press.

Wilson, E. (1985), *Adorned in Dreams: Fashion and Modernity*, London: Virago Press.

SECTION 3

IN PRACTICE

8 FROM MUSEUM OF COSTUME TO FASHION MUSEUM: THE CASE OF THE FASHION MUSEUM IN BATH

Rosemary Harden

The Fashion Museum in Bath, UK, is one of the world's great museum collections of historic and contemporary fashionable dress, with objects ranging from exquisite pieces of seventeenth-century embroidery to cutting-edge twenty-first century fashions by top international designers. The museum collection, which numbers in the region of 100,000 objects, was designated under the Museums Libraries and Archives scheme as a collection of outstanding national significance in 2000 in recognition of the breadth and quality of the collection as a whole. It is the collection that is at the heart of the Fashion Museum's operation and upon which the whole action and endeavor of the museum is based; and, consequently, both how and why fashion is presented at the museum in Bath is determined by this unique, precious, and publicly owned resource.

This exploration of how and why fashion is exhibited at the Fashion Museum in Bath is written from the point of view of a curator whose job is to present a large specialist museum collection of fragile original material to a broad and diverse audience in a small West Country city, which also happens to be one of the world's major tourist destinations. This will be a personal view; but the history of the Fashion Museum is made up of the work of the people who have been associated with the collection over the last fifty years.[1] The resources to present the museum collection are relatively modest,[2] but there is a wealth of enthusiasm and commitment from a dedicated professional team of museum workers and volunteers,[3] and a wider circle of Fashion Museum supporters, which means that everything is considered and anything, within reason, is possible. The aim of this chapter is to give a snapshot of a moment in the Fashion Museum's long and distinguished history in Bath by discussing the presentation of the museum collection in 2012, with reference to current projects and forthcoming aims. This is what the Fashion Museum team are working to achieve given the information, resources, and opportunities that are available at the moment. All of this will, of course, change. New opportunities, and also new constraints, will arise. There will be different personnel and different circumstances, which will lead to changed outcomes and a different experience for those who visit and use the museum.

Bath

The Fashion Museum, previously known as the Museum of Costume, Bath,[4] has been situated in the Assembly Rooms in the Georgian city of Bath for nearly fifty years, and the museum's location in this historic tourist city is a vital part of its identity. People have been traveling to Bath for centuries, to take the medicinal waters bubbling up from the natural springs and to enjoy the social scene, and this strong historical tradition of Bath as a destination for travel continues today. Bath was given the status of a UNESCO World Heritage Site in 1987, and every year thousands of visitors flock into the city for rest and relaxation, on holiday or on a day out. The most visited attraction in the city is the Roman Baths, a key archeological site in Britain, with over 900,000 visitors each year. But it is not only Bath's defining nature as a Roman site which attracts visitors to the city; it is also its identity as the archetypal Georgian city, with its pleasant and distinctive honey-colored stone crescents and terraces set among rolling green hills. Bath is a city much featured in film and TV adaptations (most notably of the novels of Jane Austen) and that too draws visitors to the city.

Over 100,000 of the visitors who come to Bath each year choose to visit the Fashion Museum.[5] The majority purchase a joint admission ticket when visiting the Roman Baths Museum. Visitors may not have heard of the Fashion Museum, but the lure of two visitor attractions for a saver price ticket is attractive and compelling. In practice, therefore, this means that many visitors to the Fashion Museum have little knowledge of, or indeed interest in, fashion history, but instead come as part of a pleasant day out.

There are joint ticketing arrangement between the Fashion Museum and the Roman Baths because both museums are owned by Bath and North East Somerset Council, and managed by the Heritage Services section of the Council. There is a shared economic base between the two museums as Heritage Services operates as a separate business unit within the Council and the money earned from admissions represents a significant income stream for the local authority.[6] There is therefore an economic imperative both to protect and to grow the visitor base at the Roman Baths Museum and the Fashion Museum.

As part of Bath and North East Somerset Council the Fashion Museum and the Roman Baths Museum are governed by the vision and values of the organization as a whole, which state that Bath and North East Somerset should be: "[. . .] an area with unique places and beautiful surroundings, with lively active communities, and where everyone fulfils their potential." The Fashion Museum therefore operates in a culture of public service working towards a common aim.

In the broadest sense this explains why the collection is presented at the Fashion Museum: simply put, it is because the collection is owned by the local authority, and it is the duty of the public servants who work at the Fashion Museum to present it to a wide audience. As professionally trained and experienced museum curators the challenge is to present the collection to the highest museum standards, mindful of both the origins of the museum, and the needs of all potential users, whatever their background, experience, and interest. This is the remit under which the Fashion Museum operates and it is important not only on an ideological level, but also on a day-to-day operational basis. All that we plan and do at the Fashion Museum must be tracked back to the vision and objectives of Bath and North East Somerset Council and to the Heritage Services Mission Statement: "Giving people opportunities for learning, inspiration and enjoyment through access to museum and archive collections and historic public buildings."

The Assembly Rooms

The home of the Fashion Museum is the Assembly Rooms, one of Bath's finest Georgian buildings. The Rooms are owned by the National Trust and leased to Bath and North East Somerset Council.[7] The New Rooms (as the Assembly Rooms were originally known) opened in 1771, and soon became the hub of socializing in the upper part of the town during the winter season in Bath. An assembly was defined as a "stated and general meeting of polite persons of both sexes, for the sake of conversation, gallantry, news and play."[8] The New Rooms included three principal rooms, with the grandest being the Ballroom which was able to accommodate as many as 800 dancers. Dress balls took place once a week and started at 6 pm with the minuet (a stately formal dance performed by couples alone), to be followed after a break for refreshments in the Tea Room by the more energetic country dances. The evening finished at 11 pm.

In April 1942 the Assembly Rooms were reduced to a roofless shell during a night of heavy bombing during the Second World War.[9] It took nearly twenty years to restore the grand rooms to their original eighteenth-century splendor. At this point the Fashion Museum came into the story, and the fate of the two attractions, the Georgian Assembly Rooms above, and the Fashion Museum galleries on the lower ground floor below, became incontrovertibly entwined.

Doris Langley Moore

The Fashion Museum opened as the Museum of Costume, Bath, in 1963, the time when the newly restored rooms opened to the public. The museum was founded by Doris Langley Moore, a writer, scholar, costume designer, and an inspired collector of fashions of the past who at that time gave her private collection of historic costume to the City of Bath. Mrs. Langley Moore had started to acquire what she termed "antique dress" in the 1920s and, as she said: "Now I had a collection of two, and as soon as you collect anything they breed" (Langley Moore 1949). She spoke of the relative ease of acquiring costume at this time: "I was a private collector for about twenty years before I even remotely contemplated founding a museum, and naturally, since there was no demand at all for costume in those days, and little interest in the subject, my friends, relations and acquaintances readily gave me any specimens they had." In 1949 Mrs. Langley Moore had written a book *The Woman in Fashion* which featured objects from her collection of historic dress. This was one of the key early texts of the study of the history of fashion and in the preface Mrs. Langley Moore outlined her vision for a Museum of Costume:

> There is a very great need in London of a gallery of costume—a fashion centre where designers of every métier, members of the theatrical profession, film directors, art students and interested persons in general, might have access to a reference library of dress, to pictures, and to actual clothing, under more intimate conditions than are possible in an orthodox museum. I imagine it in my sanguine moments as a place where besides historic specimens, there would be current fashions too on view, and where selected examples of the latest textiles and the best products of our tailors and couturiers would be acquired year by year, with their appropriate accessories.
>
> Langley Moore 1949

Eventually the Museum of Costume found its first home, not in London but at Eridge Castle in Kent in 1955, and it was here that Doris Langley Moore established her particular style of costume display, using realistic mannequins. She believed you needed to understand the context of the dress "[. . .] those to whom costume is an unfamiliar subject will find little interest in a sleeve with deep ruffles unless it is set off by an arm."[10] However, this was not the usual approach to the display of costume in museums at the time, where dress was generally viewed as a textile, a piece of decorative art, and not as something that was actually worn by real people.

The Museum of Costume remained at Eridge Castle for three years, and in 1958 was transferred to the Royal Pavilion in Brighton for a special exhibition.

But in 1963, it found its permanent home in the newly re-opened Assembly Rooms in Bath when Mrs. Langley Moore gave her collection to Bath City Council. She continued her association with the museum and with the City Council, off and on, until her death in 1989, and was always known as the Founder of the Museum of Costume.

The collection

Some fifty years later it is helpful to know a little about the nature of the Fashion Museum collection when examining how fashion is presented at the museum. At its most general, the collection includes fashionable dress and accessories (hats, shoes, bags, etc.) for men and for women from the eighteenth, nineteenth, and twentieth centuries. There are also embroidered Elizabethan and Jacobean accessories to dress, and a growing collection of the work of contemporary fashion designers. The collection also includes photographs, prints and drawings, magazines, and archive collections.

The Fashion Museum collection has grown considerably in size since Mrs. Langley Moore's original donation. Currently in the region of 300 new acquisitions are added each year, and collecting is governed by the Heritage Services Acquisitions and Disposals Policy.[11] In practice, by and large, the approach to collecting at the Fashion Museum is passive: objects are selected for acquisition by the curatorial staff from the hundreds of items that are offered as donations each year. Every offer is considered against a number of criteria including the Acquisitions and Disposal Policy and also the object's suitability for presentation.

In recent years the Fashion Museum has also acquired a number of wardrobe collections (a significant number of clothes worn by one person) including, in 2011, a large collection of menswear, which belonged to Mark Read, who had bought extensively from designers such as Vivienne Westwood and Jean Paul Gaultier in the 1990s and 2000s. Wardrobe collections[12] enable the museum to document systematically one person's approach to dressing, which in turn leads to possibilities of presentation and exploration of the consumption of fashion, focusing on personal stories and individual taste.[13]

British fashion designers (including Wendy Dagworthy, Sarah Dallas, and John Bates), have also donated large collections of their work to the Fashion Museum, and recently English couturier David Sassoon gave his archive of fashion drawings to the museum. Designer donations enable the Fashion Museum to present "monograph" style displays of the work of individual designers.[14] In 2010, for example, the museum displayed over twenty-five ensembles by Austrian-born designer Helmut Lang following a large donation by the designer of his work in fashion from the late 1990s to 2004.

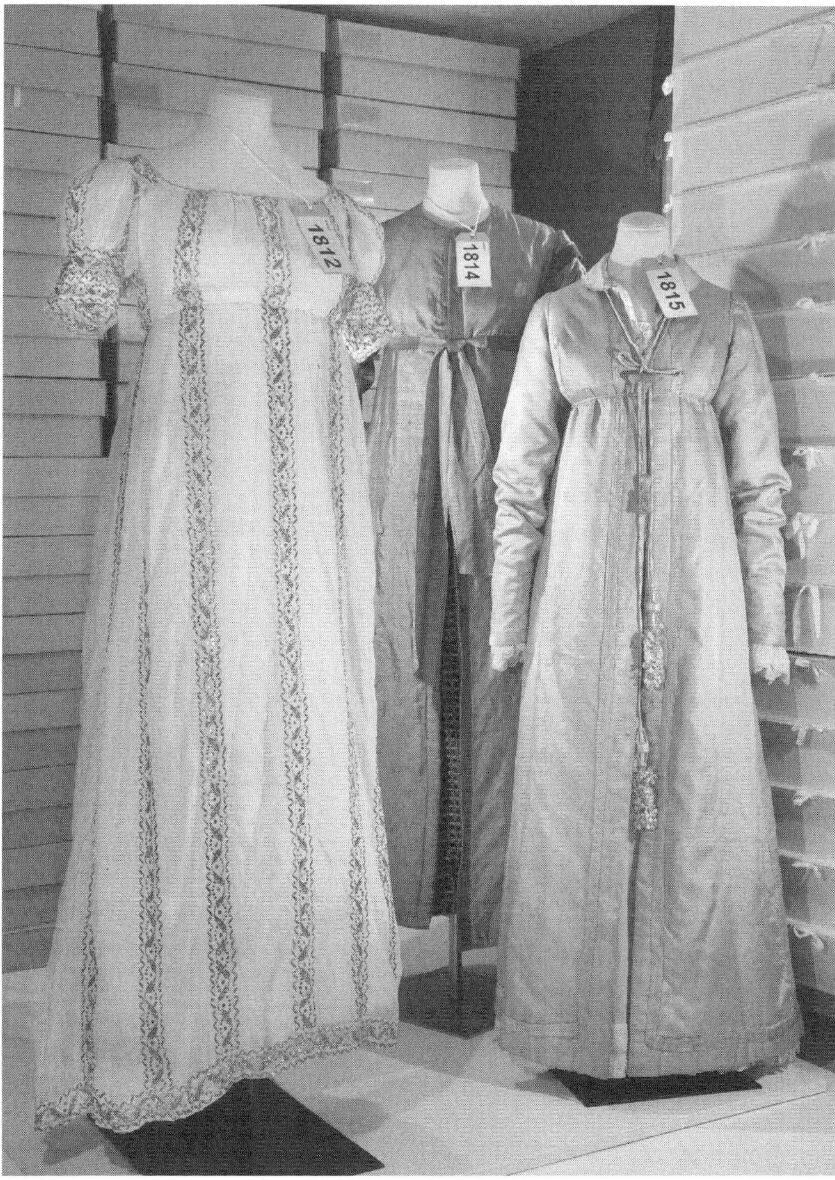

Figure 8.1 Early nineteenth-century fashions on display in the "Behind the Scenes" gallery at the Fashion Museum. Fashion Museum, Bath, and North East Somerset Council.

The Dress of the Year is the Fashion Museum's well-established scheme to update the contemporary collection on a regular basis. Each year the museum asks a fashion expert to choose an outfit that he or she feels sums up the mood or look for that particular year. The selected outfit becomes part of the

Dress of the Year collection at the Fashion Museum, a roll-call of the most famous names in international fashion. The collection includes the work of top designers who have made the headlines and set the trends in fashion since 1963 when the scheme first started in Bath.[15] The Dress of the Year removes the selection of contemporary work for the collection from the curator and instead relies on the choice of key figures from within the fashion industry; and the list of selectors reads like a Who's Who of British fashion editors in the past fifty years. The Dress of the Year for 2011 was a dress from the finale of Alexander McQueen's Autumn/Winter 2011 collection,[16] and was selected for the museum by Hamish Bowles of American *Vogue*. The dress was presented on display in the Fashion Museum galleries on a mannequin styled with the same hair and make-up as on the McQueen catwalk in March 2011. The figure was situated in a theatrical set suggesting a snow-covered landscape, which mirrors the narrative of the original catwalk show. The mannequin held aloft a tiny bird, with traces of glitter on its wings intimating that the snow princess is turning all that she touches to ice. The display at the Fashion Museum thus not only replicated a catwalk look for a museum audience, but also extended the interpretation, showing how the house of McQueen has a tradition of storytelling in the presentation of the collections.

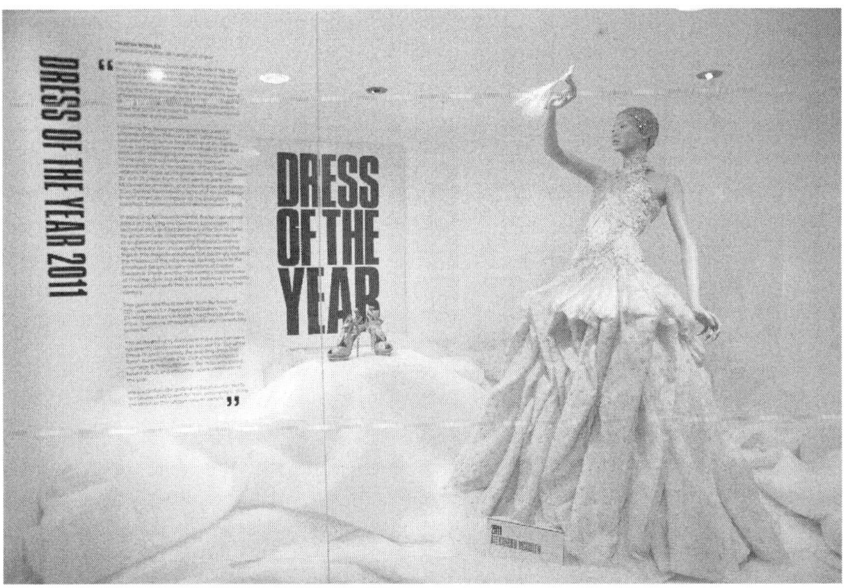

Figure 8.2 Dress of the Year 2011 on display at the Fashion Museum. Fashion Museum, Bath and North East Somerset Council.

Presenting the collection

With a wealth of material, a growing collection, and an increasing audience, the challenge for the Fashion Museum is to present the collection so that it is accessible to a broad spectrum of users with different and changeable needs. The museum's overarching display rationale is firstly that the galleries should have an editorial approach, with changes of pace and focus, rather like a magazine; and secondly that the displays as a whole should have a chronological backbone, but interspersed with thematic feature displays.

The principal display of historic dress at the Fashion Museum is the "Behind the Scenes" gallery, a display of (mainly) nineteenth-century fashion. The objects from the collection are presented chronologically, displayed on Stockman-style figures. This, however, is a display with a difference: the idea is that visitors are invited into the museum store, finding themselves literally in the midst of the collection, among boxes and boxes of stored material. This is a new display concept, neither traditional gallery display nor open storage. "Behind the Scenes" is one of the most popular displays in the museum, and appeals to a wide range of visitors, from museum professionals and those in the fashion industry to tourists with little insider knowledge of dress and museums. The key, it seems, is that the boxes are carefully arranged and set as scenes, and the impression is of beautiful, historic pieces spilling out of acid-free museum boxes, which are piled up high. The visiting experience is somewhat voyeuristic, with a feeling that visitors are being given privileged access to something not normally seen.

There is a strong linear chronological narrative in "Behind the Scenes" with information on the development of fashionable dress in the nineteenth century. The extra interpretative element is that each display case in the gallery includes selected excerpts from, and reference to, named characters in nineteenth-century novels as a way to convey information about and context for the fashionable dress on display. For example, fashions from the end of the century are presented alongside a quotation from Thomas Hardy's novel *Tess of the d'Urbervilles*.[17] The allusion is carried through with a pair of hob-nailed boots from the 1890s (similar to those the milkmaid Tess wore to walk across the Wessex Downs in a vain attempt to become better acquainted with her in-laws), displayed as a feature item on a pedestal in the display case.

The collection is deliberately presented in an anonymous way (with dresses on impersonal tailors' dummies) in the "Behind the Scenes" gallery so as to emphasize the storage nature of the displays, with the "personal" aspect of the dress tagged to the named fictitious characters in the nineteenth-century novels on the graphic panels. In contrast, much of the twentieth-century dress on display in the Fashion Museum galleries is presented on realistic mannequins, all carefully styled with appropriate accessories, hair, and make-up. The twentieth-century day-wear display carries this idea of "putting the people back into the clothes" and creating a personal context by alluding to personalities or types of wearer in the object label text displayed alongside each piece.[18]

Twentieth-century dress is presented in the Fashion Museum on display mannequins, which are given their total fashion look by Iain R. Webb, who works as a consultant to the Fashion Museum.[19] Professor Webb has also styled the figures in the display of the Dress of the Year collection, which in 2012 comprised an edited selection of the entire collection, to complement the display of the Alexander McQueen dress.[20]

The Dress of the Year section of the museum galleries also includes a display of framed album covers to show that the Dresses of the Year both inspired and drew from the look of clothes of the time. In the past, displays of the Dress of the Year collection have been seen as distant and of no relevance to clothes that visitors have worn throughout their lives. It has always been challenging to explain stylistic influence and "trickle down/bubble up" theories of high fashion and street fashion in display graphics (or on the audio guide commentary to the museum galleries, which is provided for all visitors); and in the past visitors had remarked that the displays of the Dress of the Year collection were of little interest to them. In order to alleviate these comments and to tackle these criticisms the Fashion Museum chose to display framed album covers which showed a stylistic resonance with the pieces in the Dress of the Year collection. Thus, the Mary Quant gray pinafore skirt worn with a cream silk blouse (the first Dress of the Year from 1963) is displayed opposite Barbra Streisand's first album, also from 1963, on the cover of which the star wears a strikingly similar ensemble. Often the outfits illustrated on the album covers are not quite such close fits; but they are all within the general stylistic mood of the time and show a kinship with the Dress of the Year ensemble from the same era.

Iain R. Webb's total fashion styling and the display of album covers have given context (albeit with a light touch, you hardly notice it is there) to the display and interpretation of the Dress of the Year collection, which makes for a far more attractive and engaging way of presenting the collection for visitors than lengthy text panels. The album cover display has worked well as it achieves the aim of presenting the concept of the dissemination of fashion, and it also appeals to visitors who may not be that interested in fashion, but who enjoy remembering the albums and music from their own lives.

A further challenge at the Fashion Museum is to present "everyday dress," or fashions worn by people on a day-to-day basis, rather than just garments which visitors perceive as exclusive, designer, or high-end fashion. In previous years, the museum has attempted to display dress of this type; but without careful styling and a specific context "everyday" dress can look rather dull and work-a-day in museum displays. Often too the day-to-day dress that we wear, and our forebears have worn, does not survive for posterity. It is the special garments, those with perceived value to the wearers (such as wedding dresses), that tend to be kept and which are then offered as donations to museums. The challenge therefore is to present "everyday" dress accurately and beautifully, and in ways that are appealing to a broad visitor base.

Since the museum changed its name to the Fashion Museum in 2007, everyday dress has been presented through the display of framed works in the museum galleries. The first exhibition was "1977," a photographic show of punk and new-wave bands which celebrated the thirtieth anniversary of a key year in punk history, and also illustrated how fashion is as much about a do-it-yourself ethos, putting clothes and accessories together to create a look which makes a statement about who you are and where you belong. The display showed how fashion and style is not just the premise of big-name designers, or even exclusively of well-known high street shops and brands.

In 2009 a second exhibition, in a different medium and with a different aesthetic, showed the textile pictures of contemporary embroiderer Laura McCafferty, which held a mirror up to the clothing worn in contemporary Britain, giving a snapshot of what people, both young and old, choose to wear in everyday situations. Laura said: "What I'm doing is taking the ordinary and trying to make it beautiful"[21] and this serves as a good guideline or motto for the Fashion Museum's approach to presenting "everyday" fashions to museum visitors.

In 2012, the Fashion Museum presented a further photographic display called "Buffalo," which also explored issues of everyday fashion and style. "Buffalo" was a 1980s design collective described by editor Dylan Jones as: "[. . .] street style ahead of its time,"[22] led by menswear stylist Ray Petri who worked for *The Face* and *Arena* magazines, and who brought together a group of talented young models and photographers to create a signature look, mixing elements of sportswear, such as jogging bottoms and football T-shirts, with sharp classical tailoring.

The Fashion Museum is keen to attract younger, harder-to-reach visitors, and while many teenage girls are interested in fashion, they often do not choose to visit museums. However, the "Top Trends" series of displays at the museum had an appeal for this audience. The concept behind the display was the presentation of the top five or six catwalk trends for the particular fashion season. The display showed the "looks" to be found in fashion magazines and on the high street; but all the fashions on show were historical pieces from the Fashion Museum collection. Visitors saw six contemporary looks, but all put together using historic fashions. This was also a good way for the museum to show "vintage," a trend which has become important in fashion history in recent years.

Conclusion

The aim at the Fashion Museum is to put on a good show, and to give visitors value for the time and the money they spend when they visit the museum. Display strategies are, therefore, formulated to present the museum collection in a lively and engaging way so as to appeal to the many people of different nationalities, age, gender, and cultural background who visit the Fashion Museum each year. The intention is that everyone will find something in the museum displays from which they can gain inspiration, learning, and enjoyment.

But what of future plans? Increasingly the Fashion Museum collection will be presented to users in additional ways, and not just as displays in the galleries. Traditional museum boundaries between stored collections and those on display will continue to be broken down; and the Fashion Museum collection will be regarded as one entity, with the emphasis on presentation, not just on display, and in different experiential ways, according to the needs and desires of the end-users. This style of presentation of the collection builds on the success of the Fashion Museum Study Facilities where anyone who wants to learn more about fashion history can examine objects from the collection at close quarters in a self-directed study session.

In conclusion, both why and how fashion is presented at the Fashion Museum is determined essentially by who we are, how we are constituted, how we were founded, and where we are situated. But above all, perhaps, the presentation of fashion at the Fashion Museum in Bath rests upon the nature of both this magnificent museum collection, and of the thousands of people who want to experience the collection for their own learning, inspiration, and enjoyment.

Notes

1 Doris Langley Moore founded the Museum of Costume in Bath in 1963. Myra Mines worked as Chief Costume Assistant from the 1960s to 1991. Penelope Byrde Ruddock worked as Fashion Research Officer, Keeper of Costume, and Curator, Museum of Costume from 1973 to 2003.

2 The annual budget for the Fashion Museum displays in 2011/2012 was £11,530 with an additional £10,000 available from the Heritage Services Re-investment Budget.

3 In 2012 the Fashion Museum curatorial team included Rosemary Harden (Fashion Museum Manager, full-time), Vivien Hynes (Fashion Museum Administrator, part-time), Elly Summers (Fashion Museum Collections Assistant, part-time), and Elaine Uttley (Fashion Museum Collections Assistant, full-time), plus ten part-time regular volunteers.

4 The Fashion Museum changed its name from the Museum of Costume, Bath, in 2007 following an extensive consultation exercise which found that "fashion" was the term that better reflected both the nature of the collection and visitor expectations. "Costume" was regarded as a term for dress to be put on to play a role, i.e. on the stage.

5 124,655 visitors in 2010/2011, and 132,000 visitors in 2011/2012.

6 In 2010/2011 Heritage Services made an income of £12 million, returning a profit of £3.5 million to the Council.

7 The original lease was signed between the National Trust and Bath City Council in 1938.

8 *The New Bath Guide 1766*.

9 The Bath Blitz took place on the night of April 24–25, 1942.

10 Doris Langley Moore, *Eridge Castle Guidebook*.

11 Bath and North East Somerset Council, Heritage Service Acquisition and Disposal Policy.

12 Other wardrobe collections at the Fashion Museum include those of the following: Sir Roy Strong, Director of the National Portrait Gallery in London in the 1960s and of the Victoria and Albert Museum in the 1970s and 1980s; Dr. Janet Roscoe home-made clothes, showing a particular eye for selecting woven and printed textiles from which to make her clothes; and Joan Mee, a girl who left home and joined the services during the Second World War.

13 The Fashion Museum celebrated this personal approach to fashion in a display called "Women of Style" in 2000, which featured the wardrobes of Mary Chamberlain, Lady Curzon, the Rani of Pudukkottai, Martita Hunt, Helen Gardner, and Margot Fonteyn.

14 "John Bates Fashion Designer" in 2006, and "Four 1970s/1980s British Designers" in 2007.

15 The first Dress of the Year selection in 1963 was a gray flannel knee-length button-through pinafore skirt by Mary Quant.

16 This collection was partially conceived as a "cover" for the fact that Sarah Burton of Alexander McQueen was at the time, and unknown to all, designing the dress worn by Miss Catherine Middleton at her wedding to HRH Prince William on April 29, 2011.

17 "A year had now elapsed since her sad marriage, but she had preserved sufficient draperies from the wreck of her then full wardrobe to clothe her very charmingly as a simple country girl with no pretensions to recent fashion; a soft gray woollen gown, and a black velvet jacket and hat. ''Tis a thousand pities your husband can't see 'ee now – you do look a real beauty!' said Izz Huett, regarding Tess as she stood on the threshold between the steely starlight without and the yellow candlelight within" (Hardy, 1891).

18 Labels are made up of two parts: identifying information plus a suggestion about a cultural reference point. So, for example: "Mid-1960s suit by Bonnie Cashin, *Think* . . . Anne Bancroft as Mrs Robinson in *The Graduate* (1967); Late 1960s trouser suit by Kimberly, *Think* . . . race for space and the Apollo moon landing (1969)."

19 Iain R. Webb is a fashion writer and journalist who has worked for the *Evening Standard, The Times* and *Elle*, and has twice won Fashion Editor of the Year. He is Professor of Fashion at Central Saint Martin's School of Art and the Royal College of Art.

20 The 2012 display of the Dress of the Year collection at the Fashion Museum includes the selections for 1963 Mary Quant, 1969 Ossie Clark, 1977 Jap, 1985 Scott Crolla, 1987 John Galliano, 1989 Rifat Ozbek, 2000 Versace, 2004 Tom Ford for Yves Saint Laurent Rive Gauche, 2008 Karl Lagerfeld for Chanel, and 2010 Vivienne Westwood.

21 Laura McCafferty

22 Dylan Jones.

Reference

Langley Moore, Doris (1949), *The Woman in Fashion*, London: B.T. Batsford Ltd.

9

COLLECTING PRACTICE: DESIGNMUSEUM DANMARK

Kirsten Toftegaard

Not only is a museum categorized by its exhibitions, it is also characterized by the content of the collections. This chapter is about the importance of balancing textile, dress, and fashion in collecting at Designmuseum Danmark, Copenhagen, pointing out that fashion, dress, and textile should be regarded on equal terms in the practice of collecting. During the lifetime of the museum, collecting has not been a constant practice. The change of times and changes in directors' and curators' ideas and attitudes have influenced the character of the collections.[1] For Designmuseum Danmark's textile and dress collection, the basis was formerly based on collecting textiles. Dresses did find their way into the collection; however, as in many other museums in Europe, they were considered more or less a byproduct of collecting textiles (Cumming 2004: 53). One can nevertheless say that the collection of dress and fashion originated from the textile collection.

Within the last twenty years fashion and dress exhibitions at museums have become popular, and new specialized fashion museums have emerged with a historical or contemporary point of departure. Concurrent with this development, collecting fashion and dress for permanent collections in museums has increased and the former division between the areas of textile, dress, and fashion has been challenged. For these reasons, it is relevant to shed light on the relationship between the different areas in the practice of collecting. Giving "fashion" status as a concept in the practice of collecting in a design museum does not necessarily rule out "textile" and "dress" but can be seen as complementary. Fiona Anderson states in "Museums as Fashion Media" (Anderson 2000) that fashion and dress history are supplementary to each other. I would like to extend her statement also to include textile.

The fashion, dress, and textile collection at Designmuseum Danmark and the criteria of collecting

As an art museum, Designmuseum Danmark is selective in collecting, and the overall collecting criteria constitute a combination of form, function, material, and execution seen from an aesthetic point of view. It has been and still is the intention to collect contemporary as well as historical cutting-edge or leading design, which in one way or another belongs to the avant-garde. As long as it is considered to fall into this criterion, the museum should not differentiate between for instance a piece of furniture and a dress.

In the design museum, collected textiles are either for clothing or domestic use, for example curtains, upholstery fabrics, textiles for beds, tables, kitchens, carpets for floors, and tapestries. There are periods in history where there is no distinction between the two purposes. In the eighteenth century, for instance, the same fabric was used for clothes as for home furnishing.

The textile collection of Designmuseum Danmark is one of the largest and most important collections in Denmark with a global perspective. It contains both archeological material and contemporary design for textiles and needlework, sophisticated weavings of silk from workshops in Italy and France, together with examples of folk art from Europe, the Middle East, Asia, and South America, as well as a collection of oriental carpets. The collection contains material to illustrate the history of lace in Denmark and other parts of Europe and embroideries both for dresses and for domestic use from most of the world. The museum holds a unique collection representing the Danish embroidery technique, Hedebo-embroidery.[2] However, the largest number of textiles is within the group of Danish textiles from the twentieth century, covering most areas of textile technique.

The collected textile can be made of different materials and uses many techniques. The fabric can be an example of a complex weaving or can be embellished with embroidery or print. It can be an example of exquisite material and/or a well-designed pattern or motif. Finally, it can be a combination of several qualities, all with an aesthetic value.

Not until twenty-five years ago, like many other museums of decorative art and design in Europe, Designmuseum Danmark had not decided to focus collecting on dress and fashion together with textile. Through some special exhibitions during the 1980s and the early 1990s, it became clear to the museum that the interest in exhibiting and collecting dress and fashion was growing.[3] The change of title of the collection from "The Textile Collection" to "The Textile and Dress Collection" took place in 2007. In the strategy plan for 2009–2012, it was announced that the museum would focus on collecting fashion, dress, and textile. As a consequence of this strategy, it was more logical in the future to include the word "fashion" in the title of the collection.

The museum collects dress that represents a combination of fashionable silhouette, made from valuable material and executed according to crafts rules and technological options. It can be a prototype, a unique specimen such as couture dress made with bespoke tailoring from a highly specialized fabric, or the dress can show groundbreaking details and belong to the avant-garde. This includes artistic dress and dresses made by experimental artists. Instead of following trends and pandering to target groups, which is the norm in the fashion industry, these artists often aspire to move the frontiers of our perceptions of design and clothing and aim to challenge the audience in our perception of the world around us. The fashion and dress collection holds examples of every major historical period in fashion from the middle of the eighteenth century up until today. The biggest part is Danish designed clothes from the twentieth century, both couture and ready-to-wear.

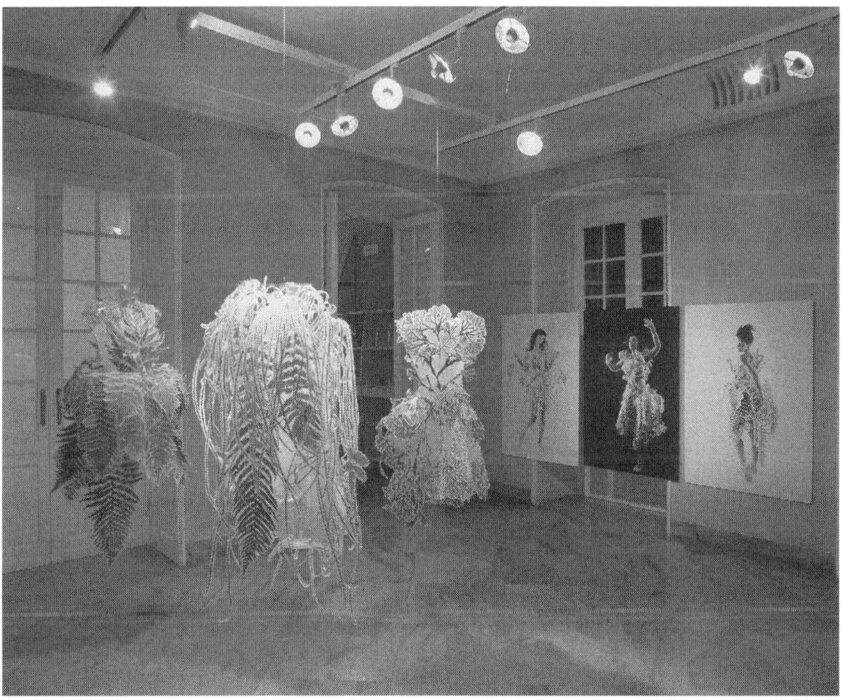

Figure 9.1 In 2007, the Danish fashion designer Laura Baruël exhibited at Designmuseum Danmark. The exhibition was called "Wilderness." The dresses were made of conserved plant material sewn between two layers of transparent fabric. As an example of artistic dress, the museum collected the dress to the right made from seaweed. Photography by Pernille Klemp.

The definition of fashion and dress in relation to the practice of collecting

The word "fashion" is used in many connections and can mean many different things depending on whether you are an average clothing consumer or a scientific researcher. And indeed within the scientific world there are several differences. To many fashion historians dealing with clothing from around the 1850s to the present day, fashion constitutes a material language connected to *identity*, whether it is an individual or a group. Other fashion historians choose the more simple definition of *change*. Both definitions are connected to the idea of the fashion system. The fashion system is defined by all the stages a garment has to pass through, from the idea of the designer, the production, the marketing and distribution, to the consumption and recycling of clothes. The fashion system is said to be responsible for the annual or seasonal change of silhouette and form, textile, material, color, and pattern in clothes and accessories according to taste, the zeitgeist, and social life (Entwistle 2004: 43–48).

The notion of dress is often linked to clothes, which are detached from the fashion system. For instance, when a dress enters a collection in a museum, very often it loses the language which the former owner used to stage or even manipulate the reading observer. Furthermore, the documentation of the fashion system, for example the design, evidence of production, and the advertising material connected to the specific dress, is lost. Or it could be an item where the designer deliberately wishes the dress to be outside the system, for instance a nun's habit or an artistic dress. The dyed and pleated Delphos dresses by the Spanish-Italian artist and designer Mariano Fortuny (1871–1949), which he made for around forty years in the same shapes, could hardly be a part of the fashion system, nor could the contemporary equivalent of the Delphos dress, Issey Miyake's (b. 1938) Pleat Please range made since 1989. Modifications in Fortuny's dresses or to a nun's habit can occur but not at the speed and with the regularity of which fashion changes in modern society. However, if an artistic dress or a nun's habit were to be a part of the fashion system, it could be as an inspiration for the couture or the ready-to-wear fashion designer. In general dress and fashion scholars are constantly discussing to which extent it is relevant to apply the fashion system to clothes from earlier centuries. No matter which historical period, some researchers are arguing that the study of fashion must also include the study of technology, economics, politics, and social context. Often evidence of the fashion system is absent, and written sources have not survived. In those cases, researchers are often left to study visual representations, for instance paintings or sculptures. In lucky cases, an actual dress has survived, and it is possible to collect knowledge from the fabric, the construction and silhouette, the stitches, linings, and the marks of use (Cumming 2004: 48; Entwistle 2004: 43–48).

As written sources become available through research, we are able to learn more about the context in which, for example, fashionable clothes in the eighteenth century were made and used. Close studies of a dress are supplemented by documental material. Collecting material reflecting the fashion system has become more and more relevant. Dress and fashion are an integral part of each other and seem to be more and more difficult to separate. But, on the other hand, one should be cautious in applying the fashion system to all historical periods.

Some examples of the relationship between textile, dress, and fashion in the collection at Designmuseum Danmark

For about a hundred years, the main focus for the collection at Designmuseum Danmark has been collecting flat textiles made either for domestic use or fabrics made for fashion and dress. In 1890, several dresses had already found their way into the collection. However, the attention was still on the fabric aspect. These dresses were interesting as collecting objects because they were examples of fabrics showing an interesting technique, a beautiful pattern, or simply because they were made of precious materials. This is underlined by the way the dresses were recorded and depicted in the hand-painted illustrations in the museum inventory and the fabric was very often the most important visual representation. Although not recorded in the inventory, some eighteenth-century dresses were bought with the purpose of using the fabrics for upholstery of furniture.

However, some of the acquired dresses escaped being cut up and made into upholstery fabrics. From about 1900 to 1985 acquisitions of dresses varied from one to eight items every ten years; however, the years from 1931 to 1935 stand out with twenty-seven acquisitions. Dating from around 1750 to 1880, the twenty-seven dresses are among the most valuable historical costumes in the collection, representing the fashion of the period. Some of them were bought from dealers, others were given to the museum as donations. Unfortunately, the dresses have no provenance, and as such are partly detached from the fashion system.

We do not know what causes this sudden interest and intensive collecting. What we do know, though, is that the National Museum in Copenhagen worked on a new presentation in its dress galleries to be opened late in the 1930s (Andersen 1938). Furthermore, there was a close relationship between the curator Ellen Andersen (1898–1989) and the director at Designmuseum Danmark, Vilhelm Slomann (1885–1962, director 1923–1949). They shared a common interest in eighteenth-century dress and in 1938, on the occasion of the

150th anniversary of the abolition of adscription, they organized a small dress exhibition at the National Museum.[4]

From the 1960s—perhaps even earlier—many opinions have been aired about the interest in collecting dress and fashion among curators at museums in general. These assertions were apparently due to many views of cultural and political significance such as the gender of leading curators at design museums (Taylor 2004). However, searching in the Designmuseum Danmark's archive for documented evidence of any interest in collecting dress and fashion or for that matter any dismissal, the different clues are unclear and somewhat ambiguous. Fashion has often been accused of close ties with commercialism and being connected to the ephemeral. This was supposed to exclude the field from being acceptable in terms of collecting in art and craft museums as art is associated with the classical. In the past, this opinion has also influenced the collecting of dress and fashion in Designmuseum Danmark.

However, in the collection of Designmuseum Danmark one type of clothes needs to be pointed out. The museum holds a sizeable, fine collection of clothes from the 1950s up to the present day, recorded over the years under the designation "craftsmen's dress." In 1958 the first craftsmen's dress was acquired by the museum. Made by the Danish textile printing artist Ruth Christensen, this was the first contemporary dress bought for the collection. For many years ahead, craftsmen's dresses were the only contemporary clothes to become part of the collection. In most cases, a common feature of all dresses is the manufacture of the fabrics as unique specimens by leading Danish textile printers and weavers. A craftsmen's dress is usually based on an integrated working relationship between a clothes designer and a textile designer. However, this may strictly speaking also be one and the same person. The textile is ordered and most often produced as hand-printed or hand-woven materials specific for the purpose in question, and the cut of the garment goes hand in hand with the pattern and/or structure of the fabric, most often cotton, wool, or silk. Models were sometimes produced in limited numbers, but most often they were unique specimens. In Denmark, the craftsmen's dress became highly popular in the 1960s and onwards through the 1970s, and many designers produced this type of clothing either alone or together with colleagues (Toftegaard 2011).

Craftsmen's dresses seemed to be accepted in the collection, and they were the only contemporary dress bought for many years ahead. The reason may be found in the fact that the clothes were considered interesting because they were made by already-known artists, and the fabrics in many ways had their own qualities. As such the craftsmen's dress was perceived as the result of a non-commercial practice. Moreover the artists of craftsmen's dresses spoke about their clothes as anti-fashion and in opposition to what the fashion industry at that time defined as being fashion. Today we look differently at the concept of the craftsmen's dress. In retrospect we realize that the attitude of anti-fashion was quite fashionable at the time and also a part of the fashion system (Toftegaard 2011).

In 2005 a friend of the museum donated a small collection of dresses, trousers, suits, and coats designed by the French fashion designer André Courrèges (b. 1923). He was known for his space-inspired clothes and for using flexible fabrics and vinyl as trimmings in the clothes and in accessories in order to add a characteristic futuristic expression. In 1961 André Courrèges established his fashion house in Paris, and in 1964 he launched the famous "Space Age" collection. Courrèges was among the avant-gardists in European fashion and it is continuously discussed whether he or the English fashion designer, Mary Quant (b. 1934), introduced the miniskirt. The combination of the fashionable clothes and the fabrics tells the story of the 1960s fashion revolution from tailored clothes to ready-to-wear, from clothes made for adult, mature women to youth fashion, from constricted clothes to streamlined fashion which did not suppress body movements.

Last but not least, in 2003, the museum acquired around ninety haute couture dresses by the Danish-born fashion designer Erik Mortensen (1926–1998). Mortensen started his career at the age of 16 by serving as an apprentice with the locally famous Danish couturier Holger Blom (1906–1965). In 1948 Mortensen settled in Paris and worked at the Parisian fashion house Balmain as the assistant of Pierre Balmain. In 1982, when Pierre Balmain died, Mortensen was appointed chief couturier of the fashion house. In 1990 he moved to another fashion house—Jean-Louis Scherrer, where he worked until 1994. Mortensen was known for his extravagant use of all beautiful, black fabrics in his haute couture dresses. All kinds of silk from the finest to very heavy quality, from plain weave to velour, but also pleated artificial fabrics, were a part of his gowns. It is as though any black fabric does his design full justice. Both designers André Courrèges and Erik Mortensen represent the higher end of fashion in the twentieth century and both reflect the importance of the collaboration between fabric and fashion.

The challenges

What would be lost if textiles within the concept that combines form, function, material, and execution seen from an aesthetic point of view were devalued, or even excluded in collecting in the future? There is fashion in textiles as well as in dress. There have been periods in fashion history where fashion-consciousness was determined not only by wearing the right gown, but also by applying the latest colored and patterned fabric. In addition, very often the configuration of a gown depends on the characteristics of the fabric applied for its creation. Also, fabrics used for contemporary dresses follow fashion trends. One year it is chiffon, another woolen tartans or corduroy. It could be paisley patterns, stripes or dots, or a new technological functional fiber or knitted textiles—the options are endless. Textiles offer knowledge in fashionable clothes as important as for instance the cut of a dress.

In fashion and dress, the textile and the designer's choice of textile can provide the clothes with different functions. It can show bodily functions: some materials work better as underwear and some as outer garments, some are suited for sportswear, and again some have strong-wearing qualities and are used as workwear. Some fabrics are more washable than others, which can prove to be an advantage. Some are better suited for summer, others for winter, some have decorative functions—the list is long. The same functions can be applied to domestic textiles: some textiles are more suited for curtains, others for upholstery. Finally, some textiles function both as domestic textiles and as textiles for garments.

In addition to functionality, fabrics communicate: Some fashion firms use a patterned fabric as signature and transmitter for the fashion label. The varied checked patterns of the two British firms Burberry and Mulberry function as logos for each firm. The width of the horizontal and vertical stripes and the space in between are so established that it has been possible to experiment with other color combinations and continuously keep the recognizable effect. The signature can be the coloring of the fabric or the pleating, as seen with Mariano Fortuny's Delphos dresses and Issey Miyake's pleated clothes. The knitted, multi-colored zigzag pattern of the Italian knitting firm Missoni is a significant fabric for the firm. And what would jeans be without denim? With success for more than five decades, the Finish textile and fashion firm Marimekko has sold simple A-dresses recognizable for the colorful great-scale patterns—the same pattern that is usable for domestic textiles. In these cases, it is relevant to discuss whether the most important thing is the fabric and its pattern, or the actual construction of the piece of clothing.

Most couture designers work with the fabric alongside the construction of the clothes. Today, young designers have started to explore and work with innovation in fabrics. Either a designer develops a fashion garment from the fabric, or develops ideas from draping directly on the dummy. This was the case for the local Danish couturier Holger Blom (1905–1965). Also, the contemporary Danish fashion designer Henrik Vibskov (b. 1972) works with draping when designing about 50 percent of his clothes. For each seasonal collection, half of the models are decided after and inspired by the purchase of the fabric; the other half is designed and then the appropriate textile is chosen. The conceptual streetwear clothes by Henrik Vibskov have innovative cuts and details; this makes them both stylish and unique compared to corresponding conceptual streetwear design. This means that a garment can be used year after year without losing its fashionability. For that reason the quality of the fabric is of great importance; it is also a great problem, expressed by Henrik Vibskov's co-designer, Maja Brix. She

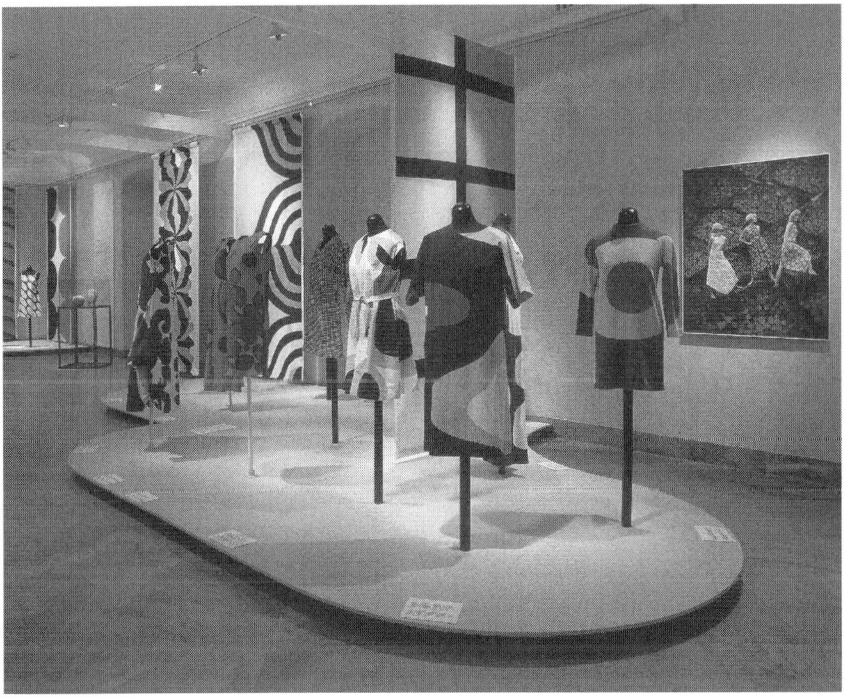

Figure 9.2 Shown at Designmuseum Danmark in 2007, the exhibition “Marimekko—the Story of a Nordic Brand” was an example of how fabric and fashion merged together both in the individual dress but also in the exhibition display. Photography by Pernille Klemp.

explains that both the manufacturer of the textile and the producer of the clothes continuously try to optimize economy with the obvious purpose of reducing costs and increasing profit.[5] This development results in reduced quality that is almost impossible for the designer or the customer to find out, but will become noticeable after a short period of use.

The Danish-born, London-based fashion designer Peter Jensen has recently relocated 70 percent of the firm’s production back to England and Scotland. According to Jensen, this was done in order to re-establish the control of quality both in terms of textiles and the production of clothes: he succeeded in doing so even if the know-how had almost vanished with the closing down of local industries. However, sales increased, although the prices went up; especially in Japan, where spending power is high, it gave status to the clothes branded as “made in Great Britain.”[6] Holger Blom is represented in the collection, and both Henrik Vibskov and Peter Jensen are contributing to the collection currently.

When the fashion designer sets out to prepare the collection for the coming season, choosing the appropriate fabric for the garments is one of the many decisions he or she has to make together with his staff of employees. It is an important part of the design process. The fashion designer's relationship with the fabric can be very personal, most visible in haute couture and the high end of fashion (Gale and Kaur 2004). Fashion and dress history is full of examples where fabric and dress melt into each other and become inseparable; such as the haute couture clothes from the French fashion designer Madame Grés (1903–1993). Inspired by antique, Greek sculptures, she draped the fabric, either jersey, thin wool, or silk directly on the live model. The tiny pleats in the thin textile and the fall of the fabric provided her classic dresses with an air of simplicity and elegance.

Introducing a new all-inclusive collecting policy at Designmuseum Danmark

Regarding the practice of collecting fashion, dress, and textile, a strategy has been developed partly in order to be familiar with previous practice and partly to be conscious about future collecting. Three areas are defined, representing either textile design, dress design, or fashion design. Sometimes two different aspects are found in a single item, other times all three aspects can be integrated in one object. But it does not have to remain a static view and seen in a retrospective perspective—the object could move from one area including one aspect to another zone where two or three aspects are incorporated. This sometimes happens when for example research in collected documentary materials changes your view. Between the 1950 and 1970s, when craftsmen's dresses were acquired, they fulfilled a combination of textile design and dress design. As the craftsmen were anxious to point out, their dresses were in opposition to current fashion, and they claimed that the clothes were outside the fashion system, hence only two aspects were covered. Today the view has changed and we realize that the clothes are a representation of an alternative, anti-fashion movement, in itself a kind of fashion statement and also a part of the fashion system—and the perspective has moved to include to all three categories.

The museum challenges previous collecting criteria by increasing the focus of collecting fashion compared with past ideas, but not at the expense of the textile and dress aspect. Within the museum, it still needs to be accepted that a broader notion of fashion can touch on everything acquired within the area of art and design.

Conclusion

This chapter has intended to argue for the importance of balancing the collecting of textile, dress, and fashion in museums on equal terms and considering all three to be complementary to each other. As a curator one always has to try not to be biased by the zeitgeist and in best cases try to predict what one believes to be future prospects. Designmuseum Danmark wants to develop in tune with the times, but not to ignore important knowledge of the study of textiles.

Some say that textiles are the hidden art of fashion (Black 2006: 6) and as textiles form the basis of the collection at Designmuseum Danmark it is time to be attentive to balancing fashion and the materiality of fashion in collecting, because it makes sense considering the collecting criteria for the museum and because the tradition has already been embedded in the museum for more than a hundred years.

In 2005, the Danish National Research Foundation's Centre for Textile Research, University of Copenhagen, was established, and a formalized research environment has been growing in Denmark. Danish researchers and a group of researchers from all over the world, not least Europe, have contributed to the study of textile, dress, and fashion from pre-historical to present times. Governmental approval for a center focusing on these topics has had an enormously positive effect on all textile, dress, and fashion research done in Denmark. The Centre is supportive at least by offering facilities to a wide range of researchers trying to include textile craftsmen in their research as well as being aware of the cost of a possible loss of knowledge.

Denmark has a very profitable fashion industry with a variety of designers operating on a spectrum from couture and designer brand level using high-quality materials and production methods to the mass market where clothes are a basic commodity sold in supermarkets at the cheapest price. The textile industry in Denmark is dominated by one big textile design company, namely Kvadrat.[7] Many textile designers barely survive as craftsmen, and many have been left alone or in groups to operate in workshops (Paludan 2003). Today, many Danish textile designers have to collaborate with bigger workshops and factories in faraway countries to secure their own production. This more economical yet insecure way of living is reflected in a constantly falling number of educated textile designers in Denmark compared with the number of fashion designers.

In Denmark, the education of fashion and textile remain separated, a sad fact that underlines the division between the areas of textile and fashion. Taking into consideration Designmuseum Danmark's collecting criteria, the combination of the design of fashion and the design of fabric is of special interest in the practice of collecting for the museum. The French haute couture designer Christian Dior (1907–1957) once said: "Fabric not only expresses a designer's dream, but also stimulates his own ideas. It can be the beginning of an inspiration. Many a dress of mine is born of the fabric alone" (Gale and Kaur 2004: 4). Other times, the designer merges the design of the fabric with the design of clothes, as is seen in craftsmen's clothes. Even to go a step further would be when the form of clothes is created simultaneously with the fabric itself. It becomes a synthesis, as for example in knitting.

Notes

1 Before April 1, 2011, *Det danske Kunstindustrimuseum* (The Danish Museum of Art and Design). Since the 1920s, the museum has been located in the former *Det kongelige Frederiks Hospital* (The Royal Frederik's Hospital), built in the middle of the eighteenth century based on drawings by the Danish architect Nicolai Eigtved (1701–1754). Designmuseum Danmark was founded in 1890 in Copenhagen by *Industriforeningen* (The Industry Association) and by *Ny Carlsberg Museumslegat* (The New Carlsberg Museum Grant).

2 The white-on-white embroidery was used to decorate homes for festive occasions, but also for women's shifts and men's shirts from the eighteenth century and over the next 150 years.

3 In 1983 "Alverdens Broderier – I Kunstindustrimuseet", in 1988 "Stjerner i Fransk Mode – Kunstindustrimuseet", and in 1991 "Pragt & Poesi – Kniplinger gennem 400 år."

4 This information has been known thanks to colleagues at the Nationalmuseum, Esther Grølsted and Mikkel Venborg Pedersen.

5 Interview with Henrik Vibskov in his studio, August 1, 2011. Interview with Maja Brix at Designmuseum Danmark, November 24, 2011.

6 Interview with Peter Jensen at Designmuseum Danmark September 26, 2011.

7 Kvadrat was founded in 1968. The company works mainly with upholstery and curtain textiles. The company holds one of the leading positions in the European market (www.kvadrat.dk).

References

Andersen, Ellen (1938), "Nationalmuseets Dragtgalerier," in *Haandarbejdets Fremme*, 13.

Anderson, Fiona (2000), "Museums as Fashion Media," in: Stella Bruzzi and Pamela Church Gibson (eds), *Fashion Cultures: Theories, Explorations and Analysis*, London: Routledge, pp. 371–389.

Black, Sandy (ed.) (2006), *Fashioning Fabrics – Contemporary Textiles in Fashion*, London: Black Dog Publishing.

Cumming, Valerie (2004), *Understanding Fashion History*, London: B.T. Batsford.

Entwistle, Joanna (2004), *The Fashioned Body – Fashion, Dress and Modern Social Theory*, Cambridge, Malden and Oxford: Polity Press/Blackwell Publishers.

Gale, Colin and Jasbir Kaur (2004), *Fashion and Textiles: An Overview*, Oxford: Berg.

Paludan, Charlotte (2003), *Vævekunst – Dansk håndvævning i det 20. århundrede*, Copenhagen: The Danish Museum of Art & Design.

Taylor, Lou (2004), *Establishing Dress History*, Manchester: Manchester University Press.

Toftegaard, Kirsten (2011), "Dansk Kunsthåndværkertøj – mellem skrædderi, konfektion, kunst og mode," in: Solveig Hoberg, Helle Leilund, Maria Mackinney-Valentin, Marie

Riegels Melchior and Kirsten Toftegaard (eds), *Snit – Industrialismens tøj i Danmark*, Copenhagen: Museum Tusculanums Forlag, Københavns Universitet, pp. 247–282.

Interviews

Interview with Henrik Vibskov in his studio, August 1, 2011.
Interview with Peter Jensen at Designmuseum Danmark, September 26, 2011.
Interview with Maja Brix at Designmuseum Danmark, November 24, 2011.

10
ENGAGING THE PUBLIC IN ISSUES OF DRESS AND IDENTITY: A CASE STUDY OF AMAGERMUSEET IN DENMARK

Ingeborg Philipsen

Attracting new groups of visitors and especially young people into the museum is a challenge faced by museums all over the world.[1] Some progressive museum administrations have, with some success, turned the museum's dress department into a fashion department and developed the museum's fashion exhibition program, which has at least attracted media attention and perhaps also had a positive influence on the number of visitors, and beckoned the younger generations as stated by Marie Riegels Melchior in the introduction of this book. Displaying what was at one point or another considered the most exclusive or most admired dresses has the advantage of representing style, the production of the new at a given time, and is therefore more appealing. This is of course even truer for those dealing with contemporary, high-end designer fashion. However, this strategy is not really an option for a small open-air cultural historic museum, located on the edge of the isle of Amager near Copenhagen in Denmark.

Amagermuseet was established in 1922 and is rooted in the small Dutch community, which by invitation of the Danish King Christian II (1481–1559) settled on the island of Amager in the early sixteenth century. The Dutch community was accorded special trading and tax privileges and therefore soon rose to an economic standard above the local Danish population. The immigrants maintained an isolated, conservative, lifestyle until the middle of the nineteenth century, which was also reflected in regional dress practices. Since 1981 Amagermuseet has been an open-air museum. Today it is part of the institution

Museum Amager which is an amalgamation of four local museums. Museum Amager owns a large and unique collection of nineteenth-century folk dresses from the island of Amager.[2]

In this chapter, I will discuss how to modernize a minor provincial museum, when fashion is not an obvious option, but dress is a key entry point to the core of the museum collection and the cultural heritage represented by the museum. Of course the peasants did pick up new dress impulses from outside the local community, but this is not the key entry point to understand the dress collection (Lorenzen 1987: 56–67). In the case of Amager, inspiration came not only from Copenhagen, but also from foreign countries, especially the Netherlands, through the lively shipping trade in the nearby harbor of Dragør. Since awareness of the community's Dutch origins was so strong in local identity, impulses from the Netherlands presumably had greater influence, as in the case of the characteristic blue floss hat, worn by men in the so-called Dutch village, Store Magleby. The blue floss hat was introduced to the local community through Dutch sailors. It was also preserved in the Dutch village at Amager as a marker of Dutch identity long after it went out of fashion in the Netherlands and elsewhere.

The folk dress collection at Amagermuseet represents primarily former dress traditions. The dresses of the collection are definitely not sexy; neither in the literal meaning of the word nor in the way the word is used among journalists today, when writing about fashion in the hope of a broad and general public appeal. Young girls and boys might visit a fashion exhibition, but only very reluctantly do they visit a folk dress exhibition. Other folk dress institutions, like the Folk Music Association and similar associations, are doing a persistent and gradually successful job with a lot of outreach arrangements appealing to young people between 16 and 30. It is characteristic, however, that they do emphasize the importance of making arrangements with "less straw in the clogs."[3] So, what can a small museum with an exclusive folk dress collection do to attract older children and young adults to visit and ultimately to show interest in our dress collection? This was what we asked ourselves in 2011, when we decided to hold an exhibition which addressed the problem that folk dresses have very little appeal outside of a small group of often elderly dress enthusiasts and research specialists. We started to look for elements in the Amager dress practice which could trigger some sort of resonance in the lives of young people today.

The answer we came up with was dress codes and identity and the outcome was the exhibition, "Dressed! From Country Bumpkin to Saggy Pants" (in Danish: "*Klœdt På! Fra Bonderøv til Hœngerøv*"). We decided to address dress as a container of identity. It reflects the identity of an individual or a group more than most other aspects of material culture. It mirrors both technological achievements and the myths, moral power, and aesthetic values of a society, whereas details of any given dress provide important information about the individual aspects of the designer, creator, or wearer of the dress. Minor museums have the advantage of close connection to the local community and identity. But to keep this position, we have to keep up with the times and include newcomers and younger generations. The basic idea of this exhibition was to make the audience recognize elements of the Amager dress as something familiar in their own lives, using the dress, and its specific dress codes, as a mirror for exploring current dress codes and relations between dress and identity today.

After a short presentation of the museum and its dress collection, the ideas behind, stages of, and elements in the exhibition, "Dressed! From Country Bumpkin to Saggy Pants" are presented and discussed.

The Amager dress collection

In Denmark we do not have a tradition of wearing regional folk dress on special occasions as they do in the other Scandinavian countries, especially in Norway (Haugen 2011). Amager, however, makes an exception for this rule in Denmark: what is known as the Amager folk dress still constitutes a central element in building and reproducing the local community's identity as does the history of the Dutch settlement. Many local men and women in this community of 11,700 citizens still pursue their Dutch origins and this group of Dutch descendants constitutes the core of the approximately fifty to seventy-five volunteers who help run the museum.[4] But there is another group, the new citizens who have moved into the community, and who contribute to the museum budget through their local tax payments. But they seem to be excluded from the representation of the dress collection. They, for one, do not belong to the group of descendants of the initial Dutch settlers. If the dress collection documents the history and presence of human life, as it has been stated, many newcomers seem to think that the Amager dresses in our collection do not represent their history.[5]

Dress codes help us to build our identity. Dress and style enables us to decode information about other people's interests, social status, etc. Few folk dresses have as many dress codes attached to them as the Amager dress. As one author wrote in 1962: "To have a well-supplied wardrobe, the Amager Dutch woman had to have no less than eight different dresses, at least 30 woolen pinafores and double as many patterned silk scarves" (Kaae 1962: 69). Although the validity of certain Amager dress codes should be questioned, and in some cases are probably of later construction based on less reliable sources (Erna Lorenzen 1987). Sometimes genre paintings have been used as a source of the "correct" use of the Amager dress. Even genre oral history, have been used. A very exhaustive study of the Amager dress was made in 1930 by the curator at the Danish National Museum, Elna Mygdal (1932), and the fact remains that the museum's dress collection is characterized by a remarkable variety of groups of dresses with different skirts and pinafores, establishing the elements in the construction of the main types of dresses or outfits described below.[6]

The museum's dress collection contains about 1,200 dress objects. The main types of outfit according to the local Amager dress practice include the bonnet dress, which was the less exclusive dress, the traditional bride's dress. The so-called *kokke* dress was, according to local dress codes, the outfit of the unmarried young girls who helped to host the wedding of a young couple. The young wife's dress, with its white skirt, was only differentiated from the *kokke* dress by other colors in the two ribbons in front of the skirt. The so-called church dress with a thick red pleated skirt is the most exclusive of the many festive dresses, but it is also the kind of dress that is most represented in the museum collection—presumably because these were the most exclusive dresses and the ones least worn and therefore have been best preserved for posterity. Finally, there is the so-called market dress with the blue cotton pinafores and the large bonnet, which protected women from the sun when they drove about six miles to the market-place in Copenhagen, where they sold their famous vegetables. Other farmers are said to have copied and used the Amager market dress deliberately as their trademark when selling their goods at the market (Møller *et al.* 1996).

Characteristic of the Amager dress is the special bonnet, known as the "duck's beak," which is decorated with Amager needlework—a dark indigo dyed variant of the Danish Hedebo Embroidery tradition which is also *glittet*: flax is rubbed with a round stone to make the oil of the flax come out and give the indigo dyed clothing a shining surface. There are also the so-called Barcelona scarves which are colorful silk scarves that sailors in Dragør brought home from Spain and which the local women decorated with extra embroideries on top of the dyed patterns. The skirts come mostly in black, but also in white with narrow pleatings or thick, red wool and even in blue or red dyed fur from a sheep.[7]

The most noteworthy part of the man's Amager dress is the black, very wide, trouser and especially the big, round, blue floss hat, which became the most important token of the Dutch community—and was as an example in 1906 chosen as the emblem of the local (since 2011, defunct) Amager Bank. The story behind the blue floss hat is further described below.

Besides the museum's large collection, some Amager dresses are also still handed down from one generation to the next or are acquired at local auctions for use on special occasions, like the annual harvest festival or other local celebrations. It is estimated that there are about ninety or more original dresses owned by private citizens.[8] This strong local attachment is both the strength and the Achilles' heel of the museum. A tendency for self-glorification and cutting off the rest of the world has been pronounced.

How we got from country bumpkin to saggy pants

The title of the exhibition was chosen due to its ability to address the negative prejudice about folk dress head on: using the term "country bumpkin" was meant as a way to comply with the fact that this was actually how many (young) people perceive folk dress collections and folk dress enthusiasts. By linking this to a very familiar conflict concerning young people's dress and especially boys' dress—the saggy pants—we hoped to catch the attention of this group.[9] However, this provocative attitude to the subject enhanced the risk of losing backing from traditional visitors and the group of volunteers in the museum community. This danger was averted, we thought, by the existence of a very popular Danish TV show about a young farmer, Frank, who is proud to call himself a country bumpkin. This show also had other communicative advantages, which we will return to later in the chapter.

At the other extreme we had the saggy pants, which represented not only something very current but also something controversial, which turned out to

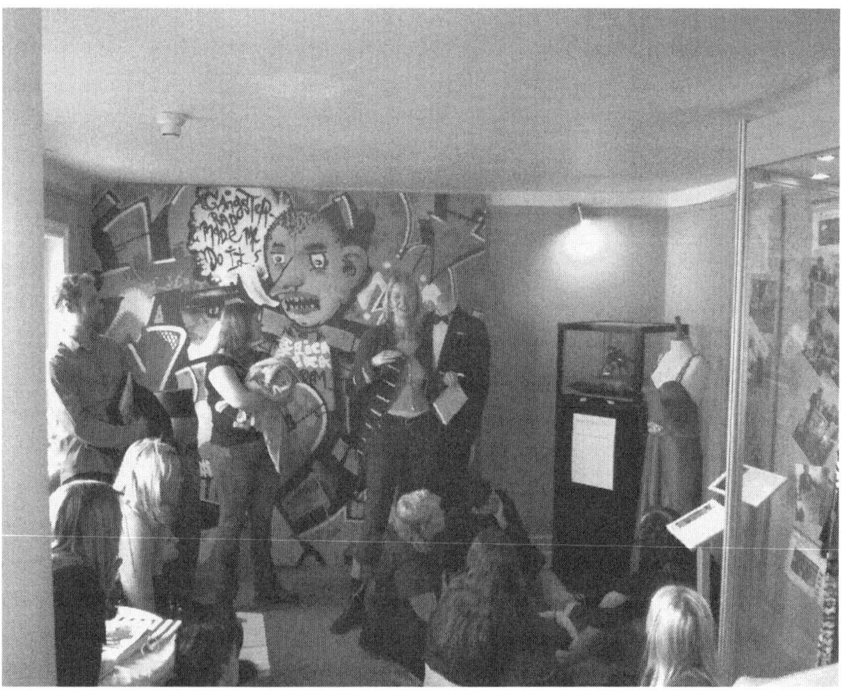

Figure 10.1 A guided tour in the exhibition "Dressed! From Country Bumpkin to Saggy Pants." The COP15 gala dress and the saggy pants on display with a group of young visitors in 2011. With permission of Museum Amager.

raise many interesting universal issues about sexual morality, respect and disrespect, personal freedom, etc. The internet and public debate was overflowing with undocumented explanations about the low-slung pants originating from the American prison environment as a result of a lack of belts or the even more problematic explanation that argued that sagging your pants and showing your underwear in prison would indicate your identification with being a homosexual.[10] These very widespread myths made the theme of the exhibition even more relevant. The challenge was, however, that the phenomenon of saggy pants was apparently still so new that it was very difficult to find relevant research literature on the subject.[11] The lack of academic literature was however counterbalanced by the information we received from talking to teenagers both before and during the exhibition.

In practice, we came from the country bumpkin to the saggy pants by dividing the exhibition into six areas representing the following themes designed to communicate with groups within the local community, which is not integrated in the traditional museum community.

a) Display of the Amager dress as an introduction to the theme of dress codes and identity. Aspects of collective identity that derived from the local connection to the origin of the Dutch settlement and individual identities reflected in the maintenance of the Amager dress practice.

b) Display of five professional uniforms with special relation to Amager, exploring different aspects of abolition of individual identification and adaptation to collective identities.

c) Display of examples of dress "scandals" and "violations" of dress codes in contemporary Danish history on the basis that it is when rules are broken that we realize that rules indeed still exist and that they generate strong feelings as well.

d) Display of alternative, contemporary "Amager dresses" gathered from local citizens based on the idea that "folk dress" is "what folk wear."

e) A display of ten large posters showing photographs of ordinary people from the streets of Amager wearing all kinds of clothes.

f) A large red wardrobe containing all kinds of clothing and an invitation to play with identity by dressing up in different types of clothes.

The physical setting dictated that we would have to separate the flow of the exhibition into two after the introduction. This meant that a–c were placed in one direction and d–f in another. Since the outreach strategy was twofold, we chose to have the first part targeted at both groups, but the second part (d–f) targeted mainly at local people. During guided tours with teenagers, they were led through the first part, but left to go through the second part on their own.

A so-called code book was part of the exhibition. Different code numbers were attached to a part of a dress or an item of clothing. The play with codes and decoding was a way of materializing the point that human beings are constantly collecting information about each other by scanning and "decoding" dress and looks. The audience were able to look up the code in the codebook, where the text "decoded" the item of clothing, its history, containment of symbolic meaning, etc. Short texts and collages of newspaper illustrations, articles, headlines, and, in some cases, mirrors with texts written with felt-tips, supplemented the dresses displayed on the mannequins.

In the following the exhibition is unfolded with the intention to illustrate and discuss the relationship between the ideas behind and the concrete configuration of the exhibition design and the outcome and response from the audience.

Dressed 1: the folk dress and the notion of the "country bumpkin"

Two types of Amager dress were introduced in the first section of the exhibition: the young wife's dress and the man's Sunday dress. Both contain many markers of individual and collective identity of the Dutch settlement of the nineteenth

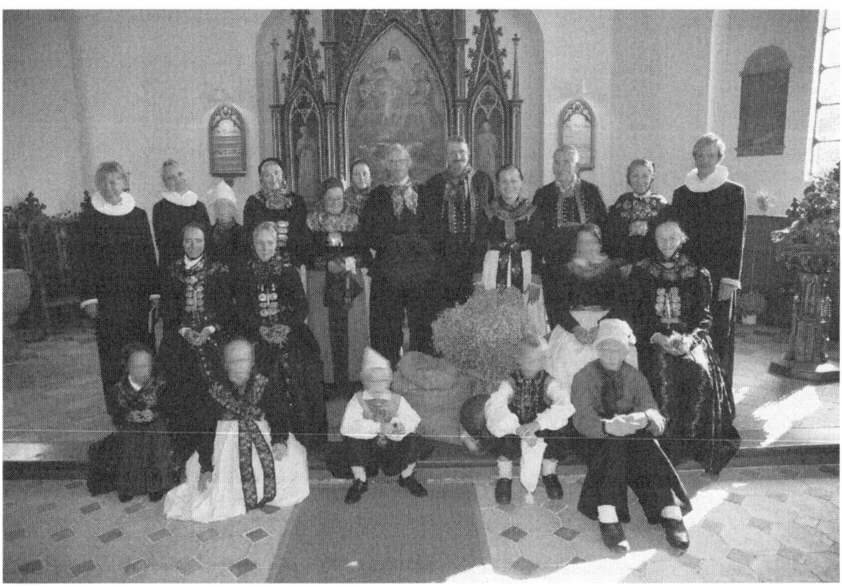

Figure 10.2 The Amager dress is still in use for instance in connection with the annual harvest festival at Store Magleby Church. Photograph by Dirch Jansen. With permission of Museum Amager.

century: the young wife's dress was the dress that the bride traditionally changed into when she removed her wedding dress immediately after the celebration. According to the local dress code, she wore this dress every Sunday until the christening of her first child.

These Amager dress forms worked as a point of departure for a general discussion about dress and identity. We would often open a guided tour for a school class of teenagers with a discussion about how the kids chose the clothes they wore that day—did they think a lot about it, did their mum choose (which to our surprise was often the case), and, did they have a favorite dress combination? Many of the teenagers were preoccupied with the dress codes in relation to the up-coming confirmation, where many of the boys would perhaps wear a suit for the first time. This again would lead to discussions about the role of clothing in relation to rites of passage from one life phase to another. This would trigger long and engaged debates, for instance about the traditions of baptism and why boys would be baptized wearing a girly christening gown, but would never wear a girly dress elsewhere; whether it is acceptable for boys/men to wear pink, etc. These debates with the teenagers clarified the fact that the subtle dress codes for most men and boys are much more restricted than those for women and girls. All these debates were linked continuously to the practice of the peasant community and the young wife's dress which she wore in the period between being a young wife without a child, and becoming a mother.

As noted above, the other dress on display was the man's Sunday dress. The peculiar blue floss hat was originally worn by Dutch sailors, who often visited Dragør harbor during the eighteenth century, and the hats remained a popular item in St. Magleby. By the end of the eighteenth century, the floss hats had gone out of fashion in the Netherlands. New supplies of hats dried out at Amager, and they became part of the festive dress for men—according to local dress codes, only to be worn by married men on festive occasions.

The floss hat illustrated the theme of dress in relation to collective identity. The point of the historical role of the museum and the collection of folk dress as an instrument in the formation of a Danish national identity was made. It is a paradox that an originally Dutch settlement, with descendants who celebrated their Dutch culture, was among Julius Exner's favorite models when he tried to fulfill contemporary requests to artists to portray the life of "common Danes" with the idea of forming a new national character. This point put the traditional narrative of the museum in perspective also in relation to current debates about the role of the local museum as an identity-building institution today. Here the earlier mentioned TV show *The Country Bumpkin* was brought in as a reference. The show follows a young man, Frank, in his efforts to build a self-sufficient farm in Denmark. Frank is the epitome of the present-day romantic discourse in Denmark: an ecological idealist striving to re-establish the values of the good old days, when the pig could wallow in its pigsty, when the farmer knew how to make his wife a new cupboard from scratch. The exhibition used this pursuit of the values and ways of the "good old days in the countryside of the 1950s" as a parallel to the efforts to establish a new national spirit in the traditional peasant culture during the so-called National Romantic Movement of the late nineteenth century in Denmark.

The question of individual and collective identity reflected in dress was further illustrated in the following section of the exhibition.

Dressed 2: the uniform

The next section of the exhibition displayed five different kinds of uniform: workmen's/women's uniforms as well as military uniforms. The basic idea of displaying uniforms was to eliminate individual identity and to form and consolidate a sense of common or unified group identity. The work uniforms or workwear displayed derived from local companies, such as the waste-collecting company R98 or the airline Scandinavian Airlines (SAS). R98 was the dominant waste-collecting company in Denmark until it closed only a month before the exhibition was opened. R98 was a very important part of the island of Amager—also known as the "island of shit" due to the fact that night soil from Copenhagen was brought out to Amager to fertilize the fields and help in the growing of the Dutch farmers' famous, fine-quality vegetables. R98 was a company with a good reputation, giving prestige to the profession and enhancing the self-assurance of its employees in their characteristic blue-gray collared workwear right to the end.

Copenhagen Airport, situated next to the museum, takes up about a sixth of the island's area, and makes the SAS-uniform an unavoidable sight in the streets of Amager. As a result it is sometimes locally referred to as "the new Amager dress." This part linked the notion of dress and identity to the concept of branding—an element of the Amager dress which is reflected in the use by the descendants of the Dutch settlers of the Amager market dress as a brand.

Guided tours in this part of the exhibition often led to discussions of uniformity—the focus was drawn to the existence of conformity, which was not only present in companies and in the military but also in social groups, in classrooms, etc. Stepping into the next area, the focus shifted from the relationship between individual and collective identity to an evaluation of the phenomenon of historical and current dress codes.

"Clothes make the man" is a Danish saying, but clothes also produce contempt, scandal, and even conflict requiring legislative action. The third section of the exhibition tried to illustrate that dress codes are at least as important today as they were in the eighteenth and nineteenth centuries, although they are such an integral part of our social structures that we often do not realize they exist. It is only when the rules are broken that their existence is really brought to light.

Dressed 3: breaking the rules

In the third section of the exhibition, we displayed a Marimekko dress with its accompanying cycling shorts of the former Danish Minister for Culture, Jytte Hilden from the Social Democratic Party, together with a traditional Pakistan dress, a *sherwani*, worn by the Danish politician Kamal Qureshi from the Danish Socialist's People's Party. Both these outfits caused "scandals" when worn at royal celebrations. Jytte Hilden wore her "cycling knickers"—which were in fact a pair of short trousers—at a royal lunch on a hot summer's day in 1993. The incident is still frequently mentioned as a "terrifying" example in fashion magazines today.

Hilden broke several rules that day: royal dress codes—at least in "public opinion"—prescribe long or short dress. Besides, women over 25 do not wear "cycling knickers." Over the black trousers Hilden wore a Marimekko dress. The Minister of Culture was, in other words, wearing a brand that could be considered the uniform of the intellectual woman of the 1970s—and she literally wore it open and casual, thus infuriating fashion journalists and other public arbiters of taste even more.

Kamal Qureshi is a former MP from the Danish Socialist People's Party. He was born in Rawalpindi in Pakistan but moved to Denmark when he was 4. As an MP he was invited to the queen's annual New Year's Reception in 2001. Instead of the traditional western European gala dress for men—white tie and tails—Qureshi decided to wear the traditional Pakistani gala dress, a *sherwani*. This upset both journalists and politicians from the ultra-conservative and nationalist right-wing party, the Danish People's Party. One member of the Party wrote that Qureshi "profoundly insulted the country, which had given him citizenship."[12] The case of Qureshi's *sherwani* at the heart of the symbol of Danish identity, the queen's New Year's Reception, bears a resemblance to the Dutch settlers and their descendants who wished to maintain their Dutch cultural markers even to the present day. It is remarkable, however, that while Qureshi's act was considered offensive in some conservative nationalistic groups, the original Dutch folk dresses are considered to be part of an important cultural heritage and are held in high esteem. The Dutch considered themselves to be "the king's chosen."[13] It is also reflected in the king's repeated invitations to them to perform and dance at court, dressed in their traditional "Dutch" folk dress (Hjorth 1986).

We had another example of royal gala dress in the exhibition, namely copies of the clothes that two Greenpeace activists wore when they managed to gate-crash the dinner which the Queen of Denmark hosted in connection with the international COP15 meeting in December 2009—plus the original red, 11-cm high-heeled shoes that the female activist wore. When the activists showed up in long red evening dress and dinner jackets, they were rushed through all the security checks to the ceremonial hall where they rolled out their banner stating: "Politicians talk—leaders act" in front of the world's press. This was a classic example of how the right kind of dress can open doors everywhere. But in fact it was in spite of their choice of dress that they managed to get in. The queen's COP15 dinner invitation prescribed "short dress" for women and "dark suit" for men. In other words, the activists were overdressed for the occasion and it ought to have been obvious to the security services that these "diplomats" had never had an invitation.

It was in this section of the exhibition that the saggy pants were introduced: a pair of worn-out saggy pants were placed on a mannequin over some Calvin Klein underwear. Two young graffiti artists provided a suitable surrounding graffiti wall.

Two myths concerning the saggy pants were addressed here: the myth that this fashion was adapted from prisoners, due to the lack of belts in prison, which made the prisoners' trousers sag. This persistent explanation was rejected based on research by Holly P. Alford from Virginia Commonwealth University and Dr. Joanne Turney from Bath Spa University. According to their research sagging started in the urban areas and was later connected to prisoners. It began in the early 1980s when men, particularly African American men, wore their pants two sizes too big because they didn't like the tight styles. The look resembled that of the prison system, when belts are taken away and the pants sag down. The community was quick to criminalize the fad, and as hip-hop continued to become popular and gangster rap gained more traction, the look began to symbolize the gangster and prison image.[14] The flow of influence, according to these researchers, was the other way around, in other words. Several attempts were made to ban saggy pants. Florida state senator Gary Siplin tried for years to get kids to pull up their trousers. In 2011 he finally had his "baggy pants bill." Another example was in Opelousas, Louisiana, where wearing saggy pants carried a maximum penalty of a $500 fine and up to six months in prison.[15]

In Denmark reactions to saggy trousers have been less dramatic. Dress codes are generally more casual and school uniforms are not used. Posters in the exhibition told the story about a school in Jutland, Denmark, which banned saggy pants. As a result, however, most of the pupils decided to deliberately violate the ban. The press picked up the story and a clothing company quickly launched a campaign against the school's ban of saggy pants, handing out badges with the statement: "My jeans—My ass—My choice."[16]

These cases were held up against the Danish kings' sumptuary laws during the eighteenth century and generated long discussions about whether dress was something that the government should be able to regulate by law. Many young people were very upset about the legal restrictions and strict dress codes in the US. But if asked whether it would be all right for their neighbor to walk around naked in their garden or even in the streets, few agreed to go so far.

Dressed 4: the alternative Amager folk dress

In the fourth section we showed alternative, modern Amager dress collected by local citizens. This was an attempt to reach out to the local people who generally thought the traditional peasant dresses were irrelevant. The idea was also to generate reflection over the meaning of cultural heritage, and the often-held notion that cultural heritage is "something very old."

The idea was to advertise for items of clothing that meant something for you in your life—to collect clothes that could be considered to be part of the local citizens' personal heritage. By putting them on display in the museum they changed; instead of being just a part of a personal wardrobe and a personal memory, they became part of the public wardrobe in line with the traditional folk dress. Each piece of clothing was displayed with an introduction to the personal history related to the piece.

The first item of clothing we received was the denim jacket of a man named Robin and the history of this jacket turned out to correspond to the intention behind this part of the exhibition: Robin is in his fifties. After he had heard the "Do you have a special item of clothing in your life?" advertisement during lunch, he turned up at the museum the next day with a very cool, very 1970-ish denim jacket, with a lot of stars and patches on it. He had bought the jacket in 1973 from a friend who had just bought it for twice as much, but was in need of cash. Robin told us that he felt wonderful when he wore this jacket. The price was equivalent to his monthly rent and his landlady said: "If you were my son, wearing that jacket, I would slap your face!" But he loved it and he had kept the jacket in his wardrobe ever since.

In fact most of the clothes that we collected turned out to be from the 1970s. Many of the donors were—in spite of the intention to involve new groups in this part of the exhibition—part of the established museum network. This was a consequence of insufficient communication with the target group outside the museum network, and the strong engagement from the local museum community, which was basically positive, and showed that they were indeed open to change.

Each item was displayed with a short text telling its personal story. The idea of this part of the exhibition was to illustrate the link between dress and identity, but it was also an invitation to reflect on "what makes cultural heritage" in the case of dress. It reflected some of the veneration for the old folk dress, only here it was the local, ordinary people's private wardrobes which were turned into public wardrobes.

In the next and final section of the exhibition, we moved from the private wardrobes into the street and then back into the wardrobe again.

Dressed 5: "I am so tired of being hot!"

A display of ten large posters showing photographs of "ordinary people" from the streets of Amager wearing all kinds of ordinary clothes was then produced. These posters were placed so that the audience would have to walk in between them to pass on, as if they had met these people in the street. The idea was simply to let the audience reflect on the many different kind of characters and dress codes which exist on the streets today.

In the final part of the exhibition we built a large red wardrobe. A mirror was placed next to the wardrobe and on it we wrote the text: "I am so tired of being hot!" This was a quotation from a 15-year-old girl, who described the extreme pressure she felt she had to face every day. The visitor could dress up in different kinds of clothes from the wardrobe: folk dress, a fireman's outfit, a *niqab*, and also some very boring and outmoded clothes. The point was not that they would necessarily dress up in the clothes—although some did—but that they were invited to play with their identity through dress.

Perceptions and responses to the exhibition

Unfortunately, we did not manage to market the exhibition to schools as much as we had originally planned. On the other hand, the special offers of free guided tours which were made twice during the summer season attracted a new local audience, who were curious about the new approach and delighted that we had at least tried to reinvigorate the exhibition. But most importantly, the dialogue with the visitors during a guided tour—especially with the school classes—was extraordinary lively and engaged the intended audience. The starting point, the folk dresses, was strange and exotic to all of them, but talking about dress and what we wear and why was very democratic in the sense that it is something everybody knows about because we all wear clothes.

Although the exhibition was generally accepted among the museum's volunteers, it was in some cases considered to be too academic. Also, we realized that one of the general museum guides, who had been attached to the museum for the season, literally boycotted the exhibition in frustration over the changes and simply avoided taking the guests into the exhibition. This was of course a blow to us since it obviously undermined our efforts to attract a new audience. It shows the strong feelings involved and therefore in itself was an illustration of the close relationship between dress and identity—as well as of the importance of a well-organized communicating strategy.

Nevertheless the exhibition offered an alternative way of actualizing the museum's folk dress collections and seemed to make sense to the young audience, who got quite involved in the debates during the guided tours. It is also noteworthy that it was more often male teachers in their thirties who took the initiative to come and see the exhibition, for example as a feature in their social science classes. To them the exhibition offered a forum for a more general debate about the role of dress and individual and collective identity. One of the challenges during the preparations was that it was very difficult for us to photograph women wearing headscarves in the street. One young girl agreed to have her picture taken on the precondition that the exhibition would *not* be focused on the question of whether or not women should wear headscarves. We had considered addressing the debate about the banning of *burqas* and use of headscarves in western societies. Instead we included Kamal Qureshi's *sherwani* in the exhibition which added another perspective to current debates about cultural differences, integration, and dress identity. Besides, it turned out that the one item of clothing that most people wanted to try in the wardrobe was the *niqab*.

During the preparation we soon realized that, being adults (even though every single one of us on the staff were parents of teenagers), we lacked the most elementary abilities to decode current trends among teenagers and thereby be spot-on in our communication with them. To take one example we wanted to make a picture of a young man looking into a mirror. The image in the mirror would show another type of person than the one in front of the mirror. The idea was to have one of them showing "a rebel" and the other "a nerd." We did some research on the subject and collected some cloth that would be suitable for the purpose, then went to see the model, a young man of 17. When we asked him and his friend about the suit for "the rebel" they suggested that he wear a polo shirt. A polo shirt for a rebel? In our opinion a polo shirt is the uniform of a nerd. They showed us a photo of their favorite rapper wearing a polo T-shirt. We thought he looked like a model pupil. In the end we dropped the polo T-shirt in the picture, although it would have been an excellent illustration of the problem of coding and decoding dress across generations.

We want to work further with the concept behind the exhibition since only a fraction of issues in relation to the subject of dress codes and identity were represented. The staff's experiences during the guided tours opened their eyes to the possibilities of using an exhibition like this as a platform for further studies and a more systematic collection of empirical data in an environment that invites and inspires the visitors/informant to answer questions in more depth. The fact is that even if it seems that dress codes are less restricted today than in the seventeenth- and eighteenth-century peasant community on Amager, they are of no less *importance*. In fact, due to the growing fragmentation of style and fashion today, the rules are less obvious and all the more subtle. Dealing with dress codes and finding identity through dress is therefore much more difficult to deal with today than when dress code rules were sanctioned by the local community.

Involving teenagers in the process of establishing our next dress exhibitions is an obvious choice.

Notes

1 "*Unges Museumsbrug*," Dansk Museer, årgang 24, nr. October 4, 2011, pp. 26–28.

2 Amagermuseet is located in St. Magleby just next to Copenhagen Airport. Besides Amagermuseet, Museum Amager runs Mølsted Museum, Dragør Museum, and the Maritime Pilots' museum situated in Dragør town.

3 Folkemusiksammenslutningen, Nyhedsbrev February 2012.

4 See for instance "De har holdt med Holland I 500 år,: *Politiken* 9/6 2012.

5 This statement is not based on scientific evidence but on observation of the sex, age, and background of the visitors to the dress exhibition at the museum and informal talks with local citizens at the bus stop on my daily ride on the bus to the museum. My fellow passengers informed me they sometimes visited the museum with their children or grandchildren, to see the animals, but expressed outright contempt for the dress collection and people who "fooled around" in old dress.

6 Marianne Zenius has analyzed Danish genre paintings including Julius Exner and documented their unreliability as representations and documentation of folk dress practice in the early or mid-nineteenth century (Zenius 1976). Nevertheless, Julius Exner is currently used as a source among dress enthusiasts in the museum community. Whether their particular interpretations of the dress codes and practices are historically correct is not crucial in relation to this particular exhibition. First of all, the lack of reliable sources is an important pedagogic point made in the introduction to the exhibition. Secondly, the dress codes and practices which have been constructed through the twentieth century have been established as authoritative in the local community whether they actually reflect nineteenth-century dress practice or not.

7 The Amager dress was very well researched in the 1930s (Mygdal 1932). In 1996 the museum published a book about the Amager dresses: *The Amager Dresses – Their History and Use* (in Danish: *Amagerdragterne – deres historie og brug*) (Møller *et al.* 1996). The account of the different Amager dress outfits above is based on this book.

8 In October 2011 we performed an Amager folk dress catwalk called "Livstrappen" ("The stair of life") based on original private items in which more than forty different dresses representing different phases of nineteenth-century life and dress codes in Store Magleby were displayed.

9 The English terminology concerning *baggy* or *saggy* pants has caused some confusion. I have chosen to use "saggy pants." In Danish, we use the term "hængerøvsbukser" about saggy pants (low-slung pants showing the top of what usually is designer underwear, while oversized "baggy pants" are not necessarily saggy). In Danish, baggy pants would mostly be known as "hip-hop-bukser."

10 See for instance http://voices.yahoo.com/sagging-pants-hip-hop-trend-prison-trend-363230.html.

11 The *Berg Encyclopedia of World Dress and Fashion*, vol. 8, which was published in 2010, for instance, does not mention the saggy pants fashion at all (Eicher and Skov

2010). Juliet Ash touches upon the subject very briefly in *Dress Behind Bars* where she writes that "low-slung jeans that revealed the bum became fashionable for young men and women in Europe and America. The style took as its inspiration the way prisoners were not allowed belts" (Ash 2010: 171).

12 "En pakistaner hos Dronningen," *Dansk Folkeblad*, nr. 1, March 2004.

13 See http://www.Dragør.dk/page1301.aspx.

14 The result of Joanne Turney and Holly P. Alford's research in this field will be published in J. Turney (ed.), *Fashion and Crime: Dressing for Deviance*, I.B. Tauris, in 2014.

15 *Los Angeles Times*, April 14, 2011 (http://articles.latimes.com/2011/apr/14/nation/la-na-baggy-pants-20110415).

16 The school was Hjerting Skole i Esbjerg. The fashion company was Kabookhi (Grunt), Urban, February 14, 2007.

References

Ash, Juliet (2010), *Dress Behind Bars: Prison Clothing as Criminality*, London: I.B. Tauris.

Eicher, Joanne B. and Lise Skov (eds) (2010), *Berg Encyclopedia of World Dress and Fashion*, vol. 8, Oxford: Berg.

Haugen, Bjørn S.H. (2010), "The Concept of National Dress in the Nordic Countries," in Joanne B. Eicher and Lise Skov (eds), *Berg Encyclopedia of World Dress and Fashion*, vol. 8, Oxford: Berg, pp. 18–21.

Hjorth, Birthe (1986), *Fastelavn i Hollænderbyen*, Dragør: Foreningen Vennekredsen.

Kaae, Harry (1962), *Dragør – Huse, mennesker, historie og historier*, Copenhagen: Thaning & Appel.

Lorenzen, Erna (1987), *Hvem sagde nationaldragt?*, Aarhus: Wormianum.

Møller, Lisbeth *et al.* (1996), *Amagerdragterne – deres historie og brug*, Dragør: Kommune.

Mygdal, Elna (1932), *Amagerdragter. Vævninger og Syninger*, Copenhagen: Nationalmuseet.

Zenius, Marianne (1976), "Genremaleri og virkelighed. En kildekritisk analyse over billeder af Chr. Dalsgaard," *J. Exner og F. Vermehren*, Copenhagen Local History Department, no. 6.

11 LEARNING THROUGH FASHION: THE NORWEGIAN MUSEUM OF SCIENCE AND TECHNOLOGY

Tone Rasch and
Ingebjørg Eidhammer

When the Norwegian Museum of Science and Technology was founded in 1914, it was as a part of the ongoing establishment of technical museums that went on throughout Europe at that time. From the beginning, the museum's mission was to illuminate technical progress in a broad sense within a Norwegian context. Much has happened since then, but still the museum communicates the history of technology, science, and medicine, and provides insight into principles of scientific and technological processes. In addition to its exhibitions, the museum has extensive collections of artifacts as well as archives. Traditionally the artifacts have been widely exhibited while the archives have represented a more silent part of the collection. In recent years there has been an increasing interest in a more active use of the archives both at the museum and among the budgetary authorities that finance much of Norwegian museums' activities. This opened the possibility to develop an educational program called "Sources of Knowledge" at the museum. The theme of the program is the Industrial Revolution in Norway, and it is connected to the permanent exhibition "The Industry Along the Aker River" (in Norwegian: "*Industrien langs Akerselva*"). This exhibition opened in 2000, and shows the establishment of different mechanical industries in Oslo in the nineteenth century. One of the most prominent branches was the textile industry.

The weaving mill Hjula Væveri was a large factory on the Aker River. The mill's archive was given to the museum in the 1970s. It is a complete and detailed business archive from the nineteenth century, unusual because of its complexities and completeness (Bruland 1989: 5). In 2010 and 2011 the museum received external funding from the Norwegian Art Council to reorganize and register the Hjula archive. This gave the opportunity to do further research on the archive. Thus, selected documents from the archive have been linked to the existing exhibition. The history of the Hjula mill has been a part of education about the Industrial Revolution at the museum for several decades, and through a more active use of the archive new issues have been brought into the teaching.

The focus of prior presentations of the Industrial Revolution had been on classic themes of the history of technology, such as transfer of mechanical technology, power transmission, and the owners' stories. These are important issues, but we wanted to try out new introductions to industrial history. Fashion is one of those. One reason was a key interest in fashion among us as a curator and a museum educator. We wanted to use our knowledge in the education program. We were also inspired by an ongoing international trend at different kinds of museum focusing on fashion in their exhibition programs. For example, the Museum für Kommunikation in Frankfurt opened the exhibition "Fashion Talks" in 2012 and the Norwegian photo museum Preus Museum held an exhibition about fashion photography in the spring of 2012 where we participated with content and photos from our museum's collection. We saw the potential to develop new approaches to understanding the history of technology within the sources of the Hjula archive through fashion. The education program opened up an understanding of fashion as a part of the history of industrialization.

Textile production is of special interest for the study of dress and fashion. Fabrics produced at the mills can be seen as raw materials in fashion production. The mills were subcontractors to the fashion system that existed in the late nineteenth century, as they are today. The textile industry was one of the first trades that was industrialized during the Industrial Revolution. The technology was imported to Norway from Britain from the 1840s onwards. Spinning mills were located in the highest populated parts of Norway near Bergen and Oslo and a few years later weaving mills were established as well. The Hjula weaving mill started production of cotton fabrics in 1856. It was one of the leading Norwegian textile factories and was a pioneer in the use of new technologies such as synthetic dyes and printing techniques. The factory closed in 1957 (Grieg 1948–1950).

Fashion is not the only focus of the education program (Eidhammer and Rasch 2013). Other themes are just as important. One theme is about the methods of being a historian and using archives: for example, the difficulties of interpreting old handwriting, or understanding old currencies and measurement standards. Other themes concern historical issues such as the roles of the owner, the immigration of skilled British mechanics, and women's positions in the mill. Even so, the fashion theme remained very suitable when discussing the influence of industrial production systems on everyday life in general and clothing in particular. Fashion and industrialization have mutually influenced each other during the history of technology, and a focus on fashion might attract a broader audience. We believed that the students would get a broader understanding of the relationship between industrialization and the overall modernization of society that took place in the nineteenth century by linking it to a theme like fashion, which is also relevant today.

The educational program "Sources of Knowledge"

The educational program is designed for history classes from the third year of high school when students are about 18 years old. It consists of a general tour of the museum exhibition that deals with the Industrial Revolution, focusing on the textile industry. Secondly, the students look at different original primary sources such as letters, an account book, and a sample book from the Hjula archive. After that the students receive a box with copies of selected sources and a question booklet related to the chosen theme. They work in groups, going through the material, and the program concludes with a presentation of what they have found out through this work. "Sources of Knowledge" is based on four thematic boxes, treating different aspects of the running of the mill. Each box contains one or two exercises on fashion and clothing. These are meant to show the students that the production as well as consumption of textiles, clothing, and accessories was an integral part of everyday life 150 years ago and that there are similarities today. There are two exercises connected to consumption. These focus on the role of clothing as a symbolic value related to social class, the professions and the economic ability to purchase luxury goods. The production exercises are directly related to the running of the mill. A price list of fabrics produced at Hjula in the 1850s shows the variety of different textiles for different uses. Some decades later the majority of the fabric produced at Hjula was gingham, i.e. chequered or striped woven fabrics for clothing. We wanted to discuss with the students the fact that the fabrics look similar today as they did a hundred years ago. In the light of these examples we want to give the students a deeper understanding of fashion and the produced goods' social and economic position. But is it correct to say that all the textiles that were produced at Hjula were fashionable? Are fashion and luxury always linked to the clothing and textile industry? With such questions our aim was to show the complexity of fashion.

Theoretical approaches

Previous research on the Hjula archive has mainly focused on the introduction of mechanical technology in Norway. Sigurd Grieg used the archive as an important reference source in his historical survey of the Norwegian textile industry (Grieg 1948–1950). The archive has also been the basis for a doctor's degree about technology transfer (Bruland 1989). Three masters theses have been written about the production and work at the Hjula mill (Wiig 1974; Gaard 1977; Wiig 1995). After 2000, Tone Rasch wrote two articles about the Hjula products (Rasch 2001, 2004). Rasch's focus has been on the fabrics and the development of the textiles.

In the educational program we use personal stories from the archive in the teaching in the same way as these are used in literature or in film. Erik Lund, who has worked with education strategies, writes that we meet stories in many forms of mass media. Furthermore, he points out that students of all ages want to meet themselves reflected in people from other times and to compare their own situation with people from the past (Lund 2011: 117–118). Stories, simulation, and role-playing expand the spectrum of learning activities (Lund 2011: 123). We have tried to make the history of technology recognizable to the students through these strategies. Various topics in the program are related to historical individuals. By highlighting the humans in the archive, it is easier for the students to identify with the subjects and thus understand historical issues.

The Hjula archive offers possibilities to explore personal stories. The archive may be fragmented, and it is sometimes difficult to find personal stories in the heaps of bills and orders, but it consists of documents with names and sometimes other information about historical persons. The owner, Halvor Schou, and his descendants are the most mentioned. But the laborers and partners are also present. We have picked out some of these personalities and presented them to the students in the boxes previously mentioned. To find out more about them, the information from the archive is linked to the censuses of the population that took place in 1865 and 1875. These are published on the web at www.arkivverket.no/arkivverket/Digitalarkivet. In this way the students can find information about age, profession, family relation, and other living conditions of the people we are talking about.

In terms of the personal stories in the education program, the focus is on the modernization of society taking place during industrialization. In this context the production and consumption of textiles made by the new industry are important aspects. There are studies about fashion and luxury related to modernization and industrialization that support the view that consumption was a driving force. An example is the book *Consumers and Luxury* edited by Maxine Berg and Helen Clifford (1999) which points out the increased consumption in the eighteenth century which stimulated industrial production in Britain. The historian Ellen

Leopold has also shown how fashion has been a result of the interaction between supply and demand (Leopold 1992). The combination of these mechanisms contributes to creating a fashion system. The examples show that fashion history can be adapted and interpreted as part of the history of technology and economic history that is the professional base of education at the museum. The archive does not directly deal with questions about fashion, but some of the selected documents reflect these issues. Our assertion is that the products, i.e. clothes, are an equally important part of the history of industrialization as the means of production and transportation of goods, which so far have been the core areas of teaching about the Industrial Revolution.

The four boxes

Each box in the education program contains a leaflet with a story, exercises related to this story and copies of documents, either prints from the digital archive or other documents that explain the themes. One box deals with the establishment of the factory and how a weaving mill in the mid-1800s worked. The factory was divided into departments for engineering, weaving, patterned weaving, and dyeing. The purchase of rights related to power supply, the building of the factory, and how the textiles were sold when the mill was in operation are also discussed. The content of this box is quite general and provides an introduction to the technical and economic development in this period. At the same time the content of the box is closest to the traditional history of technology lessons conveyed by the museum. The other three boxes are named after historical figures from the archive and tell stories about them. One box is about Halvor Schou (1823–1879). His role is first and foremost as the founder and factory owner, but he was also a family man with six children and the owner of the farm Sinsen, with many employees. Schou belonged to one of Oslo's wealthy merchant families and the box contains information about more luxurious consumption than the majority of the population at that time could afford.

The second box is about Dorthea Biseth (1819–1887), who is another person from the archive. She was head of the pattern weavers at Hjula in the 1850s and was in charge of one of Schou's tenement houses where she also lived. Dorthea Biseth was one of the few women at the factory that had a high income and high occupational position (Wiig 1974: 59). As a woman she was unusual in having a professional career at the factory. Her background was humble. Her parents were unmarried, yet she had her father's name. James Biseth's father came to Norway from Scotland in the late eighteenth century to create gardens for Bernt Anker, the most prosperous man in Norway at that time. James was also educated in agriculture. In 1847 Dorthea Biseth started to work at the weaving workshop at the prison in Oslo. She became a guardian in 1852, but soon started to work at Halvor Schou's mill, work that was better paid and maybe also higher valued than the prison work. Soon after she started to work at Hjula she became the leader of the pattern weavers.

The last person we discuss is Stephen Marmont. He came with his family from Leeds to Hjula to contribute to the development of wool production at the factory in the 1860s. He also founded another wool factory in Oslo, Grorud clothing factory, but it did not go so well and he returned to Hjula where he stayed out his career. Marmont is first and foremost a part of the teaching program because he exemplifies the knowledge that was needed to operate the machines imported from Britain. At the beginning of industrialization, very few Norwegian artisans had the necessary technical skills to operate the machinery at the factories. Therefore it was essential that professionals were brought in to instruct the other employees at the factories (Bruland 1989).

On consumption

In the Marmont box there is a picture from the Grorud clothing factory. In front of a waterfall and the wooden factory building stands a group of people. The group consists of six men and a girl. One of the men is probably Stephen Marmont, who was manager at the factory. Another man is the wholesaler Peter Petersen who was an agent for Hjula in Oslo (Grieg 1948–1950: 320, www.snl.no, accessed June 26, 2012). The girl is dressed in a plaid skirt with an apron and a light-colored hat. The men wear dark clothes, long pants, coats or jackets, and hats with brims. The dark colors are broken only by white shirt-fronts visible beneath the jackets. The clothes are similar to those a gentleman from Manchester wore in a portrait from the 1860s. The fashion historian Christopher Breward describes this photography as "an archetypical image of nineteenth-century masculinity: dark, dour and domineering" (Breward 1995: 173). Some of the men in the picture from Grorud belonged apparently to the same social class as the man from Manchester: the industrial bourgeoisie. Four of the men in the picture from Oslo wear top hats, the other two wear flat hats with wider brims. Perhaps they were artisans related to the factory. One of the questions related to the photograph is why men wore different types of hat. We want the students to reflect on the symbolic values of clothing.

The Halvor Schou box includes a bill from the merchant Lars Semb for goods purchased in 1866. It deals mainly with clothes and other equipment intended for outdoor use. Halvor Schou bought an umbrella, a raincoat, two pairs of galoshes, a pair of leggings, and a pair of gloves. In addition, he purchased a piece of clothing, braces, three ties, and cigars. The question to the students is what they think these purchases tell us about the Schou family's economic and social position. The bill shows that the family had a varied

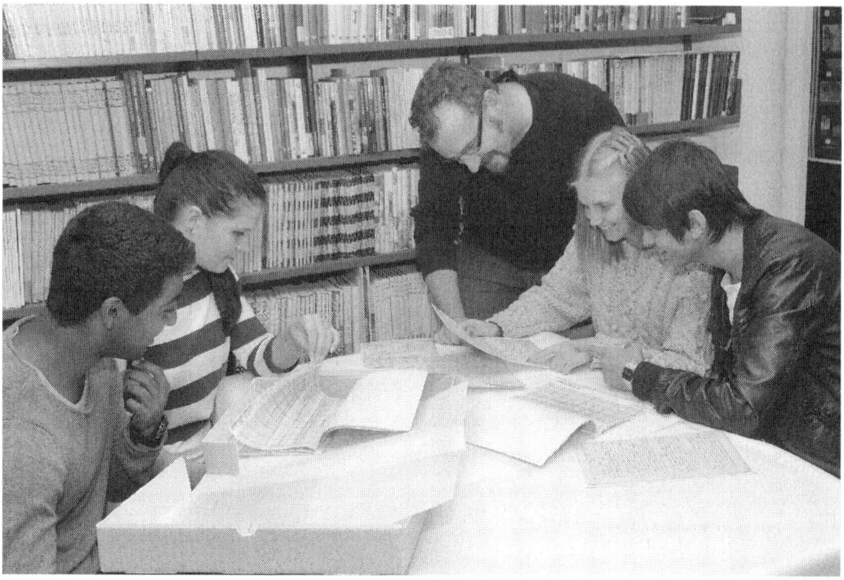

Figure 11.1 As a part of the education program "Sources of Knowledge" different issues about the Industrial Revolution and the meaning of clothing production are discussed using copies of archival documents. The museum teacher Torstein Torgner educates high-school students in old-fashioned handwriting. Photo: Finn Larsen, The Norwegian Museum of Science and Technology).

selection of clothes for different applications. Raincoats, galoshes, and umbrellas are convenient for staying dry in wet weather, but the items also show that the family could afford to have a variety of clothing for various purposes. The bill also tells the students that rainwear was used as early as the mid-1800s, though only a small part of the population had the ability to afford a wide range of clothing.

The photography from the Grorud clothing factory and the bill from the merchant assume that consumption of clothing in the 1860s was about function as well as fashion. Both hats and rainwear can be looked upon as mostly functional. At the same time the clothes indicate class differences and activities related to lifestyle that made these class differences possible. This fashion of the time was not always flashy, nor did it require frequent changes in style.

On production

The fabrics that were woven at Hjula in the nineteenth century were used for different purposes. We want to show what the textiles looked like and discuss the design with the students. The focus of the education program is on the first decades Hjula was in operation. A price list from the wholesaler and the mill's agent Peter Petersen is in the factory box. It is undated, but probably from the 1850s. It shows that there were eight different types of woven solid-colored fabrics at the factory. These were delivered in ecru, bleached, or dyed. In addition, there is a list for bed linen (bolster), and a list of fabrics within the category "Miscellaneous" where we find the patterned fabrics. The prices of the fabrics ranged from 41/4 shillings for the cheapest ecru canvas to the price of moleskin that is up to 30 shillings per yard. The prices of the patterned clothing fabrics were from 12 to 16 shillings.

The students are asked what they think determines the price of the fabrics. We want to create awareness about the meaning of techniques and materials. Although cotton was used in all these fabrics, the prices differed because of the thickness of the yarn, color effects, or complex weaving structures. All these elements made the fabrics more or less difficult to weave, and the products became more or less expensive. The patterned clothes were among the most expensive fabrics. Today it is unclear what "patterned" means: perhaps printed or woven patterns. In the nineteenth century the term meant striped or checked fabrics, usually called gingham (in Norwegian: *blåtøy*). This is explained in a textbook on weaving from 1850. Hanna Winsnes, a priest's wife, released the book *Education in Twill Diaper and Patterned Weaving by Simple Looms* (in Norwegian: *Underviisning i Dreiels- og Mønstervævning med simple Væverstole*) in an effort to professionalize housekeeping. The book describes pattern-woven fabrics as plain fabrics woven with more than two shafts in the loom. The time of the publication of Winsnes' book happened to be the same time as Hjula was established and her description suits the design of the fabrics from the mill. Winsnes' description also fits the fabrics presented in the range of sample books from Hjula called cotton samples, made from 1896 to 1922. These books are the main source from the archive that tells us what the patterned fabrics woven at Hjula looked like.

On checks

Four questions deal with patterned weaving in the Maid Biseth box. We have tried to vary the questions to the students from a simple description of a specific fabric to discussing the role of fashion. One of the documents in the box is a photo of three chequered fabrics that were woven at Hjula in 1864. We also present an advertisement from 2011 that shows a young man in a plaid shirt embracing a young woman. The advertisement is for the American clothing brand Abercrombie & Fitch. The teacher of the educational program shows the students a sample book from 1898 with patterned fabrics woven at Hjula that year. The sample book tells the students what kinds of fabrics were woven at the mill. This book contains eighteen different brands with a total of almost 1000 samples in different colors and striped and chequered combinations (Rasch 2004: 53). The book shows large variations in the striped and chequered fabrics according to color and quality. The variety of available patterns can be ascribed to the expansion and the professionalization of the mill that had occurred during the last decades of the nineteenth century. But there might also have been changes in textile production and in the demand for fashionable fabrics.

The chequered fabrics made at Hjula are quite similar to the fabrics in the skirt in the advertisement and the skirts the students currently wear. Plaids or tartans have had an important position in fashion for decades. Tartans symbolize the British upper class and country style as exemplified by Burberry checks. Young people identifying with British pop culture have used plaid clothing since the 1960s. Plaid pants were worn by punk bands in the 1970s and chequered skirts by grunge fans around 1990. The patterns have a varied history and many names. The definition of a tartan is "a woolen cloth woven in one of several patterns of colored checks and intersecting lines, especially of a design associated with a particular Scottish clan" (see http://oxforddictionaries.com/definition/tartan?q=tartan). The origins of the pattern are the woolen fabrics called tartans used by the male members of the Scottish clans. Queen Victoria and her family made tartans fashionable during the nineteenth century. This popularity led to cotton fabrics with similar designs. Tartans have a long history with no clear beginning or end. Nor is there any designer who is credited with inventing the design (Faiers 2008).

Tartan differs from the main product woven at Hjula: gingham. This is a simpler kind of fabric with only a few colors and a smaller size of checks. Another difference between the two textiles is the material; tartan is made from wool and gingham from cotton. However, it can be difficult to tell whether a pattern should be characterized as gingham or tartan. The superficial expression of the surveyed clothes may be that they look like a tartan, but the checks are smaller than the original Scottish ones and the textile fiber different. These fabrics might be called pseudo-tartans (Stillie 1970: 318). They became fashionable within the segment of cheap clothing fabrics. They were produced to a lesser cost by the mills. The industrial production of fabrics was to a great extent determined by the production costs, and the Hjula textiles competed on price.

The pseudo-tartans tell about the popularity of this design. The oldest dated sample book is from 1890. It does not present fabrics produced at the mill, but is a collection of gingham samples from the French design office I. Claude frère. This company collected samples from factories all over Europe and put them together in different kinds of collections and groups. The collections were sold to the textile industry (Sykas 2005). Hjula bought samples from the company from the 1880s onwards as inspiration for their patterns. A trend within the books is

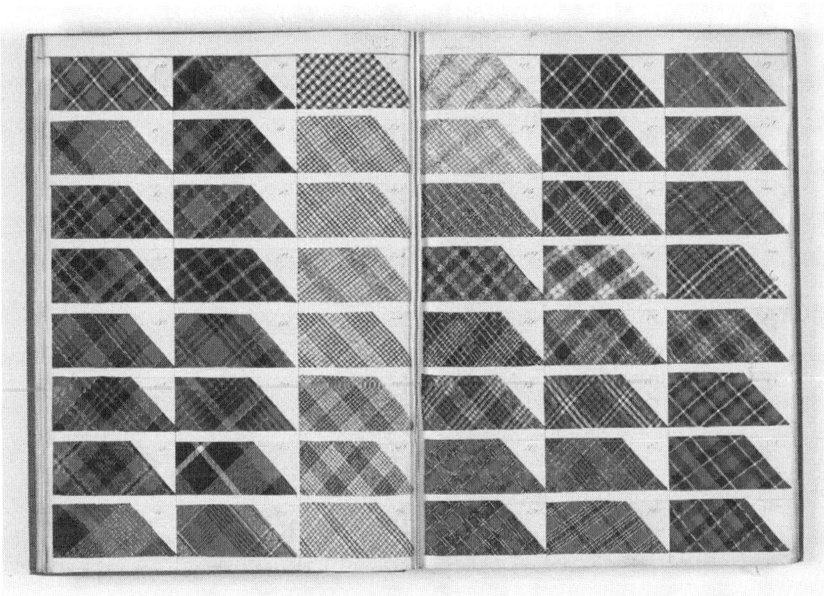

Figure 11.2 The business archive from Hjula weaving mill contains several sample books from the 1890s onwards. This tartan fabric comes from the gingham book from 1897. It is labeled "Dover" and was made in different color combinations. The pattern is still popular among the students participating in the education program. Photo: Håkon Bergseth, The Norwegian Museum of Science and Technology.

that those samples are made of thinner fabrics with more varied patterns and textures. Hjula did not copy the fabrics, but made coarser and cheaper versions inspired by the collected designs.

There are examples of plaid fabrics in all the sample books that contain fabrics from Hjula from that period. In the 1890s most varieties were available. In the pattern book from 1896 there are several examples of plaid fabrics with brand names such as Dover, Glasgow, Manchester, and Boston. At this time, the city brand names had largely taken over from the previous generalized names of the fabrics used in the price list from Peter Petersen. The sample book from 1899 has three types of fabrics with a tartan pattern, Dover, and Manchester Manila. Dover was in production until 1905 when Malta took over as the dominant chequered pattern. The various brand names applied mainly to technical differences such as weaving techniques and yarn thickness, not to patterns with similar colors, stripes, and squares. The colors of the plaid fabrics from the 1890s are typical for tartans. The samples are mainly red with white, blue, and green checks. After 1910 there was a trend towards pastel colors in the plaid.

Fashion for everyday use

Through the different exercises the teachers at the museum point out different aspects of fashion and clothing practices to the students. Fashion appears in many different ways. The sample books show what fabrics designed for everyday use in the 1890s looked like. Together with the price list from the 1850s they make it clear that the range of fabrics was big, according to us surprisingly big. It is common to believe that the supply of goods was limited, though the Industrial Revolution contributed to an increase in production. Some of the variations were intended for different uses and there were special weaves for bed linen, workwear, and curtains. The broad offer of different patterns and colors indicates that fashion was an important element for the Hjula mill in choosing which fabrics it would produce. The variation of patterns can be seen as one of the producer's ways to make the textiles more attractive for consumers and in this sense they were part of the fashion system.

The exercises about consumption open up another aspect. The bill related to Halvor Schou's shopping tells us how a well-to-do family prioritized rainwear and outdoor equipment at a time when the majority of the population had limited wardrobes. Clothes expressed social status. The examples tell us that fashion is about dress and accessories. Fashion appears in many ways, sometimes clear, other times hidden. One of our goals has been to show the students that fashion is not solely about the new. Modern clothing has a history. A surprising part of the story is that the fabrics used by teenagers today are similar to those produced by textile mills a hundred years ago. The novelty is in the way the fabrics are used. An example of this is the commercial from the clothing brand Abercrombie & Fitch. Their marketing strategy in 2010 and 2011 played on sex, presenting tartan miniskirts for girls and tartan shirts open to the navel for boys. The chequered cotton fabrics from Hjula were used in a different way in the 1890s. Young women wore long dresses completely covering the body and the men wore buttoned skirts under waistcoats. We discuss with the students the fact that the clothes in their wardrobe are no coincidence. Clothing is a part of the technological processes that have developed over the last 200 years. The history of technology, as well as fashion, is an integrated part of our everyday life.

References

Berg, M. and Clifford, H. (eds) (1999), *Consumers and Luxury: Consumer Culture in Europe 1650–1850*, Manchester: Manchester University Press.

Breward, C. (1995), *The Culture of Fashion*, Manchester: Manchester University Press.

Bruland, K. (1989), *British Technology and European Industrialization: The Norwegian Textile Industry in the Mid Nineteenth Century*, Cambridge: Cambridge University Press.
Eidhammer, I. and T. Rasch (2013), "Kilder til kunnskap – dokumentasjon og formilding av Hjula Væveris arkiv," in: H. Lange and U. Spring (eds), *Formidling for framtida – tanker om arkiv*, Oslo: ABM-media: pp. 213–231.
Faiers, J. (2008), *Tartan*, Oxford: Berg.
Gaard, E.H. (1977), *Kvinnelige fabrikkarbeidere i tekstilindustrien i Kristiania med hovedvekt på tidspunktet 1875,* masters thesis in history, University of Oslo.
Grieg, S. (1948–1950), *Norsk tekstil. Volume 1 and 2*, Oslo: Johan Grundt Tanum.
Leopold, E. (1992), "The Manufacture of the Fashion System," in: J. Ash and E. Wilson (eds), *Chic Thrills: A Fashion Reader*, London: Pandora, pp. 101–117.
Lund, E. (2011), *Historiedidaktikk: en håndbok for studenter og lærere*, Oslo: Universitetsforlaget.
Rasch, T. (2001), "Gurkemeie og anilin violet: om overgangen fra naturlige til syntetiske fargestoffer ved Hjula veveri," in: F. Weium (ed.), *Volund 2001*, Oslo: Norsk Teknisk Museum, pp. 35–68.
Rasch, T. (2004), "Blåtøy, kjoletøy og flanell: fabrikkvevde stoffer fra Hjula Veveri på slutten av 1800-tallet," in: F. Weium (ed.), *Volund 2003*, Oslo: Norsk Teknisk Museum, pp. 73–106.
Stillie, T.A. (1970), "The Evolution of Pattern Design in the Scottish Woollen Textile Industry in the Nineteenth Century," *Textile History*, 1(3), pp. 309–331.
Sykas, P.A. (2005), *The Secret Life of Textiles: Six Pattern Book Archives in North West England*, Bolton: Bolton Museums, Art Gallery and Aquarium.
Wiig, J. (1974), "Hjula Veveri: firma Halvor Schou 1849–1859," in: *Volund 1974*, Oslo: Norsk Teknisk Museum, pp. 7–82.
Wiig, H. (1995), *Produsenter, agenter og kunder: en studie av handel og salg fra Hjula Veveri 1856–1876*, masters thesis in history, University of Oslo.

12

AUTOBIOGRAPHY AS A PROPOSED APPROACH TO A FASHION EXHIBITION

Jeff Horsley

When considering collections of fashion in the museum as a "public wardrobe" it is pertinent to review not only those private curatorial activities of collecting, research, and documentation but also the very public activity of exhibiting collections. In particular, we might reflect on how museum displays interpret and present fashion in relation to other contemporary media, particularly the recent online phenomenon of personal style blogs, labeled by critics as "ego-blogs" (Oliver 2012: 219), where authors depict "not a visual self only but one whose external rendering is intertwined with autobiographical details" (Rocamora 2011: 412). This chapter[1] explores the notion of "fashion autobiography" and asks whether, inspired by internet blogs and in the spirit of the public wardrobe, it might prove a viable approach to the construction of a fashion exhibition. Central to this investigation is my attempt to construct such an autobiography, not in conventional literary form but as a proposal for a hypothetical exhibition which, like many fashion blogs, untangles its narrative threads from the interaction with my own clothing. I describe this project as a "fashion autobiography": a work in which an individual relates their life-history through clothing-associated narratives. As I will demonstrate in the first section of this chapter, such fashion narratives, while frequently published online and occasionally in literary and televisual form, are never, in my experience, realized as exhibitions.

This autobiographic exhibition project was not conceived in isolation; rather it was designed as a practice-led exercise through which to investigate a repertoire of innovative presentation modes applied to the display of fashion in the museum. I had previously identified these presentation modes through comparative analysis of exhibitionary techniques employed in almost a hundred fashion exhibitions, some of which are referred to in the first section of this chapter. While detailed explication of this review and the presentation modes subsequently identified is not essential to an understanding of the current discussion it is, however, apposite to mention the perspective from which this research was executed.

Originally trained in theater design I have for many years maintained a professional practice as an exhibition-maker. I use this definition, borrowed from art critic Robert Storr, to emphasize "the existence of a specific and highly complex discipline" (Storr 2006: 14). It also, as Storr and curator Lawrence Alloway assert, differentiates my activity, focused on presentation and display, from curatorial practice that encompasses collecting, preservation, and documentation (Alloway 1996: 221; Storr 2006: 14). Therefore, I would propose that my analysis examines '*muséographie*'—a term Gottfreid Korf, Professor of Cultural Studies, University of Berlin, uses to describe "the portrayal of a topic with the means of the museum" (Reinhardt and Teufel 2008: 39), in which "things and space are intentionally arranged as producers of meaning" (2008: 37). In relation to this chapter, particularly to the account that forms the second section where I describe the construction of my fashion autobiography in exhibition form, I would recognize my research as being focused through a *muséographic* lens.

The fashion autobiography in contemporary media

Before embarking on the construction of my own fashion autobiography, I reviewed a number of recent exhibitions for evidence of fashion autobiographic content. The majority of these exhibitions I had visited personally and documented through photography and notes, supplementing this material through reference to accompanying publications and online resources. Other exhibitions are evaluated solely through review of their catalog. While not ideal, I concluded that such publications could arguably be regarded as an extension of the exhibition experience and, for the purpose of this research, adequately represent an exhibition's curatorial thesis and content.[2] Evidence gathered through this review revealed examples of autobiographic material and autobiographic reference in exhibitions (autobiographic material meaning artifacts such as diaries, photographs, and letters, and autobiographic reference being the textual or pictorial citation of such material). I ascertained that autobiographic material and reference were generally present in one of two contexts; either related to a social or cultural history narrative, or focused on the life and personal style of a society figure or celebrity.

The social or cultural history category was illustrated by exhibitions such as "Black British Style" (Victoria and Albert Museum, London, 2004), "The London Look: Fashion from Street to Catwalk" (Museum of London, London, 2004), and "The Land Girls: Cinderellas of the Soil" (Brighton Museum & Art Gallery, 2009).

In these exhibitions, and their accompanying publications (Tulloch 2004; Breward *et al.* 2004; de la Haye 2009 respectively), autobiographic material appeared in the form of photographic images, letters, diaries, and handwritten notes, and autobiographic reference in the form of transcribed texts from oral testimony and reproductions of original images. For example the publication accompanying "Black British Style" contains autobiographic reference, similar to texts in the exhibition, that articulate particular attitudes to dress in black culture: observations such as "I think the main thing that my father enforced is just that when you are going somewhere you have to dress this way [. . .] You have to be looking appropriate everywhere you are going" (Kaiser *et al.* 2004: 59). Although selectively curated, these autobiographic statements describe particular activities, behaviors, or locations, and types of garment and styling worn, that provide illuminating contextual reference.

Examples of the society figure or celebrity category included the exhibitions "Vivienne Westwood: The Collection of Romilly McAlpine" (Museum of London, London, 2000), "Jacqueline Kennedy: The Whitehouse Years" (The Metropolitan Museum of Art, New York, 2001), and "Rara Avis: Selections from the Iris Apfel Collection" (The Metropolitan Museum of Art, New York, 2005) and their accompanying publications (Kilfoyle 2000; Bowles 2001; Bohman 2007 respectively). In these instances subjects were generally presented as arbiters of unique individual style and predominantly as consumers of fashion; Iris Apfel articulates a "personal style that is both witty and exuberantly idiosyncratic" ("Rara Avis" 2010), while Jacqueline Kennedy exerts an "enduring global influence on style" ("Jacqueline Kennedy" 2010). Romilly McAlpine is presented as a connoisseur who collects contemporary fashion as "a new art form" (McDermott 2000: 10). The catalog for "Vivienne Westwood" (Kilfoyle 2000) features an interview in which the collector of the exhibits, Romilly McAlpine, recounts illuminating anecdotes relating to the purchase, occasions of wear, and the physical and psychological effects felt when wearing garments designed by Westwood. Particularly revealing are comments describing the interaction of clothing and body, sensations that are experienced and communicable only by the wearer (Kilfoyle 2000: 19). McAlpine's contribution is supplemented by illustrated autobiographic vignettes from another twenty-two Westwood fans, illustrating interaction between Westwood's designs and a broader spectrum of her customer base (Kilfoyle 2000: 26–63).

Occasionally, the social history and society-figure narratives coincide. The exhibition "Fashion and Fancy Dress: The Messel Family Dress Collection, 1865–2005" (Brighton Museum & Art Gallery, Brighton, 2005) and associated publication (de la Haye *et al.* 2005) traced the fashion legacy of six generations of the upper-class Messel family women, over a period of 140 years. Central to the construction of the meticulously researched exhibition were family archives and autobiographic material. Both the exhibition and associated publication were enriched by the inclusion of personal scrapbooks, correspondence, photographs, and diaries painting an intimate portrait of the women's relationships with their clothing and its acquisition and history. Most enlightening were handwritten notes regarding the fabrication and wearing of certain garments, inserted into, or written on, the boxes in which they were stored (de la Haye *et al.* 2005: 19, 22, 24).

The designer monograph exhibitions reviewed, such as "Giorgio Armani" (The Royal Academy, London, 2003), "Balenciaga Paris" (Les Arts Décoratifs, Paris, 2007), and "Yves Saint Laurent" (Petit Palais, Paris 2010), focused predominantly on discussion of the designer's aesthetic or technical achievements. An exception was "Hussein Chalayan: From Fashion and Back" (Design Museum, London, 2009) which, through exhibition panels and a printed exhibition guide, articulated autobiographic narratives relating to the designer's childhood and family life such as stories of "displacement, migration and cultural identity" (Anon. 2009: 3) as intrinsically linked to the conceptualization of his design practice. It is noteworthy, however, that inclusion of an autobiographic account stemmed from its inseparable relation to the designer's process (Anon. 2009: 4) as opposed to an overt curatorial strategy.

Evidence demonstrates that, even when the exhibition narrative promoted adequate opportunity, autobiographic reference was often noticeably absent. Reviewing the exhibition "Men in Skirts" (Victoria and Albert Museum, London, 2002), Jane Malcolm-Davies (then lecturer in heritage management, University of Surrey) observed behavioral evidence that reflected a degree of disengagement among visitors which she attributed to a lack of contextual reference, for example first-hand testimony of men describing the effect and experience of wearing a skirt in western society (Malcolm-Davies 2003: 105–106). While the publication (Bolton 2003) contains many examples of designers discussing the male skirt, there is little first person account from male skirt-wearers. Similarly, the exhibition "Flowers in the Dustbin: Society and Fashion in Czechoslovakia in the Seventies" (Museum of Decorative Arts, Prague, 2007) presented an absorbing record of the production and consumption of fashion in 1970s Czechoslovakia. Of particular note was an account of the cultural clash between western fashion and pop cultures and an oppressive communist regime, to which inclusion of autobiographic reference could have added illuminating participant narratives. Although the accompanying publication discusses the impact of subcultural movements such as "hippie" and "punk," neither exhibition nor catalog related first-hand testimony from individuals who identified with subversive underground cultures and used fashion to make a political statement (Hlaváčková 2007).

As indicated, my review uncovered significant evidence of autobiographic material and autobiographic reference in exhibitions, but no evidence of an exhibition that could be described as a fashion autobiography. As a result, I widened my investigation to include other media. A review of literary, televisual, and internet sources was more successful in unearthing fashion autobiographies. Journalist and broadcaster Robert Elms' *The Way We Wore: A Life in Threads* (Elms 2005), a detailed account of the writer's early life, links his passion for clothing to music, football, style publications, and the energetic subcultures prevalent in working-class London during the last decades of the twentieth century. Alongside documenting contemporary sociocultural phenomena, Elms describes intensely personal responses to clothing, from the fetishization of the skinhead uniform (Elms 2005: 45–50) to the olfactory sensation of a pair of new shoes (p. 51). In this fashion autobiography, as the author attests, clothing is inseparable from experience and memory, where "every shape of shoe, every variety of collar has lodged itself in my brain, with a million barnacles of association clinging to its threads. I recall events by what I was wearing, a button-down, chisel-toed, fly-fronted mnemonic" (p. 4).

Fashion journalist Justine Picardie similarly traces a fashion autobiography in *My Mother's Wedding Dress: The Life and Afterlife of Clothes* (Picardie 2006). Picardie interweaves accounts of professional meetings with leading fashion designers through autobiographic narratives that express the ability of clothes as powerful triggers for memory and emotional response, tracing her life story through the legacy of her mother's wedding dress. In *The Thoughtful Dresser* (Grant 2009), novelist and journalist Linda Grant relates autobiographic an account that reflects the relationship between clothing and the construction of identity, particularly culturally determined notions of what is appropriate dress in relation to age and gender. Pertinently, Grant's illuminating recollections confirm that, though subjective and personal, autobiographic narratives are able to articulate those associations that form the foundation of our physical, emotional, and psychological relationships with clothing. These unmediated autobiographic accounts offer an emotional intensity rarely encountered in fashion exhibitions despite the presence of actual garments.

A comparative work can be found in the televisual medium, *All the Young Dudes* (Connolly 2004), in which music critic and cultural historian Paul Morley presented an autobiographic account of the various sartorial phases of his teenage years. As with Elms' account, Morley closely links his clothing narratives to contemporaneous popular music and youth movements, resulting in a narrative in which fashion is presented as an integral component of subcultural lifestyles. Both Morley's and Elms' work is noteworthy in articulating the close relationship between fashion and other cultural phenomena, such as popular music and football, in the construction of masculine identities.

To complement these literary and televisual examples, the internet offers numerous instances of autobiographic reference, where fashion as a medium for the expression of individual life stories and personal identity is prevalent. Scott Schuman's *The Sartorialist* (Schuman n.d.) publishes informal portraits that the photographer considers to be "more as a social document celebrating self-expression than as a catalogue for skirt lengths or heel heights" (Schuman 2009: 5). The site's commitment to the dissemination of personal "sartorial expression" (Schuman 2009: 5) can be seen to be following in the tradition of British style magazines from the 1980s,[3] and the "on-the-street" photographic format pioneered by veteran New York-based photographer Bill Cunningham.[4] Elisa Goodkind's website *Stylelikeu* (Goodkind n.d.) appropriates the approach of *The Sartorialist* but places subjects in their own homes, recording their wardrobe space. Again, the emphasis is on the personal, the individual's autobiographic narrative reflected through clothing, gesture, and location. As Goodkind asserts, "it's not about the clothes it's about the person in the clothes and that's the point of this site."

Although these sites reflect a contemporary web-based trend to associate fashion with the articulation of personal identity, self-expression, and individuality, often accompanied by autobiographic reference, they are, like the exhibitions previously cited, mediated and edited and demonstrate autobiographic reference as opposed to fashion autobiography. There are, however, numerous blog sites that act as personal style diaries of the author's fashion choices, including Gala Gonzalez's *Amlul* (www.amlul.com), Karla Deras' *Karla's Closet* (www.karlascloset.com), Izzy Tuason's *The Dandy Project* (www.thedandyproject.com), Katie Mackay's *What Katie Wore* (www.whatkatiewore.com), and Chiara Ferragni's *The Blonde Salad* (www.theblondesalad.com). These blogs offer unmediated fashion autobiography. UK-based Poppy Disney's site, *What I Wore Today* (Disney 2011), records each outfit the author has worn every day since January 1, 2010. Recently redesigned, the new site enables users to upload their own "what I wore today" images with the facility to tag garments with their "label," "comments," the wearer's "mood," and their "situation," introducing users' fashion autobiographies alongside that of the author, and attesting to the importance of individual identity and personal narratives in relation to young peoples' understanding of fashion.[5]

The examples cited above illustrate that fashion autobiography exists in literary, televisual, and digital media, and demonstrate an ability to communicate vital personal and cultural narratives in relation to clothing. They also provide incomparable evidence of the increasingly conscious use of fashion to construct identity in the context of wider sociocultural arenas. The narrative possibilities of fashion autobiography are effectively articulated on blogs such as those cited above, where individual style is emphasized over industry-led fashion. Successful blogs gain significant recognition, with some reaching over 25,000 hits per day (Oliver 2012: 16), with certain bloggers embraced by the fashion industry as collaborators, models, and brand ambassadors (Oliver 2012: 9, 15, 77, 139, 219). The popularity of these blogs, most importantly, serves to illustrate how bloggers and their audiences understand and construct notions of fashion, relating instinctively to the intrinsic links between fashion, personal identity, and autobiographic narrative.

Exhibitions such as "Black British Style," "Vivienne Westwood," and "Fashion and Fancy Dress" illustrate that the inclusion of autobiographic material and autobiographic reference can offer the visitor privileged insights into garments on display. These examples support the view of dress historians, such as eminent academic and curator Professor Lou Taylor, who recognize autobiographic material as an essential source of contextual information, allowing unique insight into intimate narratives of consumption, identity, and the phenomenological aspects of clothing. Taylor substantiates her argument with numerous examples that reveal how autobiographic sources provide dress historians with valuable information that supports meaningful understanding of a garment in relation to its sensory effect on the body and the sociocultural context in which it was created and worn (Taylor 2002: 102–111). She proposes that "the use of text from personal diaries, letters and autobiographies related to clothing making, selection, purchase and wearing thus offers another way to the understanding of the cultural significance of clothing" (Taylor 2002: 103).

As autobiographic material demonstrates a significant role in contextual approaches to garment histories, its place in an exhibition is, of course, dependent on its appropriateness to the exhibition narrative and the curatorial approach. As previously stated, however, examples of exhibitions that include autobiographic reference are in the minority, rendering the contradiction apparent: that while certain approaches to the study of dress advocate autobiographic source material as an important tool in understanding fashion, autobiographic material and autobiographic reference rarely appear in fashion exhibitions. I discovered no evidence of an exhibition where the curator (or author) was also the subject and, therefore, I conclude that the fashion autobiography is not to be found in the exhibition format. Despite the value of autobiographic account it is not commonly evident in exhibitions, as Taylor attests, "all too many artefact-centred studies [. . .] omit to enter into any detailed debate on life-styles, beliefs, work or personal interests of the wearers whose clothes are under discussion. The relationship between consumers and their clothes is thus almost never dealt with in exhibitions and rarely in publications" (2002: 50–51).

Considering the evidence presented above, it should not be unexpected that Linda Grant proposes, "I could write my autobiography in terms of analysing my clothes from birth to present" (Grant 2009: 16). Despite an apparent lack of autobiographic fashion exhibitions in the sample I reviewed, fashion autobiographies were evident in other media and, as expected, prevalent online. Encouraged by the wealth and complexity of narrative these instances of fashion autobiography displayed, I embarked on the construction of my own fashion autobiography in exhibition form.

Realizing a fashion autobiography in exhibition form: the "Hotel" project

My investigation began by taking a cue from institutional museological practice, with the compilation of a collection catalog of the contents of my wardrobe. The catalog took the conventional format of a chronologically structured inventory in which each garment was located in the timeline through reference to purchase receipts and recollection of occasions of purchase or wear. Once located in the chronology, garments were subjected to various interrogative processes that, I intended, would provide detailed documentation data to complete the catalog entry and reveal potential autobiographic narratives for the exhibition. Direct inspection of the garments identified information relating to fabric composition, designers' or manufacturers' branding, and signs of wear or alterations: data that would enable me to describe the material nature of each item. This inspection placed the garments within a frame of interrogation that focused my inquiry on the garment's physical composition, and the material qualities of each garment, drawing attention to those tactile sensations derived from the fabric and the structure of cut and construction. Subsequently, drawing was used as a process through which to record the interaction between clothing and the body. The drawings made were diagrammatic with annotations that described features of cut and construction and the relative effect exerted on the wearer. Drawing garments identified and recorded narratives that related the physical and emotional response provoked by certain fabrication techniques. Finally, I used photography to record garments in groups in which they might be worn. Composing these still-lives was an exercise focused on the garments' aesthetic qualities. The process of photographing the garments revealed autobiographic narratives relating to aesthetic appreciation of the garments and suggested narratives locating the garments within a contemporary design-historical context.

The inventory took the form of a series of hard-bound volumes, featuring a double-page spread for each garment. The right-hand page noted the provenance and classificatory information of the type conventionally recorded in institutional collections, while the facing side recorded the personal associations and responses each garment generated through the various interrogative processes, drawn and drafted by hand directly onto the page. A number of recurrent themes were identified during the cataloging process, such as the factors that influence choice of clothing, scenarios relating to purchase and consumption, dress and dressing as signifiers of identity and social belonging or difference, and intellectual and sensory response to the physical and aesthetic characteristics of garments, including the effects of cut, fabrication, and material qualities.

The process of refining each theme commenced with the accumulation of related textual and visual references. As this material was compiled in scrapbooks it became evident that certain themes related to specific events or locations in my life history. I selected eight of these "autobiographic episodes" and began to assemble each as a handmade volume. Each volume contained an accumulation of material related to each episode; photographs, drawings, prints from digital scans, and both typewritten and handwritten texts. The appearance of each volume became increasingly representative of the incident it embodied. The books defined the actual exhibition content for the episode each represented and through the physical qualities of the materials used for its manufacture suggested the atmospheric qualities of the autobiographic episode's *muséographic* rendering. Fabricating these handmade volumes evolved into a practice-led research process that operated as a bridge between the drafting of the collection catalog and the realization of the exhibition proposal, in which each autobiographic episode would be translated into visual and spatial constructions, executed in the form of a detailed scale model of the installation *in situ* in the exhibition gallery.

The chosen location for the hypothetical project was ModeMuseum (MoMu), Belgium, whose exhibition program had been central to the research into innovative presentation modes mentioned in the introduction to this chapter. Searching for a unifying structural element for the exhibition I was inspired by an image of the MoMu building, in its original early twentieth-century incarnation as the Hotel Central, to reinstate the hotel floor plan and to adopt it as the architectural footprint of the exhibition. Translated into the exhibition gallery, the hotel corridors once again gave physical delineation to the space, with rooms leading off the corridors housing individual autobiographic episodes. With each autobiographic episode conceived as occupying a distinct enclosure, the installation took shape as a series of spaces that could be visited in any order, in which the overall effect was intended to be an accumulative rather than a chronological autobiography. This architectural reference to MoMu's previous incarnation as a hotel suggested the title of the project, and also established a conceptual structure where, alluding to the depiction of the hotel in other contemporary sources, the surreal and unexpected are possible, as in Stanley Kubrick's film *The Shining* (1980) or David Lynch's TV series *Twin Peaks* (1990–1991), and where intimate spaces can be invaded, as in French artist Sophie Calle's mixed-media work *The Hotel* (1981) where, posing as a chambermaid, Calle photographed and published the belongings of guests residing in a Venetian hotel. The hotel location embodies the intimate and revelatory nature of autobiography, as the visitor, in the guise of hotel guest, opens the door to each room, enters, and discovers its contents. The hotel also acts as a spatial metaphor for memory, where each room reveals an autobiographic episode, with each episode linked to the next via the hotel corridor.

The first room of the exhibition, entitled "Conformity," relates to time I spent as a child in my local swimming pool, growing up in the early 1970s in a working-class area of the North East of England. The public pool was the main location for our leisure activity. From a fashion autobiographic perspective, it represents a site intrinsically linked with early memories of the act of dressing, of exposure to and growing curiosity with regard to the adult body, and an awareness of observing the clothing that others around me wore. The identification of conformity as an autobiographic episode stems from recognition, brought about through the investigative process of documentation, of clothes in my adult wardrobe that provoked recollection of similar childhood garments. This observation gave rise to the central theme of conformity: the impact of clothing choices made by our parents during childhood on our adult wardrobes, the unconscious assumption of clothing that is appropriate to gender and class, the interaction between clothing and body and the resultant eroticization of this interaction alongside fetishization of certain garment types that represent a particular construction of masculinity.

The room in which the autobiographic episode of conformity appears replicates the changing area of a public swimming pool with realistic detail. Underfoot is a tiled floor, with residual pools of water and drainage channels that end in metal covers that have leached the surrounding tiles with rust stains. The space is lit by overhead fluorescent tube lights and smells of chlorinated water. Rows of gray-walled changing cubicles stand back-to-back, forming two aisles. Fitted into the cubicles are slatted wooden benches. Screens replace the back wall of some of the cubicles, and depict slow-motion close-up footage of a figure dressing and undressing. The images focus on details that articulate the mechanics of clothing; closing buttons, lacing boots, fastening a belt. The cinematic images are intermittently interrupted, flickering to a black screen, to give the effect of the image being glimpsed surreptitiously.

At opposite ends of the space, viewed as a vista along the aisles between the cubicles, is a reproduction of a frame from Jack Hazan's film *A Bigger Splash* (1975), which documents British artist David Hockney's life in California and London during the 1970s. The images, taken from a scene that tracks a male figure swimming underwater, are digitally manipulated, their colors muted. They are reproduced as transparencies on large-scale lightboxes propped against the stud-work frame walls so that the image surface, emulating the rippled surface of the swimming pool, glows with light. A soundscape recreating the noise of a public swimming pool, water splashing and distant, echoing voices, emanates from speakers located behind each image and resounds through the space.

A number of garments are present, depicting ordinary, everyday clothes from a man's wardrobe; a faded blue denim jacket, a navy wool pea-coat, black leather boots, a striped cotton polo shirt, gray corduroy jeans, a striped webbing belt. They are not typical "fashion" garments, rather they are emblematic of garments worn by working-class men in the UK in the latter half of the twentieth century. The garments are placed as if recently discarded while undressing; they

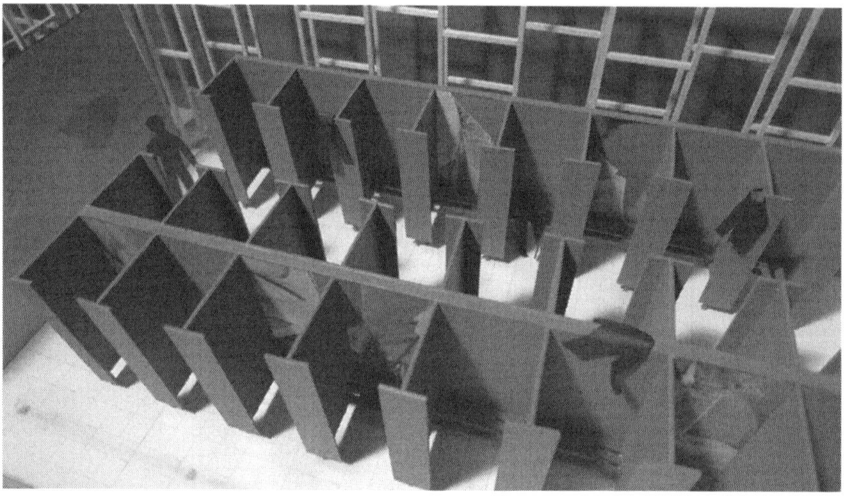

Figure 12.1 View of the scale model of the "Hotel" project depicting the room titled "Conformity." Photograph © Jeffrey Horsley.

are draped over the walls of the cubicles, lying on the floor, folded on the benches, hanging from the corner of a cubicle entrance. They are recognizable as similar to the garments depicted in the moving images presented inside the cubicles. The objects displayed in "Conformity" are not dressed on mannequins; instead the human body is represented through sound, moving image, and by the presence of the discarded garments, *in absentia* through evidence of activity.

The second autobiographic episode, presented in the room titled "Rebellion," was inspired by garments in my collection by British fashion designer Vivienne Westwood that have details of cut and structure that, when placed on the body, enforce an unconventionally disheveled appearance. "Rebellion" evokes the period at the end of the 1970s when, mainly through tabloid newspaper articles and television reports, I became aware of the punk movement then prevalent in the UK. Too young to adopt full punk regalia, aspects of punk style in a much diluted form were assumed by me and my friends. The schoolroom setting evokes the regional grammar school that I attended at this time, and represents the establishment institutions punk sought to deride and destroy. The central theme of "Rebellion" is the adolescent realization of the potential of clothing as militant expression, as a mechanism for the construction and externalization of personal identity and, through sartorially establishing cultural difference, clothing as a tribal signifier.

The room in which "Rebellion" is staged is lit with a cold, low, winter light that casts shadows of window panes onto a worn but heavily polished, dark-stained wood plank floor. Rows of black enameled metal lampshades, suspended on cords from the ceiling, hold light bulbs that emit a warmer glow. The walls of the space are surrounded by large blackboards supported on easels that lean against the surrounding stud-wall framework. They are covered in text, handwritten in white chalk, which is partly erased in places. In one corner of the room stands a portable projection screen on which can be seen footage of Peter Brook's film *Lord of the Flies* (1963) cast from a cine-projector opposite. The film, based on William Golding's 1954 novel of the same title, relates the social disintegration that befalls a group of public schoolboys marooned on a tropical island. The cine-projector loops scenes that depict the sartorial dishevelment symbolic of its subjects' societal collapse. Broken desks and chairs are strewn throughout the room, and form a chaotic pile in one corner. The space smells of dust and floor polish, and the whirr of the projector instills an unsettling atmosphere. The scene presents evidence of a recent violent disturbance.

The displayed garments are dressed on mannequins approximating the build of adolescent boys, leaning against the wall or sitting on the floor, with the main group standing *en masse* in the center of the space facing the entrance to the room. One of the group stands on a desk. They are positioned as a gang, confronting the visitor who enters as an intruder interrupting their rebellious activity. The mannequins are dressed in a combination of garments by Westwood and items typical of a British schoolboy's uniform and they are styled to emphasize an impression of disarray. In emulation of a tradition commonly practiced in British schools at the end of the summer term, some of the uniform garments are covered in handwritten texts in black pen on white shirts and white correction fluid on black trousers and blazers. These texts echo those on the blackboards,

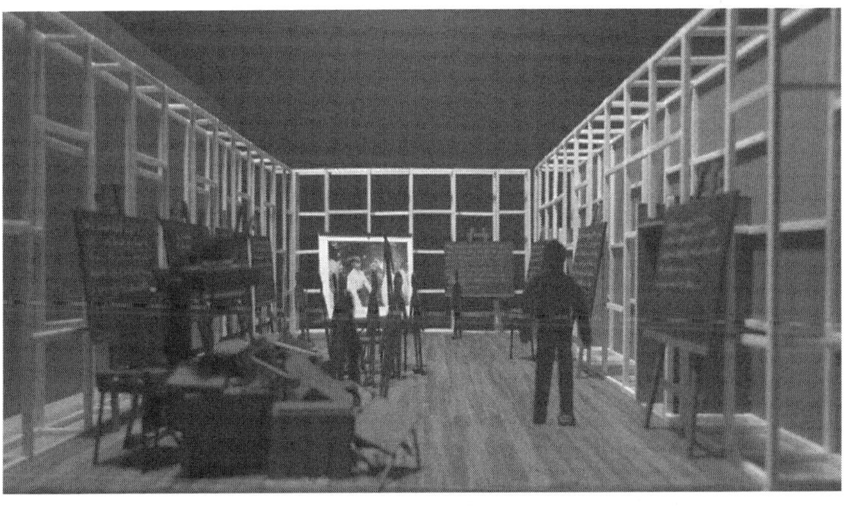

Figure 12.2 View of the scale model of the "Hotel" project depicting the room titled "Rebellion." Photograph © Jeffrey Horsley.

citing passages from various biographic sources that recount incidents of childish waywardness and teenage rebellion in relation to Vivienne Westwood's personal history and punk aesthetic.

While this chapter allows description and illustration of only two of the eight autobiographic episodes of the complete "Hotel" project, I anticipate that this is sufficient to communicate a sense of the complete scheme. While the *muséographic* style might appear overly elaborate and theatrical, I had observed comparable instances throughout the review of fashion exhibitions, that informed and influenced my approach. Exhibitions staged at MoMu such as "GenovanversaeviceversA" (2004), "Malign Muses: When Fashion Turns Back" (2005), and "Bernhard Willhelm: Het Totaal Rappel" (2007) all demonstrated comparable "immersive environments" which, as architect David Dernie notes, "absorb the visitor by the completeness of the design and bring communication to the level of drama" (Dernie 2006: 17). In fact I would argue that such *muséographic* constructions are perfectly matched to the autobiographic content, in that both realign focus to the individual: the exhibitionary techniques identified by Dernie as "anti-institutional" (2006: 15) and the autobiographic narratives which, as Rocamora notes in relation to personal style blogs, promote re-appropriation of "the power of representation" (Rocamora 2011: 418).

Conclusion

As previously discussed, my review of relevant sources indicated that while the fashion autobiography occurred in literary, televisual, and digital media it did not occur, in my experience, in exhibition form despite the acknowledged value of a first-person account in relation to the study of dress history. It was not, however, the remit of this investigation to ascertain why this should be so and therefore it would be inappropriate to hypothesize on the reasons for this situation. Through evidence gathered and experience gained through my practice-led research I can, nevertheless, propose conclusions to support the authoring of a fashion autobiography or the inclusion of autobiographic reference and autobiographic material in an exhibition.

Evidence attests, from those sources previously cited, that autobiographic narrative can tap directly into those personal experiences that dress historians indicate as invaluable in our understanding of fashion and provide a first-hand account of the relationship between garment and wearer. Autobiographic reference relating directly to the physical effects of a garment, as noted in the Vivienne Westwood customer testimonies cited in Kilfoyle (2000: 26–63), can relocate a garment distanced from the viewer by vitrine or display case, from an object of spectacle to an item understood in relation to their own experiences of consumption and wear. Astutely, Grant identifies the power of the autobiographic account to communicate those narratives that habitually fall outside the concern of much academic study:

> When academics write about the language of clothes and describe the various messages that are encrypted in the garments, they seldom include in that vast vocabulary the word *Rejoice*! Clothing as a social system is supposed to emit various significant social and cultural signals but not those piercing feelings of joy that new clothes can bring to the wearer.
>
> Grant 2009: 155

As illustrated by exhibitions such as "Black British Style," autobiographic reference can also operate as a bridge between the garment, the visitor, and complex sociocultural narratives by providing a first-hand account that situates the garment and promotes an understanding of it in the context of narratives of provenance, wear, and consumption. My practice-led research revealed the ability of autobiographic narratives to address social and cultural issues such as the impact of advertising and the media on personal identity and clothing choices, clothing and body image, the conflation of a designer's particular aesthetic and personal style, the notion of age, gender, and class-appropriate dress. As also revealed through my research, autobiographic narratives enable associative links to be made between fashion and other forms of expression, such as music, literature, or cinema. These examples demonstrate that one of the invaluable qualities of the autobiographic approach is the ability to develop narrative and thematic strategies that offer alternatives to chronological dress history.

There are evidently conditions influencing the use of autobiographic material or autobiographic reference—particularly in relation to items where no autobiographic information was collected at the point of acquisition from the owner or documented during their lifetime. This, I would propose, is an opportunity for the curator to recount their own interaction with the garment. In the museum context, where public handling of garments is generally not permitted and where fashion exhibits are commonly displayed behind glass, the curator is often the only direct link between the physical qualities of a garment and the visitor. In this instance, communication of the curator's personal experience of handling the garment can express important information relating to the item's material qualities; weight, texture, rigidity or suppleness, the noise made by the fabric, or its distinctive aroma. From the perspective advocated by American artist Fred Wilson, that "curators, whether they think about it or not, really create how you are to view and think about these objects" (Karp and Wilson 1996: 253), I would also propose that in the appropriate narrative context it would be entirely relevant for the curator to express any personal associations a garment might inspire them to recall. The public presentation of these associations I believe, as an adjunct to more conventional information, will encourage visitors to reflect on their own associations and potentially establish a more engaged connection with the items on display.

What might be the implications for fashion autobiography, or autobiographic reference in relation to the museum as a "public wardrobe"? Considering the recent prevalence, indicated by personal style blogs, to identify fashion intrinsically with the construction and expression of individual identity, it can be argued that contemporary audiences are as likely to understand fashion through personal narratives and autobiographic association as through conventional narratives of design history or technological development. Critics might read the fashion autobiography as an immense act of ego—indeed blogger Susan Lau, aka Susie Bubble, regarded her first posts on stylebubble.com as "a preposterous act of narcissism" (Oliver 2012: 7). I would counter, nevertheless, that engaging with autobiographic narrative facilitates the release of those intimate encounters invested in a garment relating to occasions of purchase and wear, emotional and psychological connections, and sensory phenomenon, that visitors will understand through associated personal experience, tapping into what Dernie terms the "memory economy" (Dernie 2006: 13). I would argue that by creating the opportunity for visitors to connect personally and emotionally to objects through the use of autobiographic material and autobiographic reference, the museum can exploit personal narratives to express itself as a public wardrobe.

It is important to stress that I advocate an autobiographic approach to the exhibition of fashion in the museum only as one of many possible strategies available to the curator, and not as a universal method. As I have demonstrated, the inclusion of autobiographic reference and autobiographic material in the exhibition of fashion is critical for a number of reasons: it enriches the visitor's experience of garments on display through its potential to relate first-hand narratives that articulate emotional response, sensory phenomena, and stories relating to provenance, wear, and consumption; it also allows the curator to voice personal experience and impressions and to develop alternative narratives to orthodox design and dress histories, and to locate garments in sociocultural contexts. Finally, for a growing generation of "digital natives" who establish a relationship with fashion via internet sources, where clothing is regularly positioned as an expression of individuality and personal experience, autobiographic narrative relates to a current sense of how fashion is consumed, disseminated, and understood—as a reflection of personal life histories.

Notes

1 This investigation comprised a significant component of my PhD research, based at London College of Fashion, University of the Arts, London.

2 A drawback of research into exhibitions is that, unlike published sources, there is no universal accessible catalog. Since completing this inquiry other exhibitions that may be relevant to my argument have come to light, including "American Women of Style" (The Metropolitan Museum of Art, New York, 1975), "One Woman's Wardrobe: The Jill Ritblat Collection" (Victoria & Albert Museum, London, 1998), and "Women of Style" (Fashion Museum, Bath, 1999).

3 British magazines such as *i-D*, launched in 1980 and still in production, featured the "straight-up"; portraits taken on the street that could be viewed simultaneously as fashion photography and social documentary.

4 Cunningham's unique work has recently been documented in the film *Bill Cunningham New York* (Press 2011).

5 For a detailed examination of blogs as a space for identity construction see Rocamora (2011).

References

Alloway, L. (1996), "The Great Curatorial Dim-Out," in: R. Greenberg, B.W. Ferguson and S. Nairne (eds), *Thinking About Exhibitions*, Abingdon: Routledge.

Anon. (2009), *Hussein Chalayan: From Fashion and Back*, exhibition guide, London: Design Museum.

Anon. (2011), "Spectres: When Fashion Turns Back," fashion installation, www.vam.ac.uk/content/articles/s/spectres [accessed May 5, 2011].

Bohman, E. (2007), *Rare Bird of Fashion: The Irreverent Iris Apfel*, London: Thames & Hudson.

Bolton, A. (2003), *Men in Skirts*, London: V&A Publications.

Bowles, H. (2001), *Jacqueline Kennedy: The White House Years*, New York: Little, Brown & Co.

Breward, C., E. Ehrman, and C. Evans (2004), *The London Look: Fashion From Street to Catwalk*, New Haven, CT: Yale University Press.

Connolly, M. (dir.) (2009), *All The Young Dudes*, State of Grace Films for BBC Four.

de la Haye, A. (2009), *Land Girls: Cinderellas of the Soil*, Brighton: Brighton & Hove Museums.

de la Haye, A., L. Taylor, and E. Thompson (2005), *A Family of Fashion, the Messels: Six Generations of Dress*, London: Philip Wilson Publishers.

Dernie, D. (2006), *Exhibition Design*, London: Laurence King Publishing.

Disney, P. (2011), *What I Wore Today*, www.wiwt.com [accessed September 8, 2011].

Elms, R. (2005), *The Way We Wore: A Life in Threads*, London: Picador.

Goodkind, E. (n.d.), *Stylelikeu*, www.stylelikeu.com [accessed September 8, 2011].

Grant, L. (2009), *The Thoughtful Dresser*, London: Virago.

Hazan, J. (dir.) (1975), *A Bigger Splash*, First Run Features.

Hlaváčková, K. (2007), *Flowers in the Dustbin: Society and Fashion in Czechoslovakia in the 70s*, Prague: Museum of Decorative Arts, Prague/NAGA Ltd.

"Jacqueline Kennedy" (2010), "Jacqueline Kennedy The Whitehouse Years," www.metmuseum.org/exhibitions/listings/2001/jacqueline-kennedy [accessed September 8, 2010].

Kaiser, S., L. Rabine, C. Hall, and K. Ketchum (2004), "Beyond Binaries: Respecting the Improvisation in African-American Style," in C. Tulloch (ed.), *Black Style*, London: V&A Publications.
Karp, I. and F. Wilson (1996), "Constructing the Spectacle of Culture," in R. Greenberg, B.W. Ferguson, and S. Nairne (eds), *Thinking About Exhibitions*, Abingdon: Routledge.
Kilfoyle, M (ed.) (2000), *Vivienne Westwood: A London Fashion*, London: Philip Wilson Publishers Ltd.
Kubrick, S. (dir.) (1980), *The Shining*, Warner Bros. Pictures.
Lynch, D. (dir.) (1990–1991), *Twin Peaks*, Lynch/Frost Productions.
Malcolm-Davis, J. (2003), "Men in Skirts," in: *Fashion Theory*, 7(1), pp. 103–108.
McDermott, C. (2000), "A Wearable Fashion," in: M. Kilfoyle (ed.), *Vivienne Westwood: A London Fashion*, London: Philip Wilson Publishers Ltd.
Oliver, W. (2012), *Style Feed*, Munich: Prestel.
Picardie, J. (2006), *My Mother's Wedding Dress: The Life and Afterlife of Clothes*, London: Picador.
Press, R. (dir.) (2011), *Bill Cunningham New York*, Zeitgeist Films.
"Rara Avis" (2010), "Selections from the Iris Barrel Apfel Collection," www.metmuseum.org/exhibitions/listings/2005/iris-barrel-apfel [accessed August 4, 2010].
Reinhardt, U.J. and P. Teufel (eds) (2008), *New Exhibition Design 01*, Ludwigsburg: Avedition GmbH.
Rocamora, A. (2011), "Personal Fashion Blogs: Screens and Mirrors in Digital Self-portraits," in: *Fashion Theory*, 15(4), pp. 407–424.
Schuman, S. (2009), *The Sartorialist*, London: Penguin.
Schuman, S. (n.d.), *The Sartorialist*, www.thesartorialist.com [accessed August 4, 2011].
Storr, R. (2006), "Show and Tell," in: P. Marincola (ed.), *What Makes a Great Exhibition*, Philadelphia, PA: Philadelphia Exhibitions Initiative.
Taylor, L. (2002), *The Study of Dress History*, Manchester: Manchester University Press.
Tulloch, C. (ed.) (2004), *Black Style*, London: V&A Publications.

IN CONCLUSION: MUSEUMS DRESSED IN FASHION

Birgitta Svensson

In advertising the exhibition "Hollywood Costume," The Victoria & Albert Museum (V&A) in London stated as the meaning of the exhibition that "Costume designers are storytellers, historians, social commentators and anthropologists" and we do in this volume agree; besides we take it a bit further and believe that fashion museology can throw new light on both social conditions in society and historical change. As the different chapters of this book show, the growing interest among museums for fashion is not just a matter of new and renewal in common but also a willingness to reach new groups in society. However, reflecting on fashion and museums, past and present, we have seen a controversy growing up between past and present and between dress history and contemporary fashion. By presenting the controversy as one between dress museology and fashion museology it might be possible to overcome it.

This last chapter considers why there is an ongoing international trend at different kinds of museum focusing on fashion in their exhibition programs and what has been discussed throughout the book about the meaning of identities in fashion heritage constructions, whether as collections, exhibitions or bodily experiences, city branding, or simply attracting new visitors.

Why has fashion become important in Swedish museums? The power of fashion (cf. Eldvik 2010) can be understood as an answer to what has been called the Swedish wonder with the growing international reputation of fashion brands like Acne, J. Lindeberg, Filippa K, Cheap Monday, and H&M. The exhibition at Moderna Museet in Stockholm in 2004 reflected the view of fashion's enhanced status which has since been prevailing in museums, by presenting the mutual fascination between the worlds of art and fashion. It has been discussed what is characteristic to the Swedish fashion wonder. It is said not to be a question of national aesthetics, but rather portability, functionality, the feminine in men's fashion, and the masculine in women's fashion, not to mention the plain and easy (Falk 2011). Maybe it is the absence of luxury, the commonplace and practical design mantra that H&M has long advocated? Anyhow, this is what has been highlighted when the cultural history museums have come to be interested in fashion. Moving from dress museology to fashion museology, they focus on the impact of how people get dressed, while the art museums focus on designers.[1] Still, these museums tend to have more in common today when fashion is in focus. They do consider it as important to be fashion museums, maybe as a part of the Swedish wonder. Besides the Swedish cultural history museum, Nordiska Museet in Stockholm is claiming the title of Sweden's fashion museum.[2]

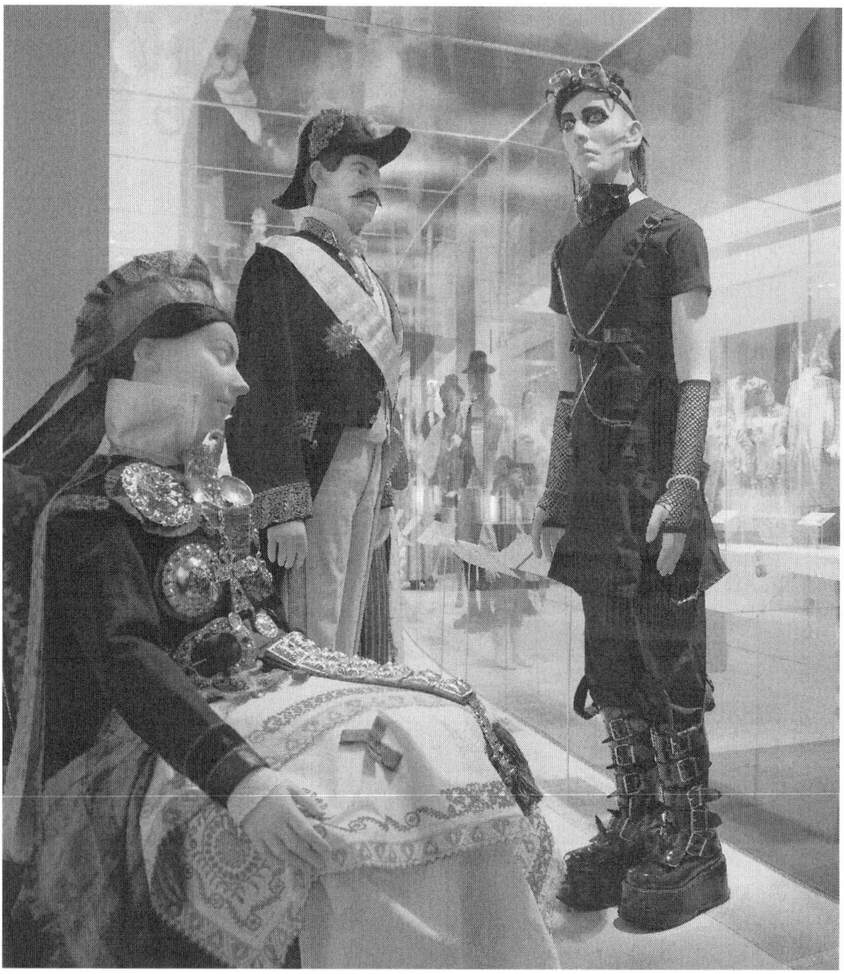

Figure C.1 Entering the exhibition "Power of Fashion," you meet a mixture of traditional costume and fashion. Photo: Karolina Kristensson, Nordiska Museet.

City branding and tourism

Museums tend to adapt to management strategies to survive by attracting the growing heritage industry and the tourism economy. When visiting Lisbon in 2011 I found it strikingly easy to find the new fashion and design museum MUDE—Museu do Design e da Moda. It was located in a spectacular architecturally designed building in the very busy city center and shopping district, among the main tourist attractions. The museum tries to convey an image of both historical perspectives and of the contemporary fashion trends and industry, though its main collection is from a single designer, the Francisco Capelo Collection, bought in 2002.[3] The fashion exhibited is mainly international haute couture. On the website the museum claims to use a historical context. However what is being exhibited is mainly contemporary, showing fashion design's new trends and directions in the twenty-first century. The contemporary perspective is further strengthened by designers as collaborators and key agents in addition to being partners. This is more trend than tradition and fashion museology could be said to be its main focus. Besides, MUDE proactively promotes Lisbon as a cultural tourism destination, reinforcing its status as a new design capital. In advertising the museum it is emphasized that the museum enjoys the cultural dynamic of the Bairro Alto District, predominantly visited by youth and subcultures seeking alternative stores, nightlife, and art/exhibition galleries (see www.mude.pt).

As easy as it was to find MUDE, just as difficult was it to find a totally different museum on the outskirts of the city, which hosts a huge dress and costume collection under the name of the National Museum of Costume and Fashion (Museu Nacional do Traje e da Moda). It is located in Lumlnar, a suburb far away from the city center. And even when you got to the building it was hard to find the entrance. Inside you got a feeling of being taken back several years in museum history, though the fashion actually exhibited was quite interesting.

This might show the difference between dress museology and fashion museology. Even if you do find dresses that show how fashion has changed over a long time and an abundance of fashion dresses in the national costume museum, the approach in costume and not fashion does not attract the visitor (cf. the chapters of Koda and Glasscock and Teunissen in this book). Exhibitions done within dress museology tend to be seen as uninspiring (cf. Steele 2013). Besides it is beyond interest when located far away from other urban attractions.

Even in Bath the Fashion Museum plays an important role in attracting visitors. In fact tourists come there with combined tickets to the famous ancient natural thermal baths. There is interplay between two important heritage institutions that strengthen each other, both locally and globally. However in other places like the Guggenheim museum in Bilbao it is simply attraction to a new audience that is in focus and not at all the local history of the steel industry (cf. Zulaika 2002).

Visibility and bodily image

Fashion's popularity can be attributed to the growing interest in the body (cf. Grosz 1994; Sennett 1994). As Anne-Sophie Hjemdahl notes, it is an important objective to give the exhibited dress a bodily form so that it appears as more than just clothing. It is equally important when the exhibited is connected to and even brings to mind a certain person or even a fashion designer. When the exhibition "Power of Fashion" was opened in 2011 at Nordiska Museet in Stockholm, a vivid discussion took place about deceased fashion designer Sigsthen Herrgård. It was said that the mannequin did not give Herrgård a trustworthy corporeality.

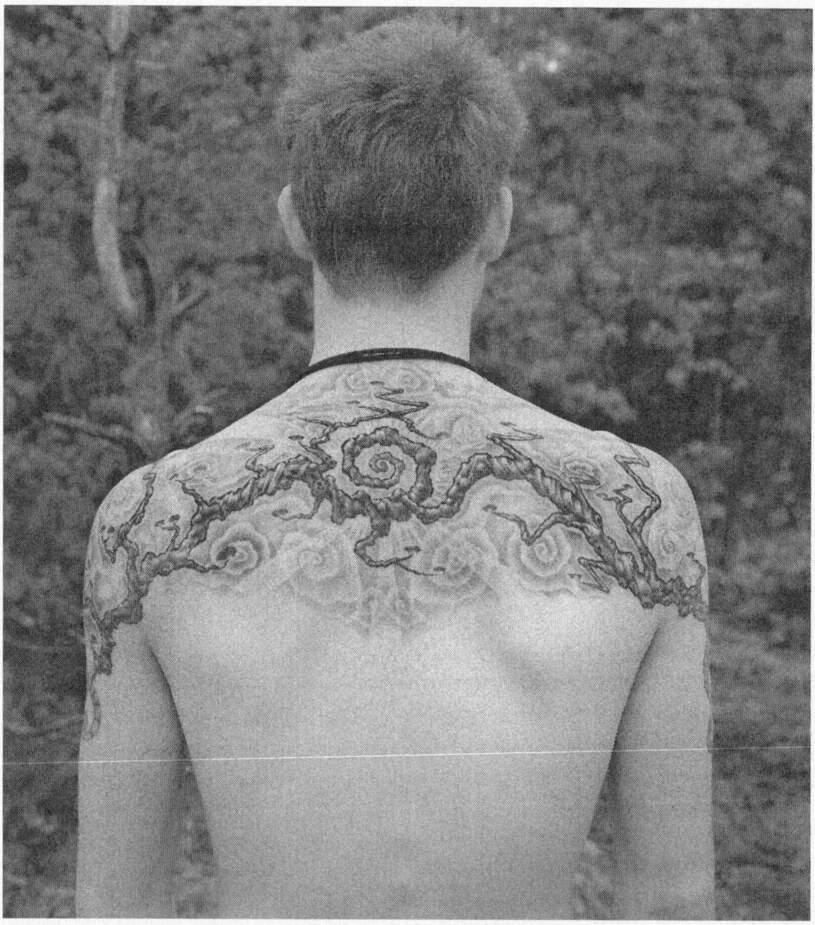

Figure C.2 The body with tattoos is a growing fashion entering the museum world. Photo: Peter Segemark, Nordiska Museet.

The discussion centered around his back/butt being represented as so tiny that his exhibited, authentic trousers were hanging in a way that would have been impossible on the living Herrgård. Maybe it would have been better to use the old “Swedish System” described by Hjemdahl in her chapter?

Marie Riegels Melchior noted in the introduction that fashion is eye-catching and as such not just about attracting new visitors, but also attracting media and getting their attention. This was especially the case when Nordiska Museet had an exhibition on male bathing clothes.[4] Every radio and TV channel ran it and every newspaper wrote about it, even *The Times* in London (Abrams 2011). This in turn of course attracted new visitors. Maybe it was also a matter of curiosity about the male body being exposed in an unusual way?

Fashion is no longer simply about dress; even the body itself has become fashionable to an extent. Bodily exposures have become an especially privileged fashion object or even a field of power. Tattooing has for some twenty years now been of growing importance in postmodern urban life as materializing an idea of contemporary visual culture. Art museums as well as cultural history museums have started to have tattoo exhibitions in order to attract new audiences. In Amsterdam, a tattoo museum opened in 2012. Some tattoo studios are calling themselves museums. In 2000 over 1,500 people with tattoos visited the museum on the first V&A day in order to be photographed for its digital archive of tattoos.

Along with a growing interest in the body in general and clothing and fashion in particular, tattoos have also come to be used on the catwalk. In many haute couture shows lace and tattoo is combined as a way to alternately highlight, sometimes hide, the body. Both have in different ways the ability to show and hide the naked skin. Just as the media and celebrities paved the way for increased use of tattoos, the fashion world has played a big role in that tattoos have become common. Sometimes garments tattoo designs and sometimes a fashion creator’s body is tattooed. Marc Jacobs is himself tattooed but also uses the tattoo designs in his design of Louis Vuitton bags.

Visibility and bodily exposures can also be studied in fashion collections as such, whether exhibited or not. As Marianne Larsson shows, women’s emancipation in the last century was reflected in the body and clothes. For a long time women were forced to mask certain body parts in their sporting performances, despite all the trouble it caused. But what had previously been hidden could slowly and eventually appear, which even came to highlight the interplay between free time and free body movements.

In late modern societies freedom seems to be equivalent to expressing individuality, which in turn more and more is shown in tattoos. Museums do not only exhibit tattoo images, they have tattoo artists who allow people to get tattooed in connection with openings or other special events. This has come to be very successful.

Dress museology

I believe that one of the main distinguishing traits of museum research as dress museology is connoisseurship. However in the cultural history setting it is a special variant of connoisseurship (Svensson 2008). There you are not interested in separating a false from an original piece of art but in distinguishing what kind of skill is connected to the artifact. With the help of construction, color, and form you can learn something about variation and the special knowledge needed in the museum setting. It is telling something about skill, provenance, origin, and authenticity but also about manufacturing conditions and processes. You study the artifact thoroughly to find out about its details. Detail is an important distinguishing trait with museum research as dress museology. It is the small traces, the seemingly insignificant, that could make the difference and also make it possible to discover something about the bigger issues in history. This kind of tacit knowledge is common in museums. Even if research perspectives have changed, much of the research in the cultural history museum is still done within the traditional fields of dress codes, textiles, and techniques. However these research perspectives simply reflect the collections with all their limitations. Kirsten Toftegaard notes from her experience with collecting in the Designmuseum Denmark that the balancing of fashion, dress, and textile is important, since fashion and dress supplement each other. She shows the importance of seeing the materiality of fashion through the textile. As for many other researchers, fashion is by her understood through the fashion system and she shows why collecting material reflecting the fashion system is crucial.

Fashion museology can transform even educational practices in museums. In the Norwegian Museum of Science, Technology and Medicine, Rasch and Eidhammer show how fashion is used for understanding the history of industrialization. This was their way of attracting young, new audiences. Their focus is on textile, since textile industries have been subcontractors to the fashion system and so modern clothing has a history. A surprising part of the story may be that the fabrics used by teenagers today are similar to fabrics produced by textile mills a hundred years ago. The novelty is the way the fabrics are used. Using an understanding of the role of textile is in line with what Kirsten Toftegaard notes in this book. As the British design historian Judy Attfield describes (2000), fabric is a very special form of material culture by which you can communicate social relationships and create fashion. It helps to create identification in the room the same way that clothing not only reveals the fashion but also follows and even creates body motion patterns. Attfield believes that textiles mediate between the inner woman, her body, and the outside world while contributing to the creation of identities. She stresses that the fabrics' ability to follow and shape, contain and simultaneously signal something to the outside world, means they can also be used to analytically understand so much more than plain text can convey.

Fashion museology

To sum up, as stated by Riegels Melchior, fashion museology is connected with audience-friendly contemporary designers, creativity and imagination, but also commerce and branding. It is strategically used to attract new visitors and in that sense it is front-stage, while dress museology has become back-stage, handling museum collections. In a way fashion museology has made museum collections redundant or at least secondary to the exhibitions. As for all museums nowadays, the Fashion Museum in Bath is keen to attract young visitors and Rosemary Harden explains the use of album covers in contextualizing how similarities of fashion are disseminated into personal music memories. Another convincing way of turning from dress to fashion museology, or even better, combining them, is shown by Ingeborg Phillipsen who discusses how her local museum met the challenge to attract new groups, especially young people, by making an unexpected use of saggy pants to discuss old-time costumes. She highlights that to adapt fashion museology in a setting where dress is the key entry to the museum collection demands something really new and different. By making the hip-hop connection the museum suddenly becomes interesting for the young audience.

Julia Petrova not only addresses the importance of understanding how gendered fashion exhibitions are, but also underlines the importance of exhibiting a diversity of dressed experience: men, women, children, subcultures, etc. A contrasting perspective is used by Jeff Horsley in showing that using a museum as a platform for fashion can be a medium to express life stories and personal identities.

Perhaps fashion as dress is something perishable? If so, the answer to why fashion museology becomes important could be seen through the prism of tattooing. Something engraved on your own skin, directly on the body, is both a lasting value and a changing fashion. Fashion tattoos are distinguishing symbols and as permanent corporeal inscriptions they characterize the person. Newness in many museums has, as stated above, lately showed itself in a growing interest in exhibiting the intensive growth of tattooing, which means both including a new audience and an interest in documenting through photography. Tattoo photography is widely exhibited in museums.

Overcoming the controversy

The chapters in this book present different ways to overcome the controversy between dress museology and fashion museology, the past and the present, theory and practice. In the periods when museums were dominated by dress museology, upper-class women's fashion was in focus. The central question addressed in Teunissen's chapter is how and why museums have become established as ideal for fashion. Surprisingly enough, the answer she gives is that it is because exhibiting fashion through broader sociocultural historic narrative can reveal societal processes as well as contextualize gender and global and local identities. It is the democratization of clothes culture that has paved the way for fashioning museums. New visions and new approaches have made it interesting for fashion not to use the catwalk but a less commercial environment like museums, at the same time as the museum strategy has been to find newness in more visibility and exhibitions that attract new visitors.

Parallel to the development from dress museology to fashion museology is the change of museum collections presented as costume collections to collections of fashion and at the same time a change in the museums' names. This is what has happened in, for example, Antwerp, New York, and Bath. In his chapter on the ModeMuseum (MoMu) in Antwerp, Marco Pecorari shows what he calls a new museology, that can be understood as Riegels Melchior's fashion museology, which has guided the development into a fashion museum. MoMu blurred the boundaries between museum and industry and invited designers to curate exhibitions. However MoMu also used contemporary design as a tool to understand fashion history. Pecorari also recognizes the possibilities for fashion museums to enlarge their field by focusing on mass production and consumption.

We have throughout this book seen that fashion is a subject that engages non-standard museum visitors which can open up possibilities to use fashion as a prism through which society can become visible. Key research questions that have been answered in different ways are a wish for an inclusive museum with visitors from different ages, classes, and genders, and on the other hand a wish for fashion to leave the exclusive catwalk and be a part of an inclusive society.

Notes

1 For an interesting discussion of how the distinction between dress, costume, fashion, and clothing can be taken even further, see Maynard (2004). In this book, however, our focus is on how fashion has come to take over dress in the museum context.

2 They do have the largest collection of dress and fashion in Sweden and they have a library with an extensive collection of books and magazines on the cultural history of fashion. The library is now part of The Europeana Fashion project that started in March 2012 (www.europeanafashion.eu).

3 The museum was originally founded in 1999 as a design museum, but when it was reopened in 2009 it had added fashion to its name, now being a design and fashion museum.

4 The exhibition was the result of a research project, also presented in a book (Larsson 2011).

References

Abrams, Melanie (2011), "Men on Show: From Philadelpia to Stockholm, Curators of Menswear Exhibitions are Promising Much More than Suits and Shirts," *The Times*, Saturday May 14.

Attfield, Judy (2000), *Wild Things: The Material Culture of Everyday Life*, Oxford: Berg.

Eldvik, Berit (2010), *Power of Fashion: 300 Years of Clothing* (trans. Alan Crozier), Stockholm: Nordiska museets förlag.

Falk, Karin (2011), *Det svenska modeundret*, Stockholm: Norstedts.

Grosz, Elizabeth (1994), *Volatile Bodies: Toward a Corporeal Feminism*, Bloomington, IN: Indiana University Press.

Larsson, Marianne (2011), *Män i baddräkt: En kroppslig kulturhistoria*, Stockholm: Nordiska museets förlag.

Maynard, Margaret (2004), *Dress and Globalization*, Manchester: Manchester University Press.

Sennett, Richard (1994), *Flesh and Stone: The Body and the City in Western Civilization*, London: W.W. Norton.

Steele, Valerie (2013), *Fashion Designers A–Z*, New York: Taschen.

Svensson, Birgitta (2008), "Facts and Artefacts in Cultural History Museums: The Material Turn in Research," in: *Research and Museums: Proceedings of an International Symposium in Stockholm 22–25 May 2007, Nationalmusei skriftserie*, 20, pp. 175–191.

Zulaika, Joseba (2002), *Guggenheim Bilbao Museoa, Museums, Architecture, and City Renewal*, Reno, NV: University of Nevada Press.

INDEX